THE NORTHEAST QUESTION

This book explores the idea, psychology and political geography of Northeast India as forged by two interrelated but autonomous meta-narratives. First, the politics of conflict inherent in, and therefore predetermined by, physical geography, and second, the larger geopolitics that was unfolding during the colonial period. Unravelling the history behind the turmoil engulfing Northeast India, the study contends that certain geographies – most pertinently, fertile river valleys and surrounding mountains that feed the rivers – are integral and any effort to disrupt this cohesion will result in conflict. It comprehensively traces the geopolitics of the region since the colonial era, in particular: the Great Game; the politics that went into the making of the McMahon Line, the Radcliffe Line and the Pemberton Line; the region's relations with its international neighbours (China, Bhutan, Myanmar, Bangladesh and Nepal); as well as the issue of many formerly non-state-bearing populations awakening to the reality of the modern state.

Lucid and analytical, this book will be of great interest to scholars and researchers of Northeast India, modern Indian history, international relations, defence and strategic studies and political science.

Pradip Phanjoubam is the Editor of *Imphal Free Press* and is based in Imphal, Manipur, India. He began his career as a journalist in 1986 as a sub-editor at *The Economic Times*, New Delhi. He has written extensively on affairs of the Northeast for many reputed publications, both in the mainstream media as well as academic journals. He was a Fellow at the Indian Institute of Advanced Study, Shimla (2012–14) at the time of writing this book.

THE NORTHEAST QUESTION

Conflicts and frontiers

Pradip Phanjoubam

LONDON AND NEW YORK

First published 2016
by Routledge

2 Park Square, Milton Park, Abingdon, Oxfordshire OX14 4RN
711 Third Avenue, New York, NY 10017

Routledge is an imprint of the Taylor & Francis Group, an informa business

First issued in paperback 2017

Copyright © 2016 Pradip Phanjoubam

The right of Pradip Phanjoubam to be identified as author of this work has been asserted by him in accordance with sections 77 and 78 of the Copyright, Designs and Patents Act 1988.

All rights reserved. No part of this book may be reprinted or reproduced or utilised in any form or by any electronic, mechanical, or other means, now known or hereafter invented, including photocopying and recording, or in any information storage or retrieval system, without permission in writing from the publishers.

Notice:
Product or corporate names may be trademarks or registered trademarks, and are used only for identification and explanation without intent to infringe.

British Library Cataloguing-in-Publication Data
A catalogue record for this book is available from the British Library

Library of Congress Cataloging-in-Publication Data
A catalog record has been requested for this book

ISBN: 978-1-138-95798-5 (hbk)
ISBN: 978-0-8153-9588-1 (pbk)

Typeset in Galliard
by Apex CoVantage, LLC

For Ima and Pabung, who made this possible.

CONTENTS

	Introduction	1
1	Geography of conflict in the Northeast: rivers, valleys, mountains as integral regions	8
2	History of militarisation of the Northeast: search for a liberal response to radical civil unrests	31
3	Eastern frontier of Northeast India: State and non-State	67
4	Inner Line as Outer Line I: making of the McMahon Line	108
5	Inner Line as Outer Line II: the Empire and its colony	135
6	Linguistic nationalism versus religious nationalism: Partition trauma and the Northeast	159
7	Conclusion: in the end is the beginning	195
	Bibliography	211
	Index	215

INTRODUCTION

This book was written during a fellowship at the Indian Institute of Advanced Study (IIAS), Shimla, during 2012–14, and I express my sincere gratitude to the institute for accepting my proposal to research on what I call the birth pangs that went into the evolution of the idea of the Northeast region of India. I have chosen to focus on the seeds that shaped the tumultuous modern history of the region and not on its current myriad crises. On the latter, a reasonable amount of scholarly literature is already available. I have, instead, tried here to study the less-explored areas of the influences the geopolitics of the time – in particular, the Great Game – had in the shaping of the Northeast, its physical features as well as its psychology. In this exploration, my approach is, to a great extent, informed by the popular theory that geography and politics are vitally linked. The axiom I build my argument on, as outlined in the first chapter, is that certain geographies – in this case, those of contiguous mountains and the river valleys below them – are integral, and any attempt to disrupt or dismember this integrity will result in political unrests and even deadly frictions. I have also tried to show how from the time the British entered Assam in 1826, the approach to the Northeast has been one of evolving mechanisms for administering a frontier in which large tracts of territory were allowed to remain beyond the ordinary reaches of law, and simply as un-administered buffers. This legacy lives on to a great extent.

Another point I insist consistently on throughout this book is that the Northeast cannot be understood solely within the parameters of Indian nationalist historiography, which zealously expect every historical urge and aspiration occurring within the geographical territory of the nation to be explained as emanating from intrinsic reasons born within the national boundaries only. That is to say, Peter J. Taylor's 'the State as a container, from which nothing spills out, and conversely, nothing from outside spills in', as Taylor himself notes, is no longer enough in defining a nation and its history.[1] Indeed, the conceptualisation of the State as a cultural container is extremely problematic in the context of a multilingual, multi-ethnic and multireligious country such as India. This inadequacy becomes profound when we consider a region such as the Northeast, which shares only approximately 2 per cent of its boundary with subcontinental mainland India via the Siliguri corridor, and the remaining 98 per cent with countries other than India. An understanding of the histories of Tibet, Myanmar, Bangladesh and Bhutan, at least to the extent they intersect with those of the Northeast, therefore, is vital. I have tried to do just this in this volume.

I have to also concede I have had little or no direct access to archival material relevant in most of these discussions. The IIAS fellowship does not support such studies. However, I do use quotes of archival material quoted by other more resourceful authors with proper attributions. Adding to the difficulty, the Indian archives have been shut to the public from 1913 onwards despite several appeals by well-known Indian scholars. Most of the archival files of the period I write about, hence, had to be accessed in London, Beijing, Rangoon and elsewhere. Even the General Henderson Brooks–Brigadier Prem Bhagat 1963 report on the 1962 India–China war, which would have been another important document for this book, has still not been made public. I have had to, therefore, in some cases, depend on information available in controversial books such as Neville Maxwell's *India's China War* to build some of my argument, though after putting the information in perspective. Maxwell's book is interesting, nonetheless, because the author is the only writer to whom this report was leaked and this book is said to be, for a good part, a paraphrase of the report.

These are some of the broad frameworks within which I worked. The following paragraphs are a gist of the chapters in this book. The chapters sequence is deliberate, and to the maximum extent possible, ideas are made to flow from one to the next. Except for Chapters 4 and 5 – which are recommended to be read together – the rest, though bound by the larger themes of geopolitics and geography, can be read in any order without much compromise to the overall integrity of the book. Together, they should give a broad picture of the Northeast in all its diversities, but individually, they would still stand as separate and complete arguments.

Chapter 1

In the first chapter, 'Geography of conflict in the Northeast: rivers, valleys, mountains as integral regions', I outline one of the assumptions on which this book rests – that many of the conflicts we witness today have always

INTRODUCTION

been embedded in their geographies. I begin with Kashmir, and there have been some who queried why there was any need to bring in Kashmir in a book on the Northeast. The answer is pretty straightforward. Profiling the Kashmir case here is only meant as a foreground, as this conflict theatre is much better known to the world, and its example would be much more familiar and, therefore, easier for the average reader to visualise the idea I am trying to convey. Kashmir, therefore, is not the central issue, and I only want to use it as an illustration of a more abstract notion of how geography predicates many endemic conflicts.

Kashmir, which is either the source, or else, a major catchment area for the rivers that nurture the fertile river valleys below it, is important to these valleys. Any attempt to disrupt this integral geography will be seen as a civilisational threat by these valleys. When the British were gifted with Kashmir in 1846, after they defeated the Sikhs in the First Sikh War, as Kashmir's then rulers were under the Sikhs; this geography remained untouched, and therefore, there was little trouble of the nature we are witnessing today. It was the 1947 Partition and rupturing of this geography that has led to all the havoc. The World Bank–brokered Indus Water Treaty of 1960 somewhat reflects a realisation of the integral nature of this hill–valley geography.

In the Northeast, Arunachal Pradesh is similarly placed as Kashmir; therefore, the claim over Arunachal Pradesh by China has a much bigger implication than just territory coveting. This is the thrust of my argument in this chapter. Arunachal Pradesh is the source of all major tributaries of the Brahmaputra River, and therefore, controlling Arunachal Pradesh would virtually amount to controlling the entire Northeast and Bangladesh. This would be in consonance with China's quest for an outlet to the Bay of Bengal. The state also has huge hydroelectric potential. Arunachal Pradesh's importance, therefore, is not just from the historical standpoint, but also due to its geography. In most of the rest of the book, though the discussions necessarily do not anymore dwell on geography, there is always the geography element in the security assessment of the location.

Chapter 2

In the second chapter, 'History of militarisation of the Northeast: search for a liberal response to radical civil unrests', I trace the history and pattern of militarisation of the Northeast in the colonial and postcolonial periods. After comprehensively defeating the Burmese in 1826 in Assam and Manipur, and the signing of the Treaty of Yandabo, the British annexed Assam,

INTRODUCTION

but allowed Manipur to remain a protectorate state. The chapter then analyses how, having thus eliminated possibilities of external aggression from the east, the British felt continuing to deploy the military in Assam was no longer cost-effective, and so, started withdrawing their forces to be used more gainfully on other fronts of their Indian Empire. To fill the vacuum, the British administration came up with the idea of raising a civil militia, less paid than the military, but better armed than the civil police. The Cachar Levy was thus born in 1835. Reciprocal to the rise in British interest in Assam, especially with tea gardens expanding, this civil militia too continued to grow till the end of World War I; for the service rendered, it was rechristened the Assam Rifles, a paramilitary force, of civil constabulary, but staffed by officers of the Indian Army, carrying out military as well as civil duties.

The chapter also discusses two very obvious trajectories by which militarisation of the Northeast has taken place in independent India. The first is a response to perceived external threats. This is quite evident in the political geography of the Northeast as a whole, practically surrounded on all sides by foreign countries. The Partition of India in 1947, the war with China in 1962 and then with Pakistan in 1965 and 1971 ensured a concentration of the military in the Northeast.

The second reason is the more controversial one. It pertains to the use of the army in fighting radical civil dissents. I discuss the controversial Armed Forces Special Powers Act (AFSPA), 1958, promulgated in the Northeast, and the various high-powered inquiry commissions' recommendations on the matter – none of which has been implemented so far. The chapter, therefore, also has a related discussion on human rights, its nature and progress as an international movement.

Chapter 3

In this chapter, 'Eastern Frontier of Northeast India: State and Non-state', I discuss the British efforts to secure the eastern boundary of their newly acquired territory. I therefore talk of the present Indian states of Nagaland, Manipur and Mizoram. Manipur was a kingdom at the time the British annexed Assam in 1826. Nagaland, then known as the Naga Hills, and Mizoram, then known as the Lushai Hills, became parts of the British province of Assam. I talk about how the British used its protectorate state of Manipur to control the non-state spaces of the Lushai Hills and the Naga Hills, inhabited by 'wild tribes', known to the British for their violent raids in the plains of British-administered Assam.

INTRODUCTION

The chapter also reflects on the pre–British Ahom policy of dealing with these tribes by evolving a mechanism called 'Posa', in which the hill tribes were entitled to a percentage of agricultural produces from nearby villages in the plains for the return guarantee of not conducting raids on them – a system of shared sovereignty in which the hill tribes acknowledged Ahom suzerainty over them, but were, in turn, given local suzerainty on some plains villages in the foothills – a conflict resolution mechanism that the British would level as 'blackmail', but nonetheless would continue to use to their advantage after they took over Assam's administration.

The chapter also touches on another mechanism introduced by the British to contain the non-state spaces in the hills. This was the Inner Line system, which came into existence in 1873 by the Bengal Eastern Frontier Regulation. This line divided the British revenue provinces in Assam from the un-administered hills, and restricted British subjects from entering the territories beyond the Inner Line. The chapter further has a discussion on the extremely relevant but controversial notion of 'Zomia' of James C. Scott, in which he says, among others, that the hill–valley frictions seen in the Northeast is a pattern throughout the South-East Asian massif, beginning from the Northeast and stretching across much of South-East Asia and into South-West China.

Chapters 4 and 5

Chapters 4 and 5, 'Inner Line as Outer Line – I: Making of the McMahon Line' and 'Inner Line as Outer Line – II: the Empire and Its Colony', were one chapter initially, but were separated later. Most of the discussions on the internal issues relating to the Inner Line is in the earlier part, and in the latter, the external consequences are analysed, especially the mistaking of the Inner Line as the international boundary. These chapters also study the complex relations between Imperial Britain, Tsarist Russia, China and Tibet, which led to the Simla Conference 1913–14 and the drawing of the McMahon Line. There are, therefore, some small overlaps of ideas. These few overlaps are, however, in the nature of an idea being introduced in the first part and elaborated in the second. They had to be introduced in the first to ensure narrative flow, but often, explaining them there itself tended to be digressive. Together, the two chapters trace how and why the Simla Conference became urgent. They also trace how much of the controversies were consequent upon the Anglo-Russian Convention of 1907, and how indeed, if not for the 1907 Convention, China's presence in the Simla Conference may not have been necessary at all.

5

INTRODUCTION

The Tawang issue also features in the chapter. Tawang was like a dagger pointed at the heart of Assam, and this was reminded dramatically to the British after botanist Kingdon-Ward's misadventure in 1934, when he strayed into Tibet without realising it. Ward likened India's leaving Tawang unguarded to allowing the enemy to live within her gate.

These chapters also touch upon the clash of interests between the British Empire and its Indian colony. While British India saw security from the point of view of India, the Empire viewed the colony's interest differently and as secondary to the Empire's interests. For instance, Calcutta saw Tibet as important for its security, but London saw this as secondary to the British strategy of containing Russia and other European powers, and so, was worried that the concessions the British seek in Tibet may lead to demands for similar concessions by Russia and other European powers in Mongolia, Afghanistan, Persia and so on. In the end, the colony's interest ended up sacrificed on the altar of the Empire's supposed larger interest. However, after the Empire dissolved, the colony was left to shoulder the legacies left behind by a dead Empire's omissions and commissions. India's 1962 war with China is one of these.

Chapter 6

In Chapter 6, 'Linguistic Nationalism versus Religious Nationalism: Partition Trauma and the Northeast', I discuss the traumatic evolution of the Northeast's southern boundary and how because of a peculiar politics at the time of Partition, Sylhet district and the Chittagong Hill Tracts came to be included in Pakistan and not India. The narrative begins with the manner in which the British land revenue policy, after their takeover of Assam in 1826, alienated Assamese peasantry, and how their immigration policy further marginalised the Assamese peasantry as well as its emerging middle class, culturally and demographically. The chapter scans the triangular equation between the Hindu Bengali immigrants primarily from Sylhet, the Muslim Bengali immigrants also from Sylhet and other East Bengal districts and the Assamese, and how this shaped the peculiar and explosive politics in Assam of the time, with far-reaching consequences still felt in profound ways even today.

Concluding chapter

In the short concluding chapter, I very briefly sketch the histories of a few typical cultures of protest and the dynamics behind them that ultimately

INTRODUCTION

led to the outbreak of insurgencies. The attempt is to show how these rebellions were caused by a mix of a fundamental sense of difference to the idea of Indian nationalism on the one hand, and on the other, a knee-jerk response to the insensitivity of the early, insecure, independent Indian state administration. It is not, in any way, an exhaustive account of the phenomenon of insurgency in the region, and I am aware that many who have read the manuscript of this book were initially expecting the book to be about insurgency. This expectation is informed by the stereotypical image of the Northeast so long nurtured by the media and academia, together with the other image of the region as the homeland of exotic tribes. Although insurgency is important and would have to be researched in more depth, I felt it is equally important to let people know there are other lenses through which the Northeast can be, and should be, seen. In fact, these stereotypes are today major retarding factors in any fuller and more meaningful understanding of the region. There is much more to the Northeast and its experience in history than mere insurgency and tribal feuds. In this book, therefore, partly out of choice and partly out of the fact that this volume would have become too large, I have kept the insurgency question in the margins. Hopefully, in the near future, I will get to do another project to explore this phenomenon in much sharper and intensive focus.

Note

1 See Peter J. Taylor, *The State as Container: Territoriality in the Modern World-System* (University of Newcastle, 1994), online version published by Sage Journals, http://www.sagepub.com/dicken6/Sage%20articles/Chap%206/CH%206%20-%20Taylor.pdf (accessed 30 December 2014).

1
GEOGRAPHY OF CONFLICT IN THE NORTHEAST
Rivers, valleys, mountains as integral regions

Comprehending conflicts has never been easy. If this was not so, much of the conflicts witnessed in Northeast India today would have been – to use a cliché – history. Here, they have not only lingered, but become progressively more complex as well. There would obviously be many reasons for this, as indeed all complex human issues would, and the modest object of this chapter, and the book, is to try and size up some of the vitally important ones, particularly those that often have gone unnoticed, largely because of their intangible natures. One of the hurdles in the effort to understand the dynamics behind conflicts has been the tendency to oversimplify, using – in most cases – only tangible barometers available. Unfortunately, this strategy, which, for the sake of simplicity, I refer to as the bureaucratic approach, is not just a bane of the state's bureaucracy alone, but also the mindset of a greater section of the intelligentsia. What is forgotten in the process are the intangible factors, which seldom register on the accustomed radars that feed the cognitive faculties of the state, as also its various official executive apparatuses of governance.

Tangible indexes, such as unemployment rates, income, education, GDP growth rate, road connectivity and so on, are, no doubt, very important, but they are by no means everything there is about the problems of conflicts of the nature the Northeast has become stymied by. It is the contention of this study that they may not even be as fundamental as the intangibles that remain unnoticed, or else sidelined as secondary and insignificant. This introductory chapter, then, is meant to sketch the broad conceptual framework within which the rest of the chapters of this book will be located.

The nature of relationships between rivers, river valleys and the mountains where these rivers originate and the way they shape the psychology of inhabitants of their geographical reaches is one of these intangibles, and this study shall take a survey of some well-known cases in the Indian subcontinent, the logics of which will help in understanding some of the internal dynamics of the conflicts in the Northeast too. The proposition, then, is river valleys and the surrounding mountains form an integral geography and any effort to disrupt this integrity will cause political and social turmoil.

In a deliberate twist of the familiar piece of trite but insightful observation, English geographer W. Gordon East, once said 'nature imposes and man disposes', thereby 'man's actions are limited by the physical parameters imposed by geography'.[1] While geography is a given, and politically value-neutral, humans who come to settle in any particular geographical region have to come to terms with the interrelatedness of different regions, not just from the ecological point of view, but much more importantly and immediately, from their own primal outlook to security and survival. They, therefore, attribute values to geography. Most of the time, these values exist at the level of instinctual understandings, manifesting in myths and legends, religions and beliefs, superstitions and taboos. But very often, they have also showed up as very tangible political issues with tremendous potentials for triggering deadly conflicts. Indeed, such politics predetermined by geography have more often than not been behind many intractable conflicts all over the world.[2] History is replete with examples – the Nile basin and the Mekong basin, to cite just two – but the list can go on. The Mekong example is interesting, for here, the Asian Development Bank (ADB) has actually taken cognisance of the significance of viewing the entire river basin as an economically, ecologically, psychologically and politically integral, therefore inseparable, region. Its ambitious Greater Mekong Sub-region (GMS) project is the articulation of this philosophy, and the degree of success this project has met in integrating the economy of the entire region – Laos, Cambodia, Vietnam, Thailand, Myanmar and the Yunnan region of China – fostering a new level of cooperation between what, in recent history, have been mutually hostile, though culturally related, largely impoverished nations, is a vindication of this postulate. But even within the same country, these conflicts over river waters and river valleys can get bitter, as India has seen in the Cauvery water dispute.

Aksai Chin

Before taking on the issues of the Northeast directly, a tour of another much more known conflict theatre – Kashmir – would be illustrative. Though Kashmir south of the Karakoram would form the core of this discussion later in this chapter, the drama that played out north of the Karakoram ranges in the Karakash and Yarkand river basins and their contiguous territory, the Aksai Chin plateau and beyond, is fascinating from this same outlook of how geography determines conflict. Moreover, the political drama here, which resulted in an unsettled boundary between India and China in this sector, is a close parallel to the other unsettled boundary between the two countries in the Northeast sector, which will be discussed in greater detail in later chapters. It cannot be a coincidence that although located physically on two different extremes on the Indian map, Kashmir and the Northeast are the only two regions where the draconian Armed Forces Special Powers Act (AFSPA) is applicable by Indian law. This cannot again but be an acknowledgement, consciously or unconsciously, by the Indian establishment of a similarity in the political predicament of the two regions. To go too much into detail of the political intrigues on this front during the colonial days, ever since Kashmir came into the hands of the British after 1846, would be a digression; nonetheless, this conflict theatre is also interesting and relevant to be ignored altogether.

The crux of the British dilemma centred around where they wanted their boundary to be in this vast, barely populated and largely frozen wasteland, of which the Aksai Chin is a part. Broadly, the choices before them were to have the boundary either on the watershed ridge of the Karakoram ranges, thereby forsaking the Yarkand valley and the Aksai Chin, or else, draw the boundary on the ridge of the Kuenlun ranges to the north of the valley, thus incorporating this narrow strip of land between the two mountain ranges. The clash of interest on this issue even within the British administration is fascinating. On the one hand, from the point of view of establishing a secure defensive position, the Karakoram watershed boundary seemed the most logical, but on the other, the British at the time had another fear to tackle. If they left the Yarkand valley and Aksai Chin strip of flatland unclaimed, they were sure the Russians would claim it, thereby establishing for themselves a passage to the Tibetan plateau. Still, the British were also acutely aware that to opt for a boundary along the Kuenlun watershed would be to have a border logistically too stretched and impossible to defend. At one stage, there was even a suggestion that the Chinese should be encouraged to claim the territory so Russia could not have it, but the Chinese too showed no interest in the British game, and the ownership of the land was destined to remain as uncertain as the British found it when they took over Kashmir. They would also leave the boundary ambiguous, coming up with several suggested alignments, but never one definitively.

This strip of territory is now disputed and has attracted plenty of political rhetoric and posturing whenever skirmishes happen and tensions develop along the India–China border, but has not attracted a matching volume of scholarship in India, for many reasons – not the least of these is the non-accessibility of archival documents related to this dispute at the Indian National Archives from 1913 onwards. However, this is not to say that the issue is totally bereft of quality academic probes. There have been dedicated studies by many authors of renown, who had the resource to access the same archival documents locked up in the Indian National Archives, from its counterparts in London and Beijing. This chapter will rely a great deal on the data they collected and interpreted, as well as on the insights they provided into the problems, not necessarily to draw the same conclusions they did, but to throw light on issues specific to the theme of this book – the Northeast.

The Yarkand valley is a relatively narrow strip of flatland wedged between the Karakoram ranges and Kuenlun ranges in China's western province of Xinjiang (formerly Sinkiang). To its south-west are the Hindu Kush and Pamir ranges. To its east is the Aksai Chin, and further on, the Tibetan plateau. There were no definite linear boundaries that demarcated the region when the British entered the scene, and as Lord Curzon of Kedleston, viceroy of India from 1899 to 1905 – an explorer in his own right – noted, 'In Asiatic countries it would be true to say that demarcation has never taken place except under European pressure and by the intervention of European agents'.[3]

Very briefly, Kashmir was a princely state in the British Empire in India from 1846 to 1947, ruled by a maharaja. The state was created after it came to be in the possession of the British after their victory in the First Anglo-Sikh War in 1846. Kashmir at the time was under Sikh suzerainty.[4]

Ever since this new acquisition was made, the British were uneasy about Kashmir's un-demarcated boundaries, and began almost immediately thereafter to put in efforts to fix its boundaries. Two boundary commissions followed one after the other. The first, consisting of two members, was set up in July 1846 and given the mandate of defining the boundary between the British territories in the districts of Lahaul and Spiti in the south and those of Ladakh in the north and also Ladakh's boundary with Tibet.[5] This effort came to nought as China did not cooperate, largely by refusing to respond to British entreaties to set up corresponding surveys, and finally, to conclude a treaty on the matter. The governor general of India at the time, Henry Hardinge, did not, however, give up on the British quest for a defined boundary. He appointed a second Boundary Commission on 10 July 1847, this time, consisting of three members.[6] This effort also was in vain as the Chinese still did not respond to a request for a joint determination of the boundary from Spiti to Pangong Lake.[7] The British still did not give up. Failure of the two boundary commissions halted the efforts to define the boundary with China, but they did not terminate the efforts. From the point of view of this study, however, more than how far the British effort was successful or at what ends, the significant question is why the British came to consider the matter as urgent.

North of the Karakoram ranges is the Yarkand valley, flanked to its north by the Kuenlun ranges. Why and how did this narrow strip of inhospitable, virtually uninhabited land become so important for the British to make it persistent in the effort to draw a definite boundary and not leave it as a no man's land – as it always had been from their point of view? On numerous occasions, in various official correspondences within the British administration as well as those of the British administration with the Chinese authorities, the land was indeed referred to as no man's land. All the while, before the advent of the British interventions after their acquisition of Kashmir, China and, indeed, none of the smaller principalities and their tributaries in and around the region – Tibet, Kashmir, Ladakh, Hunza and more – were certain, or probably cared much about where their exact boundaries were.[8]

After many more such surveys, the unresolved debate remained as to whether the Karakoram watershed or that of the Kuenlun should be the boundary of India. If the boundary was to be made purely by the application of the internationally accepted boundary-making principle of the main mountain watershed of river systems, then, as Karunakar Gupta points out, in 'the Imperial Gazetteer of India (1908) Chamber's Gazetteer (1962), Columbia Encyclopaedia (1963), the Swedish explorer – Sven Hedin, Owen Lattimore – all agree that the Karakoram Mountains (and not the Kuenluns) are the main water-divide in this region'.[9]

Yet, the answer to this increasingly desperate concern came to be determined not by any standard principles of cartography, but by the appearance of Russia in the political horizon. Imperial Russia was, at the period, expanding and pushing south, absorbing all the small *khanates* and other principalities in the area. The urgent question for the British, therefore, came to revolve around which of these imagined boundaries would be most defensible, and at the same time, serve the purpose of keeping Russia at bay. An advocate of extending India's boundary to the Kuenlun ranges, T. D. Forsyth of the Great Trigonometry Survey of India, thus wrote in his report to the government:

> In the present state of our knowledge it would be very unsafe to define the boundary of Cashmere in the direction of the Karakorum,

and if it must be put down at all, it should run as near the lower Karakash River as possible. Between the Karakorum and the Karakash the high plateau is perhaps rightly described as rather a no man's land, but I should say with a tendency to become Cashmere property. It might prove hereafter very inconvenient to put the Cashmere boundary on the Karakorum ridge, and thus exclude us altogether from any benefit which might arise from having the high plateau under our control.[10]

Forsyth clearly outlines in his report of 21 September 1874, on his Second Mission to Kashgar, sent from Simla, and warned that if Russia extended any further, it 'will be within a few miles of touching Kashmir'.[11]

Two dangers appeared on the horizon, writes Parshotam Mehra. 'At the outset there was the threat – actual or potential – from Tsarist Russia: The Great Game posed problems, both strategic and, even more dangerously, psychological. Doubts also began to be raised about the bona fides if Kashmir's rulers.'[12]

> The conquest of Khiva and the rapid steady approach of Russia to the Oxus cause the natives of Afghanistan, and of the Punjab too considerable anxiety . . . The general idea is that Russia is the rising power, that she is destined to advance still further, that England is afraid of her, and will do nothing to oppose her progress, or to help those who would preserve themselves from being swallowed up . . . If we persist in shutting our eyes to Russia's advances, we must at all events prepare ourselves for internal trouble . . . [13]

The strongest of the opposite viewpoint came from Ney Elias, an explorer. Elias expressed the view that the maharaja of Kashmir should wind up his post at Shahidulla,[14] a seasonal township on the edge of the Karakash valley. He further was of the opinion that 'even though he (Maharajah of Kashmir) had never seen it, he understood that it was never a position of any strength, and that it is now in such a state of disrepair that it may be considered entirely useless from the point of view of defence . . . under these circumstances, I see no advantage in the Maharajah reoccupying Shahidulla either as a defensive post or as a demarcation of the border'.[15]

The officer on special duty in Kashmir who scrutinised Elias's proposal for transmission to the Supreme Government was favourable to this view, and he noted that the 'region between say the head of the Nubra Valley and the post of Shahidulla is a kind of no man's land, only frequented by passing traders, peopled by the skeletons of men and horses, and as real a boundary between the Indian Empire and its northern neighbours as would be a vast and waterless desert . . . Why should we dispel such innocent imaginings (on the part of the Dogras) and seek to demarcate by pillars or piles of stones a Line which nature has already defined? It would be time enough to do so when the first symptom of a tendency to encroach becomes apparent'.[16]

Elias's views were paid close heed to by the British India administration's higher authorities. Mehra reproduces the annotation by the Foreign Secretary (A. C. Lyall) in which the Governor-General (Lytton) endorsed without qualification: 'These papers refer to the question of demarcating and strengthening the frontier of Kashmir toward Kashgar, and beyond the Karakoram. I think the matter may stand over – if Kashmir is threatened at all, it will be from the north-west'.[17]

But this development notwithstanding, the other camp continued to push their views. Captain H. Ramsay, then British joint commissioner at Leh, pleaded in a memorandum: 'It was to our interest that this frontier should be now demarcated . . . it should, if possible, be placed as far north as Shahidulla'.[18] This was endorsed by the resident in Kashmir, who wrote: 'adjustment of the whole northern and north-western frontier of Kashmir should not be further postponed . . . (that it was) undesirable longer to defer the settlement of this boundary'.[19]

It was at this stage that a young British Army officer and explorer, Francis Edward Younghusband, entered the scene. The officer would come to be more remembered for the 1904 British expedition to Tibet. In 1886–87, on leave from his regiment, Younghusband made an expedition across Asia. With a senior colleague, Henry E. M. James (also on leave from his Indian Civil Service position) and a young British consular officer from Newchwang, Harry English Fulford, Younghusband explored Manchuria, visiting the frontier areas of Chinese settlement in the region and the Changbai Mountains.[20]

> Parting with his British companions, Younghusband then crossed the Gobi Desert to the Chinese Turkestan, and pioneered a route from Kashgar to India through the uncharted Mustagh Pass. In 1889, the year he was made Captain, Younghusband was dispatched with a small escort of Gurkha soldiers to investigate an uncharted region north of Ladakh, where raiders from Hunza had disrupted trade between Yarkand and India the previous year. In 1890 Younghusband was sent on a mission to Chinese Turkestan, accompanied by George Macartney as interpreter. He spent the

winter in Kashgar, where he left Macartney as British consul. In 1891 he returned to India through the Pamirs. At Bozai Gumbaz in the Little Pamir he encountered Russian soldiers, who forced him to leave the area.[21]

Younghusband provided some of the most detailed and vital information of the land beyond the Karakoram to the British for them to make an assessment of the security situation in the region, particularly in view of what was believed as an impending arrival and threat to Kashmir and the Indian empire, from the expanding Russian empire. The belief was that Chinese Turkestan or West Sinkiang (now Xinjiang) would fall into the hands of the Russians. The fear was that after Sinkiang, the Russians would grab the land between the Karakoram and Kuenlun ranges. From there, the logical expansion would be to the Tibetan plateau after traversing the Aksai Chin plateau. In such a scenario, Russia would have driven a wedge between India and China and have the upper hand in controlling the trade routes between the two countries. India's immediate northern neighbour would, in such a circumstance, be Russia.

Younghusband was of the opinion that the Karakoram ridge would be the most defensible position as India's boundary. However, he also had an answer to the vexing question of keeping the Russians from taking possession of the Yarkand basin, and this was to encourage the Chinese to take possession of the place:

> We must either take our frontier up to the Kuenlun mountains to include Raskam or else we must induce the Chinese (to provoke them as we have at Shahidulla) to assume an efficient control over that country . . . therefore we should use China as a buffer state in these parts with the object of keeping the Russians off our Northern frontier, and should use every endeavour to make her boundaries meet with those of our other buffer state – Afghanistan.[22]

Viceroy Lord Lansdowne sized up the debate thus:

> The country between the Karakoram and Kuenlun ranges, is, I understand, of no value, very inaccessible and not likely to be coveted by Russia. We might, I should think, encourage the Chinese to take it, if they showed any inclination to do so. This would be better than leaving a no-man's land between our frontier and that of China. Moreover the stronger we can make China at this

point, and the more we can induce her to hold her own over the whole Kashgar-Yarkand region, the more useful will she be to us as an obstacle to Russian advance along this line.[23]

This equation would soon take a radical turn in 1912, when the Manchu (Qing) dynasty in China fell following the outbreak of the Republican Revolution in China, and would make the perceived threat of Russian aggression seem even more desperate. By the middle of 1912, the collapse of Chinese power in Central Asia led Outer Mongolia to declare independence. Tibet too threw the Chinese out of Lhasa and Central Tibet. In Sinkiang, Russia gained ascendancy over China. Foreign Secretary Sir Arthur Henry McMahon's letter to Viceroy Lord Hardinge, dated 9 September 1912, bears testimony of this:

> If we consider the existing boundary between Chinese dominion and India, it will be seen that a Russian occupation of Chinese territories in the New Dominion will bring Russia within 150 miles of Srinagar and within 300 miles of Simla. In other words the Russians frontier will be nearer to Simla than Rawalpindi, Multan or Lucknow and about the same distance in Agra . . .[24]

Urgent exchanges of communication between Simla, Delhi and London on the matter summarised the uneventful end of the episode. Hardinge agreed with McMahon's proposal the very next day – 10 September 1912. When reminded the next day that the same proposal had been made in 1897, but had been turned down by the Military Department, Hardinge drafted a telegram to the Army Department 'as the question of frontier is very important', he wrote on the same day – 11 September 1912. He wanted a response by 'tomorrow evening. There is urgency and the matter must be dealt with rapidly'.[25]

The General Staff Branch replied the very next day, on 12 September.

> From a military point of view, I think the extended frontier would be an advantage provided we have not to occupy the portion beyond our present frontier by posts; but merely aim at keeping it undeveloped. This would keep Russian influence further away from India.[26]

Thus, the extended frontier of India came to be the Kuenlun watershed by a unilateral decision. This was the boundary alignment suggested by Sir

John Ardagh in 1897. The place was to be claimed, but not occupied, by military 'posts'.

Lord Hardinge's plan was 'never accepted by the Home Government, nor was it rejected out of hand'. It remained a plan, like many others before it. It is, at best, a document which did not result out of any treaty or agreement with China, but merely stating a unilateral intent. Behind the shapes of the different current political maps claimed respectively by India and China is such a history: one which, in the end, left the future of the affiliation of this river basin uncertain and even more complicated than what it was before the entry of the interests of these imperial powers. However, though a formal boundary was never to be drawn, by the first decade of the twentieth century, there were to be several suggested alignments of the border of India on this frontier. The most popularly remembered being:

> (1) Sir John Ardagh Line (1897) which showed a boundary alignment which took the crest of the Kuenlun range and placed within British territory the upper reaches of the Yarkand river and its tributaries and the Karakash river, as well as the whole of the Aksai Chin plateau; (2) Macartney–Macdonald Line (1899), which put forth a less ambitious territorial claim north of the Karakoram ranges. East of the Karakoram Pass, it left to China the whole of the Karakash Valley and almost all of the Aksai Chin proper. It followed the Lak Tsang range, the Lingzi Tang salt plains and the whole of the Change Chenmo valley, as well as the Chip Chap river further north; and (3) The Karakoram Line which was based on the watershed principle.[27]

The picture that emerges establishes once again the importance of geography as a major determinant of conflict. Here is how a barren, arid, inhospitable stretch of white desert, which neither the British were keen to have nor the Chinese interested to take possession of, suddenly became vitally important when a third party, Russia, walked into the arena. This interrelatedness of geography and politics is what this study will continually refer back to in the exploration of the conflict scenarios in the Northeast in the chapters to follow.

Before the focus is taken to the Northeast, however, it would be pertinent to examine another arena of conflict, not very far from this one physically, but unique in its own ways. This theatre is also in Kashmir on the other side of the Karakoram ranges.

Kashmir: water politics

Punjab, as the name implies, is the land of five rivers – Chenab, Beas, Ravi, Jhelum and Sutlej. It should have been six, but the sixth, Indus, is considered on the far frontier of this land, marking its border with Afghanistan. But all the earlier named five rivers further downstream confluence with the Indus to flow together as the mighty Indus river. Punjab, irrigated by these rivers, is a vast alluvial, fertile plain. The turn of politics in the mid-twentieth century being what it was, this land is today divided between two countries, India and Pakistan. Roughly a third of the territory falls within India, while a larger area of it is in Pakistan.

Pakistan's portion of the Punjab is prosperous and, therefore, the most influential, politically and economically. The region and its people determine the shape and texture of politics in the country. In India too, the Punjab region (the undivided Indian Punjab constituted of the present-day Punjab, Haryana and Himachal Pradesh) is an important granary of the country. This is where India's Green Revolution was launched in the 1980s before spreading to other corners of the country. Its rivers have given it many bounties through the ages. These alluvial plains also nurtured the ancient 5,000-year-old Indus Valley Civilisation. Whether the modern Indian civilisation is a continuity of this ancient one or whether later civilisations were built over the ruins of the older ones is another question, but the important point is the river basin of the Indus river system, which includes the Punjabs, has through history been the cradle of an important civilisation.

While there aren't likely to be many in the Indian subcontinent who have not heard of the Indus Valley Civilisation, it is more than likely many who know of this ancient civilisation have not ever asked where all these vitally important rivers, which nurture this civilisation, either originate, flow through or else, are fed by. The answer is Kashmir. Kashmir is the major catchment area for this river system. This answer itself should have already changed the complexion and texture of how the problem of Kashmir is understood.[28]

Kashmir is today a disputed territory, with India and Pakistan controlling a part of it each. There is a raging separatist insurgency in the Indian Kashmir. The goal of this insurgency comes primarily in two shapes. One, it is a movement for Muslim Kashmir to secede from India and merge with coreligionist Pakistan, a mindset inherited from the logic of the Partition of India at the end of British colonialism in 1947, and the two-nation theory of the Muslim League, which saw an irreconcilable and irreversible clash of civilisations between Hindu and Muslim India that preceded Partition, a cataclysmic event marked by unprecedented communal hatred and violence. Two, it is a movement by Kashmir to self-determine its own political future, independent of both India and Pakistan. India is for united Kashmir to be a part of India, and believes the state was always a part of India, though legally speaking, Kashmir became a part of British India only in 1846, after the British defeated the Sikhs and annexed their territories to its expanding Indian Empire. Pakistan supports the insurrection in Indian Kashmir and is for the whole of Kashmir to come under its folds. It is, however, very doubtful if Pakistan would lend the same support if Kashmir were to demand total sovereignty for itself rather than become a part of Pakistan. Kashmir is too important for Pakistan and India to let the region go outside their spheres of influence. Arguably, this is more so for Pakistan than for India.

The importance of Kashmir to the vast, fertile, prosperous, alluvial plains of Punjab and the rest of the Indus basin is determined precisely by the rivers that originate from its mountainous terrain. Deep down in their archetypal cultural memory, it is unlikely Punjab and the entire Indus valley – and, therefore, Pakistan and, to a lesser extent, India – would not see the eventuality of Kashmir going outside their direct spheres of influence as a 'civilisational threat'. This deep threat perception is arguably the same insecurity all riparian valleys would have at the thought of losing control of the hills and mountains where their rivers take birth and where their mountain passes are. Similar frictions are played out in so many different conflict arenas across the globe. Those familiar with the hill–valley tension in Manipur state in Northeast India, for instance, would vouch for this. Likewise, that the most vocal protests to India's plan to build a multipurpose dam on the Barak river at Tipaimukh in Manipur should come from Bangladesh tells of the same friction caused by disruption of the integral hill–valley geography. The Barak river irrigates the fertile valley of Barak in India and the contiguous Surma valley in Bangladesh. These hill–valley tensions are, as James C. Scott points out, one of the most distinctive features of ethnic relationships and politics in the entire South-east Asia.[29]

But these subterranean apprehensions exist in the realm of memory, often as cultural archetypal, therefore intangible. This is quite unlike 'history', which operates on the tangible plane, and indeed as Pierre Nora so provocatively said, 'history is perpetually suspicious of memory, and its true mission is to suppress and destroy it'.[30] This being what it is, it is presumable that 'history' and most historians would not have taken serious cognisance of such intangibles, and attempted factoring them in their interpretation of this history. Indeed, the tangible history of the postcolonial conflict in Kashmir tells a very different story. The familiar narrative is of this conflict being a continuity of the traumatic Partition of India at the end of British rule in mid-1947. Very briefly, Kashmir, then a princely state, was under a Hindu king, Maharaja Hari Singh; however, the majority of his subjects were Muslim. The king preferred an independent Kashmir, but under desperate duress of an invasion by an army of militant tribesmen from the Pakistan side, opted to join India, thus laying the seeds for the present unrest in the state. The preoccupation with the objective and verifiable has been such that not too many have ever tried to see the other story – in particular, Kashmir's importance in the river equation.

This is not to say the water issue in the region and its potential for triggering deadly conflicts – even wars between nations – are not recognised at all. In recent times, these intangible frictions have tended to encroach into tangible territories. A news item in the *Hindustan Times* on 27 March, 2012, for instance, says, 'A classified US report listed India's three major river basins – Indus, Ganga and Brahmaputra – among the world top 10 water conflict zones in ten years from now'.[31] The 'report based on National Intelligence Estimate on water security said the chances of water issues causing war in next 10 years were minimal but they could disrupt national and global food market and cause tension between states'.[32] The news further quotes the US report that 'Beyond 2022, use of water as weapon of war or a tool of terrorism will become more likely particularly in South Asia (India), the Middle East and North Africa'.[33] In the same vein, *National Geographic* carried a news report, as part of the *National Geographic* News series on global water issues, titled 'India and Pakistan at Odds Over Shrinking Indus River', which clearly saw a threat to peace in the issue. 'One of the potentially catastrophic consequences of the region's fragile water balance is the effect on political tensions'.[34]

Other than internal discords between regions within the same states, the report also clearly saw conflict potential between states – in this case, India and Pakistan: 'But the issue also threatens the fragile peace that holds between the nations of India and Pakistan, two nuclear-armed rivals. Water has long been seen as a core strategic interest in the dispute over the Kashmir region, home to the Indus headwaters. Since 1960, a delicate political accord called the Indus Water Treaty has governed the sharing of the river's water. But dwindling river flows will be harder to share as the populations in both countries grow and the per-capita water supply plummets'.[35]

The reasons for this depletion of water volume in the river are many, and these include climate change, which is feared to be speeding up the melting of the glaciers that feed the river. While climate change is neutral to this politics and no blame can be attributed to any single country, there are others where this is alarmingly the case. 'Both countries are also racing to complete large hydroelectric dams along their respective stretches of the Kashmir river system, elevating tensions. India's projects are of a size and scope that many Pakistanis fear could be used to disrupt their hydropower efforts, as well as the timing of the flows on which Pakistani crops rely'.[36] The *National Geographic* report further quotes a Pakistani security analyst that 'Many in Pakistan are worried that, being in control of upstream waters, India can easily run Pakistan dry either by diverting the flow of water by building storage dams or using up all the water through hydroelectric power schemes'.[37]

Likewise, a brief report in *The Guardian*, London, dated 3 June 2002 also indicated the same underlying conflict scenario, saying 'the tense stand-off between India and Pakistan has cast the shadow of nuclear conflict across the globe. But, even if both see sense and pull back from the first war between nuclear powers, there are concerns that relations are so soured that Delhi and Pakistan might resort to conflict by other means. In particular, there are worrying reports suggesting that India could cut off Pakistan's water supply. The Indus water treaty, drawn up in 1960, under the auspices of the World Bank, divided the distribution of water from the six rivers that run down from Tibet through India to the shared Indus Basin. India did not revoke the accord during either the 1965 or the 1971 war with Pakistan. In raising the treaty as an issue India may be signalling how deeply angry with Pakistan it is'.[38]

Pakistan's apprehension in the regard dates back much earlier and this had resulted in the signing of the Indus Water Treaty on 19 September 1960 between the two nations, represented by the then Indian prime minister, Jawaharlal Nehru and the then Pakistan president, Mohamad Ayub Khan, and brokered by the World Bank (then the International Bank for Reconstruction and Development).[39] This apprehension on the part of Pakistan is despite India most generously allowing Pakistan to have a major share of the river waters of the Indus river system:

'No other water-sharing treaty in modern world history matches this level of generosity on the part of the upper-riparian state for the lower-riparian one. In fact, the volume of water earmarked for Pakistan from India under the Indus Treaty is more than ninety times greater than what the United States is required to release for Mexico under the 1944 US–Mexico Water Treaty, which stipulates a guaranteed minimum transboundary deliver of 1.85 billion cubic meters of the Colorado river water yearly',[40] writes

Brahma Chellany. He sums up the underlying principle of the Indus Treaty thus: 'Without the need to redraw the British-set political frontiers, the treaty split the Indus River basin into northern and southern parts by tracing a "fictitious line" from east to west that severely limited the sovereign rights of India on three key upper rivers in order to bestow quasi-exclusive rights to Pakistan over those rivers. India's full sovereignty rights were thus confined by the treaty to the lower three rivers'.[41] By this treaty, Pakistan was entitled to a share of 167.2 billion cubic metres of water a year, leaving India with only 40.4 billion cubic metres water a year. Among the reasons for this water-sharing formula was 'the water-use patterns up to 1947, when the irrigation system under the colonial rule was much better developed in the Indus basin area of what became Pakistan'.[42]

Surely, the Kashmir conflict – or equally appropriately – the conflict over Kashmir between India and Pakistan is more complicated and deep-seated than merely the politics of religion and national identity.

Northeast: why Arunachal Pradesh is important

Having made quick surveys of two well-known conflict theatres to note the importance of a peculiar and often ignored conflict dynamic, a reassessment of the conflict situation in the Northeast from this vantage should provide new insights. This will particularly be appropriate considering the rising decibel in the debate over dams and development in the region. But first, a brief sketch of the geography of the Northeast would be pertinent.

The region's political map is unique. It shares an estimated 98 per cent of its borders with countries other than India, and only a thin corridor – often referred to as the Chicken's Neck or the Siliguri Corridor, at some point only about 20 km in width – connects the region to the rest of subcontinental India. Almost all its present boundaries were created during British colonial times. The McMahon Line, drawn in 1914, marks its northern boundary with Tibet Autonomous Region of China, the Radcliffe Line drawn in 1947 marks its southern boundary with the former East Pakistan, now Bangladesh, and the line that emerged out of the Treaty of Yandabo in 1826, but modified three times in later years and ratified by independent India and Burma (Myanmar) in 1967, defines its eastern boundary with Myanmar. The history behind each of these colonial lines is interesting, but inadequately explored.

With the discussion of the geography of conflict over Kashmir between India and Pakistan as well as between China and India earlier in this chapter as the foreground, I will now try and place the water issue in the Northeast within a similar frame. In all, 157 dams of various sizes are being planned on the rivers in the region for hydro energy generation, flood control and irrigation of farmlands, according to the Ministry of Power's 2011–12 report.[43] Though it is not known how many of these will actually see light of day, considering opposition from various quarters among civil society, it is anticipated that most will ultimately be pushed through by the government. A majority of these projects will be located in Arunachal Pradesh, where almost all of the tributaries of the region's most major and important river, the Brahmaputra, originate or pass through.

This being the case, like Kashmir, it cannot be a coincidence that Arunachal Pradesh has once again come into prominence as a disputed territory. China has been claiming the entire state for a long time, calling it South Tibet, but in recent times, this claim has been consistent, persistent and even aggressive. Till about the 1930s, or for as much as 20 years after the making of the McMahon Line, although China did not ultimately sign the agreement, it did not officially question its validity. The controversy over this boundary will be looked into in more detail in Chapters 4 and 5, but the relevant point here is, as in Kashmir, it would be prudent to not sideline the intangibles behind this dispute too. For, here too, there are indeed issues of rivers and the river valleys, and how these geographical regions are closely bound to security issues.

What is significant is that the geography of the place determines that controlling Arunachal Pradesh, where practically all the tributaries of the Brahmaputra either originate or pass through, would ultimately amount to controlling directly or indirectly the Northeast, and further on, Bangladesh. China's push for a route to the Bay of Bengal would suddenly become within reach and India would quite obviously want to prevent this from happening under any circumstance.[44] One more point needs to be remembered while assessing the importance of river sources in the mountains. From elementary science, we know that gravity dictates that the flow of water follows the path of least resistance; therefore, river ways in the mountains are also usually where mountain passes are. From this same vantage, the contest for control of these rivers is also a contest for control of the mountain passes. Travellers and explorers know this too well as the following line from a description of the terrain in Arunachal Pradesh by S. Butler tells us: 'Traversing such a country where the route follows the course of the rivers must naturally be difficult in the extreme'.[45]

Burma as bridge

China's quest and need for easier access to the Indian Ocean is obvious and evident. Its ever growing energy needs demand easier reach to the oil-rich Arabian Peninsula and Africa, making it possible to avoid the traffic bottleneck of the tedious and long sea route to the Bay of Bengal though the Strait of Malacca. It has been seeking a land route to the Indian Ocean through Myanmar, and it, in August 2014, completed an ambitious oil pipeline from the Myanmar deep sea port of Kyaukpyu (Sittwe) to Kunming, capable of transporting 12 million tonnes of crude oil per year.[46] India's security strategy think tank, the Institute of Defence Studies and Analysis (IDSA), also reported this while the project was still under construction:

> In order to meet energy demands in its resource-crunched eastern, southern and central parts, China is constructing oil and gas pipelines in Myanmar, almost reaching to the seashores of Bay of Bengal. Currently, the China National Petroleum Corporation (CNPC), in agreement with the Myanmar Oil and Gas Enterprise (MOGE) and the Myanmar state security forces, is engaged in laying a 982 km (620 miles) long crude oil pipeline from Kyaukpyu Port on the western coast of Arakan State linking Kunming after entering the border city of Ruili in Yunnan Province of China at a cost of US $2.5 billion. Concurrently, they are also constructing another gas pipeline, capable of delivering 12 bn cm of natural gas per year, from Shwe Gas off the Arakan coast up to Kunming. At the same time, a deep underwater crude oil unloading port and oil storage facility is being constructed at Maday Island (Arakan Coast) to serve as terminus for the tankers coming from West Asia and Africa.[47]

The importance of Myanmar in this context, as historian Thant Myint-U writes, hinges on its location in this globally significant junction between two emerging superpowers of the near future. China looks to Burma as a land bridge to the Bay of Bengal to avoid the Malacca Strait.[48] Ever since Myanmar's junta agreed to initiate a process of transition to democracy, there has literally been a rush of Western investors into the state to match a reciprocal spurt of political interest by the West in the country. If the former are attracted by the country's untapped resources, the latter see Myanmar as a lever to counter-balancing China's growing influence in the region. So far, the strategy seems to be paying off, as Myanmar, it is evident now, all along was wary of the unchecked growth of China's influence on its soil, which it was – till as recently as 2011 – compelled to allow as the West, in particular the United States and the European Union, had imposed very tough sanctions on the country for its disregard of democratic norms and human rights standards. But the country, now led by a hybrid military–civilian government after its November 2010 elections, has begun introducing various democratic reforms ever since it assumed power in March 2011, softening Western attitudes. Moreover, the country's charismatic democracy icon, Nobel Peace Prize winner, Aung San Suu Kyi, is today part of the establishment as the elected leader of the opposition in the country's parliament.

Floodgates of the Western sanctions are beginning to lift in dramatic fashion, ostensibly to check China's free run in expanding its military as well as economic influences in the country and beyond. The media has provocatively named the new power equation between the US, China and Myanmar in Myanmar as the new Golden Triangle, and some even predict the country as the new-generation Cold War front.[49] It is significant in this regard that not much after the reform process began taking root in the country, Myanmar's response to these new developments is curious. It is warming up to the West rather enthusiastically, and in a warning signal to the Chinese president, Thein Sein, a retired general who took the world by surprise initiating the country's unprecedented opening up to the world, suspended construction on a Chinese-funded mega hydroelectric project, the Myitsone dam, in Kachin state in the country's north. With the increasingly liberal environment in Myanmar, locals too are speaking out more forcefully against Chinese projects. At Monywa, thousands rallied against a copper mine partly owned by a subsidiary of a Chinese weapons maker.[50]

After the initial rush to embrace the West, understandably, Myanmar now is showing signs of being cautious not to make the battle lines drawn in such black and white terms, thereby rebuffing China altogether. Even Nobel Peace Laureate Aung San Suu Kyi stepped forward to assume the role of the pacifier. In the Monywa mine case, for instance, while castigating the lack of transparency in the implementation of such projects, she also added that if Myanmar kept cancelling these contracts, the country stands to lose international trust.[51] At other times, President Thein Sein has also said, rather ambiguously, that the Myitsone dam was only suspended, but not cancelled. Popular American weekly *Time* reported the development in these words: 'In Burma, too, the reformist leadership has taken pains not to alienate China. After all, Beijing was a key ally of the junta – some of whose retired members still rule the nation – when few other nations were willing to stand by the army leaders.'[52] Before Thein Sein visited the US in September (2012) for the opening of the UN General Assembly, he made sure to pop by China for a visit to a trade fair. 'Myanmar is at present in a transitional phase, but it pays great attention to developing relations with

China.'[53] Thein Sein also made a point in a statement while in southern China: 'Its policy of seeing China as a true friend has not changed.'[54]

Whatever the case may be, the fact of the matter is China cannot any longer have a free run in Myanmar. It now has competition. It may still be a conjecture, but not one that is altogether wild to suggest that China's need to have a lever in the Northeast, if it can, is all the more important now. China's new aggressive stand on its claim over Arunachal Pradesh would also have to be viewed through this lens. For, as much as Myanmar is important because it is located between India and China, the Northeast, which is contiguous to Myanmar, is similarly located. All the more reason why India's Look East Policy, so far pushed rather half-heartedly, and which often tends to overlook the Northeast, is vitally important. Lest the point is missed, India's Look East Policy must look east through the Northeast. In other words, to see the policy as more profitable as a maritime enterprise may be prudent from the point of view of immediate business gains, but such an approach would be nothing short of political short-sightedness.

Much before the Look East Policy, however, India always understood the importance of the Northeast region intuitively. India's takeover of Sikkim in 1975 through a controversial referendum,[55] which was till then an independent kingdom, is significant from this consideration. Bhutan and Nepal are close allies too, and obviously, India treasures these alliances, and therefore, though small and weak, they are hardly its minor partners. It is difficult not to see a parallel between how the barren Yarkand river basin suddenly came to be urgently important when an expanding imperialist Russia appeared on the horizon with how these states wedged between giants India and China gained their leverage power. Sikkim's merger with India in 1975 was frowned upon by China, which till 2003 considered it as an independent kingdom occupied by India, before finally deciding to end the posture, marking what observers at the time believed was the beginning of a thaw in the relationship between the two emerging Asian economic and military giants.[56] And soon, India, in turn, formally recognised Tibetan Autonomous Region as an integral part of China.[57] Diplomatic friction resulting out of China's need to gain better access and control of the Indian Ocean, and India's opposition to this, is seen even at the South Asian Association for Regional Cooperation (SAARC). China now wants to be a full member of this association – which India is not too pleased about.

Not only is this an issue about a lever to control the rest of the Northeast and Bangladesh by controlling Arunachal Pradesh, but the rivers of this state, which accounts for nearly all of the tributaries of the mighty

Brahmaputra, are extremely important resources on their own. 'As per the Central Electricity Authority, hydro potential in India is estimated at 145 gigawatts (GW), of which installed capacity is around 34 GW and another 12 GW is under construction, or around 32 percent of the estimated total potential'.[58] Of this, 145 GW potential, the Northeast's share is estimated to be about 45 per cent, or to be more precise, 57.6725 GW, as per the projection of the Ministry of Power in its 2011–12 status report on power. Of this, Arunachal Pradesh accounts for 46.9775 GW.[59] The installed capacity to date, however, accounts for only 8.977 GW from 13 completed hydroelectric projects.[60] To tap the rest, the Ministry of Power has been pushing for 157 hydroelectric projects along the rivers of the Northeast. In all, 96 of these will be in Arunachal Pradesh.[61] Other than the estimated 38 per cent of the national total of hydroelectric potential (together with other Eastern states, the figure quoted is 45 per cent), the Northeast and Eastern states together are also estimated to hold 75 per cent of India's coal reserves, according to a paper brought out by the Indian Chamber of Commerce at its 3rd Northeast and East Power Summit 2010.[62]

China's own thirst for power is well-known. As an upstream country, it has been causing concern with the dams it has built or plans to build on a number of international rivers, including the upper reaches of the Mekong, Salween and the Brahmaputra. China too has plans to harness the water of Yarlung Tsangpo, the river in Tibet that becomes the Brahmaputra after it takes a 'U-shaped turn to form the so-called Great Bend in the Nyangtri Prefecture of the Tibet Autonomous Region'[63] and enters Arunachal Pradesh. 'In all, China intends to build 40 dams on the river and its tributaries. Of these, 20 dams on the Brahmaputra will generate 60,000 MW of power, while 20 smaller dams upon its tributaries are expected to generate another 5,000 MW. Eleven of the 20 projects on the Brahmaputra will be located between its source and the Great Bend where the Brahmaputra turns northwards, executes a huge "U" turn and falls from 3,500 metres on the Tibetan plateau to 700 metres in the undulating hills of Arunachal Pradesh in India. These will generate 20,000 MW of power, while the balance of 40,000 MW will be generated at the Great Bend itself'.[64] Between the two countries, then, if all the plans get to be executed, the Yarlung Tsangpo/Brahmaputra river will be dammed at numerous places all along its course to generate 97,000 MW of power.[65]

The environmental consequences of this race to dam the natural flow of the river are only imaginable. But the picture is also one that confirms why and how Arunachal Pradesh has become such a contested geography.

Notes

1 Robert D Kaplan, *Revenge of Geography: What the Map Tells Us about Coming Conflicts and the Battle against Fate* (Random House, New York, 2012), p. 29. The original proverb is 'Man proposes, God disposes', a translation from *The Imitation of Christ* by the German-born Thomas à Kempis (*c.* 1380–1471).
2 Ibid.
3 Lord Curzon, *Frontiers*, Romanes Lecture of 1907, full text of lecture available at: https://www.dur.ac.uk/resources/ibru/resources/links/curzon.pdf (accessed 4 March 2014).
4 See J. C. Aggarwal and S. P. Agrawal, *Modern History of Jammu and Kashmir, Volume 1, Ancient Times to Simla Agreement* (Concept Publishing Company, New Delhi, 1995); and A. G. Noorani, *India-China Boundary Problem, 1846-1947* (Oxford University Press, New Delhi, 2011).
5 A. G. Noorani, *India-China Boundary Problem, 1846–1947* (Oxford University Press, New Delhi, 2011) p. 21.
6 Ibid., p. 25.
7 Alastair Lamb, *Britain and Chinese Central Asia*, pp. 79–80 (as quoted in Ibid., p. 25).
8 See Noorani, *India–China Boundry Problem*.
9 Karunakar Gupta, *Distortions in the History of Sino-Indian Frontiers, Economic and Political Weekly*, 26 July 1980, http://www.jstor.org/stable/4368898 (accessed on 3 March 2014).
10 Foreign Political A, September 1873 (as quoted in A. G. Noorani, *India-China Boundary Problem*, p. 39).
11 Confidential Report by Sir Douglas Forsyth, 21 September 1874 (as quoted in Ibid., p. 42).
12 Parshotam Mehra, *Essays in Frontier History – India, China and the Disputed Border, India's Imperial Legacy and China's Frontier Gains* (Oxford University Press, New Delhi, 2007), p. 44.
13 Forsyth's 1874 report (as quoted in Ibid., p. 44).
14 Parshotam Mehra, *Essays in Frontier History*, p. 45.
15 Exerpts from memorandum by Ney Alias dated 23 November 1878 in *Foreign Department*, Secret F. (as quoted in Ibid.).
16 Demi official by F. Henvey, Officer on Special Duty in Kashmir, forwarding copy of Elias's memorandum to A. C. Lyall, Secretary, Foreign Department, 23 November 1878 in *Foreign Department*, Secret F. (as quoted in Ibid., p. 46).
17 Note by A. C. Lyall, 3 December 1897 (as quoted in Ibid.).
18 Captain Ramsay's recommendation on 17 September 1886, *Foreign Department* (as quoted in Ibid.).
19 Colonel R. P. Nisbet, Resident in Kashmir to H. M. Durand, Foreign Secretary, 8 January 1889, *Foreign Department* (as quoted in Ibid.).
20 Wikipedia, http://en.wikipedia.org/wiki/Francis_Younghusband (accessed on 15 June 2013).
21 Ibid.
22 Excerpts from Younghusband's detailed 'Memorandum on some measures to be taken to check Russian encroachment towards our northern frontier',

in K.W. No.3 *Foreign Department* Secret F (as quoted in Parshotam *Mehra, Essays in Frontier History*), p. 49.
23 K.W. Secret F., October 1889, Nos 182–97. K.W. No.1 (as quoted by A. G. Noorani in *India-China Boundary Problem*, p. 156).
24 As quoted by A. G. Noorani in *India-China Boundary Problem*, p. 156.
25 A. G. Noorani, *India-China Boundary Problem*, p. 157.
26 Ibid.
27 Karunakar Gupta, *Distortions in the History*, EPW, 26 July 1980.
28 The arguments on water politics is a summary of a paper by Pradip Phanjoubam presented at the third two-yearly conference organised by the Asian Borderlands Research Network, the Netherlands, held at Singapore, 11–13 October 2012.
29 See James C. Scott, *The Art of Not Being Governed: An Anarchist History of Upland Southeast Asia* (Orient Blackswan 2009).
30 Pierre Nora, *Between Memory and History: Les Lieux de Memoire*, No.26, Special Issue: Memory and Counter-Memory (Spring. 1989), University of California Press, http://www.jstor.org/stable/2928520 (accessed on 6 August 2008).
31 Hindustan Times, *Water: New weapon of mass conflict*, 27 March 2012, http://www.hindustantimes.com/India-news/NewDelhi/Water-New-weapon-of-mass-conflict/Article1-831287.aspx (accessed on 7 November 2013).
32 Ibid.
33 Ibid.
34 National Geographic, 12 October 2011, http://news.nationalgeographic.co.in/news/2011/10/111012-india-pakistan-indus-river-water/ (accessed on 13 September 2013).
35 Ibid.
36 Ibid.
37 Ibid.
38 Guardian, *War over Water, It could happen with India and Pakistan*, http://www.guardian.co.uk/world/2002/jun/03/kashmir.india1 (accessed on 13 September 2013).
39 Wikipedia, http://en.wikipedia.org/wiki/Indus_Waters_Treaty See also http://siteresources.worldbank.org/INTSOUTHASIA/Resources/223497-1105737253588/IndusWatersTreaty1960.pdf for full text of the agreement. (accessed on 13 September 2013).
40 Brahma Chellany, *Water: Asia's New Battleground* (HarperCollins 2011), pp. 77–78.
41 Ibid., p. 77.
42 Ibid., p. 78.
43 The Hindu, http://www.thehindu.com/news/national/centre-pushes-for-157- power-projects-in-ne/article3480635.ece (accessed on 7 October 2013).
44 Pradip Phanjoubam, Seminar paper (unpublished) presented at the third two-yearly conference organised by the Asian Borderlands Research Network, The Netherlands, held at Singapore, 11–13 October 2012.
45 S. Butler, A Sketch of Assam (1847) (as quoted in P. C. Chakravarti in *The Evolution of India's Northern Borders*, Asia Publishing House, London).

46 Wikipedia, http://en.wikipedia.org/wiki/Sino-Burma_pipelines (accessed on 25 December 2014)
47 http://idsa.in/idsacomments/ChinasPipelinesinMyanmar_shivananda_100112 (accessed on 7 October 2013).
48 Thant Myint-U, *Where China Meets India, Burma and the New Crossroads of Asia* (Faber and Faber, 2011), p. 136.
49 Time, http://world.time.com/2012/11/23/golden-triangle-after-obamas-visit-to-rangoon-whats-next-for-relations-between-burma-china-and-the-u-s/ (accessed on 27 October 2013).
50 Bertil Lintner, Yale Global, http://yaleglobal.yale.edu/content/burma-trou ble-brewing-china (accessed on 17 August 2013).
51 Mizzima, http://www.mizzima.com/news/inside-burma/8451-suu-kyi-speaks-out- on-monywa-copper-mine-project.html (accessed on 17 August 2013).
52 Time, http://world.time.com/2012/11/23/golden-triangle-after-obamas-visit-to-rangoon-whats-next-for-relations-between-burma-china-and-the-u-s/ (accessed on 17 August 2013).
53 Ibid.
54 Ibid.
55 Wikipedia, http://en.wikipedia.org/wiki/Sikkimese_monarchy_referendum,_1975 (accessed on 3 October 2013).
56 http://www.hindu.com/2003/10/09/stories/2003100906740100.htm (accessed on 3 October 2013).
57 BBC, 24 June 2003, http://news.bbc.co.uk/2/hi/south_asia/3015840.stm (accessed on 3 October 2013).
58 Northeast Today, http://www.northeasttoday.in/national-news/hydro-power-key-to-indias-energy-security-study/.
59 The Hindu, http://www.thehindu.com/news/national/centre-pushes-for-157-power-projects-in-ne/article3480635.ece (accessed on 9 October 2013).
60 Ibid.
61 Ibid.
62 Indian Chamber of Commerce report 2010, http://www.pwc.in/assets/pdfs/Publications-2010/Energy_and_Utilities_9_Feb.pdf (accessed on 9 October 2013).
63 Brahma Chellany, *Water: Asia's New Battleground*, p. 142.
64 Prem Shankar Jha, in *The Third Pole* web magazine, http://www.thethirdpole.net/why-india-and-china-should-leave-the-brahmaputra-alone/ (accessed on 1 November 2013).
65 Ibid.

2

HISTORY OF MILITARISATION OF THE NORTHEAST

Search for a liberal response to radical civil unrests

From what was seen in the previous chapter on geography as a determinant of conflict, it is clear the vexed question of militarisation of the Northeast can never be simple. It is also clear the issue of militarisation of the Northeast will have to be considered from two broad perspectives. The first of these is the political as well as the physical geography of the region – a landmass wedged between China, Bangladesh, Bhutan and Myanmar. This extremely vulnerable physical location would have predetermined the nature of this militarisation of the region to a great extent. That there is still an unsettled border dispute between India and China in the region, which even led to a brief war in 1962 between the two countries, in which India suffered a humiliating defeat, has only added to the urgency of the matter. It must also be remembered in this context that till 1971, Bangladesh, the Northeast's southern neighbour, was East Pakistan, the eastern wing of independent India's sibling and bitter arch rival in the postcolonial era, out to purge each other's bitter memories of a bloody Partition in 1947.

The second factor determining the militarisation of the Northeast is the unresolved question of nationality among many ethnic populations in the region, which have continually spawned violent separatist insurgencies since the dawn of Indian independence in 1947. While the legitimacy of the former reason for militarisation will remain beyond questioning, it is the latter which has been expectedly at the centre of many controversies. This chapter will take a look at the patterns and logic behind the history of this militarisation – which began in the colonial era – seen from both these two vantages.

For obvious reasons, the issue of militarisation cannot but be viewed from the perspective of state building, and therefore, it is also always invariably linked with the notion of development, as determined and defined by the state building project. This implies, in an ideal situation where a state grows from the bottom, informed by the needs and pressures for changes among its subjects alone, that these development projects would have little friction with the people they preside over. This unfortunately has seldom been the case, especially in former colonies, which are modelled on the states their former colonisers built. The state, in these cases, therefore, has always had the tendency to be a hegemon.

There is thus, as a matter of rule, a ritual nexus between the military and development in all nascent postcolonial states today. The possession of a national military has almost become a validation certificate for claims to modern nationhood. It is noteworthy here that the European model of the modern nation state does rest on a foundation of violence, having been the direct cause behind two devastating world wars and numerous other ethnic, racial and ideological genocides across the globe, resulting in over 100 million dead in the span of the twentieth century, making this century arguably the most violent century in human history.[1] This fact itself is almost a demonstration of the need for a nation to keep a military and flaunt violence potential to qualify to be a modern nation state. This is true even where a military seems totally and obviously redundant for many small, weak and poor nations. Bhutan and Nepal in India's immediate neighbourhood are good glaring examples to illustrate this. These two countries, sandwiched between rising economic and military superpowers, India and China, cannot ever imagine a situation where they have to fight a war with either of their two only neighbours, but they religiously keep a military each. At best, their militaries can be used against their own citizens, which they, like many other nations, have indeed been doing so, during the anti-Maoist campaign during 1996–2006 in the case of Nepal, and the eviction of Nepali settlers in the 1990s in the case of Bhutan. The rest of the time, these militaries have no more than ceremonial duties, evoking in a way the notion of the Theatre State, which rely on spectacular and ceremonial displays of symbols of the state to confirm the sinews of their nationhood.[2] This psyche, which links the military with nationalism, however, is not confined to just the state institution as such, but also shared, discretely and openly, by a large section of the citizenry of any nation.

For instance, in opinion polls in the wake of India's first nuclear test at Pokhran in 1974, in particular, one by the popular *India Today*, to a question on what was the one event that made the respondent proud to be an Indian, the answer was quite sweepingly 'Pokhran', and therefore, India's entry into the nuclear club. This is the psyche which has always condoned, and will always continue to condone, the use of the military to any military challenge to the nation, real or perceived, from within or without. The militarisation of the Northeast region is also supported, overtly and tacitly, by such official as well as public national psyche. Perceived external threats from neighbouring countries have resulted understandably in the current unprecedented military build-up in the region, while the internal military challenges from various violent ethnic insurgencies have ensured the promulgation and continued imposition of draconian legislations, such as the AFSPA 1958, which gives the military virtually unrestrained powers to crush these insurgencies, seriously compromising the human rights of citizens of the region. The ethics and the constitutionality of the latter will be discussed in more detail later in this chapter. Arguably, state violence seems to be everybody's destiny, at least till the notion of the nation state gets an overhaul and comes to be redefined in its very essence.

The genesis and pattern of the militarisation of the Northeast region in modern times testifies to this trend and logic of state building. It began with the long shadow of colonialism falling on it towards the beginning of the 19th century. The element of inevitability of this phenomenon, coming as it did as a replacement of one kind of violence by another, is intriguing. This crucial transition, in the case of the Northeast, is almost perfectly coterminous with the historical raison d'être for the birth and maturing of the oldest paramilitary force in India – the Assam Rifles.

If the British inherited a boundary problem when Kashmir came into its possession in 1846 following its conquest and annexation of the Sikh empire, the same could be said of the NE sector. In 1826, when the Treaty of Yandabo was signed between the British and Burmese after the First Anglo–Burmese War, ending the Burmese occupation of Assam, Manipur, Cachar and Jaintia, as well as Arakan and Tenasserim, the British were left facing a similar predicament in the Northeast. At the end of this war, the kingdom of Manipur was allowed to retain its independence, though with a British residency established in its capital, Imphal, but Assam – including Cachar and Jaintia – was to become part of the British province of Bengal. Only on 6 February 1874 was Assam, without Sylhet, made a separate minor British province under a chief commissioner, with its capital at Shillong.[3] On 12 September of the same year, however, Sylhet was incorporated into the new province.[4] As its administrative tentacles grew in the Northeast, the British soon discovered that the notion of a hard linear boundary, with well-delimited and demarcated boundaries, was as much, if not more, alien here, as in Kashmir. This was especially so in the mountainous territories, inhabited by numerous aboriginal tribes. The problem, as they soon found out, would remain a festering one as far as the northern boundary with Tibet was concerned, unlike its eastern boundary, where the British eventually annexed Burma, thus eliminating somewhat any extreme urgency to demarcate an exact boundary.

In Alastair Lamb's words, 'the British swallowed Burma in three gulps'.[5] Briefly, the chronology of the annexation of Burma would run in the following sequence. Various portions of Burmese territories, including Arakan and Tenasserim, were annexed by the British after their victory in the First Anglo–Burmese War; Lower Burma, including Pegu and Rangoon, was annexed in 1852 after the Second Anglo–Burmese War. The annexed territories were designated as a minor province (a Chief Commissionership), or British Burma of British India in 1862. After the Third Anglo–Burmese War in 1885, Upper Burma was annexed, and in 1897, the province of Burma in British India was created, thus becoming a major province (a Lieutenant-Governorship). This arrangement lasted until 1937, when Burma began to be administered separately by the Burma Office under the Secretary of State for India and Burma. Burma achieved independence from British rule on 4 January 1948.[6]

South of the Northeast region at the time was East Bengal, now Bangladesh, and also very much a British territory; therefore, the boundary problem here too lacked immediacy.

A vast tract of mountainous territory of the sub-Himalayan ranges, also often designated as a no man's land, formed a buffer between Tibet and Assam. This no man's land buffer was punctuated by two well-established pre-modern feudal states, namely, the kingdoms of Bhutan and Sikkim. But they too formed a different buffer zone, what would often be referred to as neutral zones or protectorate states.[7]

The evolution of the northern frontier of the Northeast, corresponding with the northern frontier of the present state of Arunachal Pradesh, therefore, is of special interest. In 1914, some tribal-majority areas were separated from the erstwhile Darrang and Lakhimpur districts of Assam province of British India to form the North-East Frontier Tracts (NEFT).[8] After Indian independence, Balipara Frontier Tract, Tirap Frontier Tract, Abor Hills district, Mishmi Hills district and the Naga tribal areas were together renamed as the North-East Frontier Agency (NEFA) in 1951.[9] The innovations with which the British proceeded to tackle these frontiers – not giving them away, but also not absorbing them altogether – is part of the administrative annals that, in their own ways, defined the idea of the Northeast then, and continues to a great extent to do so now. Under the British administration, thus, would be born the instruments of governance, such as 'administered area' and 'un-administered area', the 'backward tracts', the 'Inner Line' and, by implication, the 'Outer Line', the 'excluded area' and the 'partially excluded area' and so on. It will also be seen how the evolution of these ambiguous administrative notions and strategies are intricately linked with the pattern of securitisation of the Northeast region. Curiously, starting from the colonial days, there has seldom been an occasion when the security issue of the region has not been juxtaposed with concerns for development, creating, in the process, very intriguing subterfuges. A consideration of two cataclysmic events in the region, which amounted to serious threats and possible compromises to the nation's security, will be illustrative. The first of these is the region's experience of World War II during 1942–44, and the second, the Chinese aggression of 1962. The first was essentially a British India experience, and the second, that of independent India. To these two, a third may be added – that of the Partition of India in 1947. Of the first, Nari Rushtomji, a civil servant and statesman of the time who dedicated his entire career to the Northeast region, has this revealing remark:

> Assam was known as the Cinderella of the provinces, and was so remote and neglected by the Centre that many people did not even realize that it was part of India – it was thought of more often as an adjunct of Burma and Siam! It was when the Japanese threatened to invade India through Assam that our Cinderella began at last to receive the attention due to her. Money, all of a sudden, was of no consideration, roads and bridges started springing up out of nowhere, and, a new but significant development, a crop of air-strips emerged in practically every district.[10]

More significantly, he adds: 'We owe it to the Japanese invasion that civil air-lines could start operating in Assam, in Manipur and in Tripura almost immediately on conclusion of the war, as it is doubtful whether Government would, under normal peacetime conditions, have ventured for many, many years to come, to incur the heavy expenditures involved in air-field construction.'[11]

Indeed, as in Assam, the tiny state of Manipur owes its six airstrips to World War II, three of which are all-weather, of which one has transformed into the currently used Tulihal civil airport at Imphal. The other two are occupied by the security forces – one at Kakching, fully, and the other at Koirengei, partially. Three other fair-weather airports have since been reclaimed by the Imphal valley's green carpet of paddy fields. All of them, together with a network of new all-weather roads and other wartime infrastructures, were built with unprecedented pace and scale by the British forces in preparation for a showdown with Japanese troops, who had then swept South-east Asia and, having taken Burma, were advancing rapidly towards India.

These war preparatory activities and the huge infusion of troops and funds into the state also meant new business openings, sowing the seed for the emergence of a crop of new elites of wartime contractors and businessmen. Indeed, the roots of many of the current generation of local businessmen in Manipur are traced to this period.[12] No demonstration of the curious relationship between the military and development could have been more stark and dramatic. It is also an uneasy relationship destined to remain a consistent and often controversial theme in the modern annals of the Northeast. In the same vein, much of the infrastructural developments in Arunachal Pradesh can be attributed to the 1962 war with China.

The Assam Rifles

For a closer understanding of the administrative drive and pattern of militarisation of the Northeast region, a careful study of the history of the Assam Rifles would be invaluable. The paramilitary force began as a civil militia upon the entry of the British in Assam, and its growth corresponded intimately with the growing interests of British businesses in the region, in tea first, but soon, coal, timber and other forest produces, and much later, oil. Thankfully, for researchers, the Assam Rifles itself has published several autobiographies. The earliest of these was by Colonel L.W. Shakespear in 1929 under the title 'History of the Assam Rifles'. Subsequently, the paramilitary force has published two more; one was commissioned on the occasion of its completing 150 years of existence in 1985, though the book was published in 2003, and another on its completion of 175 years in 2010. These books, especially the earliest by Col. Shakespear, have become rich sources for lay readers and researchers alike, to get an insider's view of the history of this paramilitary unit, and its role in the evolution of the political shape and psychology of the Northeast as it is today.

This story can be said to begin with the discovery of tea in Assam. An East India Company employee, Robert Bruce, learned tea was native to the northern hills of Assam and realised the revenue potential it would command if it was systematically grown and marketed. He saw such an industry could rival the tea industry of China. He began doing the spade work to open the gate to a great industry, but did not live long enough to see it fructify. His brother, Charles, however, picked up the initiative where he left it and established, for the first time, tea nurseries in 1834.[13] In Col. Shakespear's words, 'the tea industry started by Mr. Bruce in the first tea garden at the mouth of the Kundil River near Sadiya about 1832 spread over Assam, to be taken up later in Cachar, where the first garden was laid out in 1855, until both valleys became covered with flourishing tea concerns. Coal and oil were discovered, the forests were found to be a source of valuable timber produces, and with improved communication Assam gradually became a very different country from what it was in 1826'.[14]

There is, however, a rival claim that it was not the Bruce brothers, but another man, Lieutenant Charlton, who was behind the discovery of tea and the pioneering of the tea industry in Assam.[15] This controversy, however, is unimportant to this chapter, and what is significant is only the fact that tea was discovered, opening up a whole new gamut of commercial interests, and this, in turn, radically transforming the security perception and administrative environment of the region.

This was at a time when surface communication was still very difficult in Assam and 'for many years the only means of entering and travelling about the province was by large country boats up the two great rivers, by smaller ones and "dug-outs" in the lesser streams, and by the roughest of roads, bridle-paths or tracks in the interior'.[16] Quite predictably, this scenario was about to change radically thereafter and the magnitude of this change is spell-binding.

> The rise of the tea trade brought steamers on to the two main rivers in 1850, while railway enterprise did not start till 1883, and then to connect Dibrugarh and the river with the coal-fields of Margherita and Ledo. This was followed by the Assam and Bengal Railway, some 600 miles in length, to connect the port of Chittagong with Dibrugarh, the first survey in connection with this undertaking taking place in 1893. Construction was begun about 1897, and the whole line with an exception to Gauhati from Lumding, was open by 1901. About 1910 the Eastern Bengal Railway extended its line from Santahar to Amingaon on the Brahmaputra, nearly opposite Gauhati, and the principal stations of the province were brought into direct and easy touch with the outer world.[17]

The British administration, in later years, 1895–96, even considered linking up Burma with Assam by railway lines to facilitate its trading activities in the region, thereby quite remarkably anticipating the idea of a 'Look East Policy' independent India began toying with only in the 1980s.

It had for some time past been under consideration to link the Burma railway systems to Prome, in the centre from Lumding via Berima in the Naga hills to the Mayangkhong valley and so through Manipur to Tammoo and Monywa, in the north from Margherita over Patkoi range down the Hukong valley and on through Maiankwan to Mongoung on to the present Shwebo-Myithkyina line.[18]

This quantum increase in commerce invariably meant a matching increase in the security establishment. Inevitably, the British administration began exploring the surrounding country. The British already had a strong security presence in the entire Northeast region then, most of which came under its Assam province. These were mostly the troops brought in during the First Burmese War, 'these being stationed at Goalpara, Bijni, Gauhati, Golaghat, Nowgong, Tezpur, Jorhat, Sibsagor, Lakshimpur and Sadiya in the Assam valley, and at Sylhet, Cherrapoonji, Jaintiapur and Silchar in the Surma valley, in both cases with a large number of detached posts'.[19] The administration also had a police force 'belonging to Bengal, divided into the armed Civil Police for protection of jails, treasuries, and for guards and escorts, and into the ordinary Civil Police for criminal administrative purposes'.[20]

After the Burmese had been conclusively defeated, the administration began to feel the financial pinch of maintaining regular troops in the region. With the threat perception of an external aggression somewhat removed, the role of the military was then turned to the maintenance of internal order. The breaches to this internal order at the time had largely to do with occasional raids into what was considered British-administered areas in the fertile productive plains, by fierce tribesmen who would swoop down from the surrounding mountains to plunder, loot and take captive British subjects. These raids were, as scholars have pointed out, unlike the presumptions of colonial writers, driven by necessity rather than the tribesmen's inherent savagery and bellicosity: 'more plausibly, they raided the plains out of sheer necessity, given that technical backwardness and poverty of resources kept the tribes dependent on adjoining areas for the supply of essential commodities'.[21] In other words, these raids happened 'because the uplands were less productive than the more fertile plains, plundering may have been their last resort'.[22]

Regardless of the causes for these raids, the British administration soon began to feel that reserving and engaging its large military presence solely to meet the challenges of these raids by the hillmen was becoming unnecessarily costly. After a review, the British administration first tried cutting down the number of military force, 'which about 1840 was brought down to four regiments, viz. the 1st Assam Light Infantry at Gauhati, the 2nd Assam Light Infantry at Sadiya, the Sylhet Light Infantry in Sylhet, and a Bengal Infantry Battalion at Silchar'.[23]

After this decision to reduce the presence of regular military in Assam, a need was felt for increasing the strength of the armed civil police. It was about 1830 when this pressure led to the idea of raising a 'levy' or civil militia. This civil militia was to be a separate force under the civil government, but not the same as armed police as this proposed civil militia was to perform military duties, and would replace the troops in certain parts of the border. Initially, the militia was officered by civil police officials, but in later years, its officers would come to be drawn from the military, therefore becoming a hybrid of military and police. 'It was to be a cheap semi-military body, clothed like the Civil Police and armed with the old Brown Bess, but it was badly paid, though slightly better than was the case with the ordinary police. The men were to carry out arduous duties, often involving fighting and danger in what were then most unhealthy jungle localities, and they were drawn from the armed Bengal Police at first comprising all classes, chiefly from Bengal.'[24]

The first of these militia units was raised in 1835 under the name 'Cachar Levy' by a civil officer E. R. Grange, and with a strength of 750 personnel of all ranks, namely, inspectors, head constables and constables.[25] Three years later, the Cachar Levy was followed by a similar unit, but of lesser strength, called the 'Jorhat Militia'. This unit later would come to be merged with the Cachar Levy. This amalgamated Cachar Levy was to undergo several transformations until eventually it developed into 'the fine force of the five Assam Rifles battalions'.[26]

The Assam Rifles remains as a paramilitary unit even today. Its soldiers are its own cadres, but its officers are from the Indian Army on deputation from their parent regiments for a stipulated few years. In recent years, some structural changes have been introduced and the Assam Rifles now have, besides the Indian Army officers who come on short deputations to provide the overall command, some permanent officers of its own, but with relatively limited promotional avenues. The force comes under the operational command of the Indian Army, however, although assigned military duties of a similar nature that the British administration spelled out for it – namely, keeping civil order in a hostile internal environment – it is not under the Defence Ministry. It instead comes under the umbrage of the Ministry of Home Affairs, like the civil police. This has often been a subject of internal friction, especially at the time of awards of the decadal 'Pay Commissions for Central Government Employees', for the Assam Rifles employees find themselves neither fully in the category of the police nor the military, though they are expected to shoulder the responsibilities of both in good measures. Despite these hiccups, it remains to this day, as the British defined it in the years of its inception, a fine fighting force. The controversies it enters into in civil law-keeping is not so much a reflection on its fighting quality or discipline, but the very nature of the responsibilities it was initially conceived to handle, and still handles. Its sins lie in its very inception and not so much born out of its discretion. This will be discussed in more detail later in this chapter when the issue of the propriety of sustained use of the military in situations of civil strife and the question of human rights is analysed.

Indeed, in many ways, it can be said the raising of the Cachar Levy in 1835 and its ultimate transformation into the paramilitary force, Assam Rifles, was a stroke of genius on the part of the British India colonial administration. Interestingly, the idea and convenience of a civil militia to be used in aid of civil administration is still not a redundant policy strategy of even the modern Indian state in meeting administrative needs in situations of radical internal dissents, which the nation is unwilling to either call a war or a simple internal law and order problem. In the colonial era, the administration could afford to be a little more forthright about their resort to legally dubious measures, but a democracy's unease in adopting similar measures is substantially different. The democratic states have had to excuse these conditions as 'states of exception' resulting from extreme and threatening internal dissents, therefore deserving extraordinary measures, including those that fall in the grey areas of constitutional law and ethics.[27] The creation of the Salwa Judum militias in the tribal belts of Chhattisgarh in central India to fight a raging communist insurgency is an example. The Salwa Judum has since been officially discontinued after a Supreme Court ruling in August 2011 that declared it illegal. Similarly, in Manipur, a civil militia unit called Village Defence Force has been created to fight insurgency. Its personnel are given the title of 'Special Police Officers' and although their service conditions are far inferior to personnel of the state's regular police constabularies, they are given the semblance of regular government employees as part of an extended police family, ostensibly to avoid challenges to their legality in the courts of law.

But alongside the remarkable history of the Assam Rifles, a profile of the security establishment in Assam at the time of its creation would be invaluable to understand the milieu in which the militia was raised. Many of the military units engaged in Assam at the time were also raised from the same recruitment base as the militia, and this being the case, an umbilical cord continued to connect them long after they began to follow independent trajectories of growth and responsibilities. The histories of these military units are interesting on their own too. Many of them were raised in Bengal, Assam being part of the British province of Bengal till 1874, and after many nomenclature changes, depending on where their services were pressed, many of them ultimately were turned into various regiments of the Gurkha Rifles. A description of this history by Col. Shakespear is illustrative and is quoted at some length below:

> Two battalions of the Assam Light Infantry started life as follows: The older one was raised in 1817 as the 'Cuttack Legion' at Chaubiaganj for the protection of the Cuttack district to the south of Calcutta, and in 1823 it was moved to Rangpur in Eastern Bengal, where it was renamed the 'Rangpur (Local) Light Infantry'. Four years later, after service in Assam, it became known as the '1st Assam Light Infantry' and with its headquarters at Gauhati remained in the province as such till 1864, when its title was changed to that of the '42nd Bengal Infantry (Goorkhas)' and in 1903 to that of the 6th Goorkha Rifles, as at present. The younger battalion, raised at Gauhati in 1835 for service in the province and later moved to Sadiya, was known as the 'Assam Seebundy Corps (Irregulars)' and was stationed in Sadiya district, where eight years later its title was changed to that of the '2nd Assam Light Infantry' on being brought on to the strength of the Bengal Army. In 1864 it became known as the '43rd Bengal Infantry (Assam Light Infantry),' and after two other slight changes received its present title of the 2/8th Goorkha Rifles. The Sylhet Local Battalion was raised in 1824 in Sylhet for the protection of that portion of Assam when the first Burmese war broke out. In 1864 its name was changed to that of the '44th Sylhet Light Infantry' on being incorporated into the Bengal Army, in 1901 this Regiment became known as the '44th Goorkha Rifles,' and in 1907 this was changed again to the 1/8th Goorkha Rifles, which it has since retained. All these regiments served entirely in Assam and Burma until 1899 taking part in every border expedition, after which year

they were sent to serve in other parts of India, the 43rd Goorkha Rifles being the first to be moved to garrison Chitral.[28]

Col. Shakespear also points out that 'for many years they were recruited locally or from Bengal, until, about 1870, they began to enlist Nepalese in increasing numbers'.[29] The recruitment bases were also among the various communities of Assam and other Northeast states, and even among the Shans and Kachins, the British colonial map of India being much bigger than the map of India that post-independence generations in India are accustomed to. Hence, the Assam Light Infantry, a corps of about 1,000 men, which had been raised in Cuttack in 1817, under the name of Cuttack Legion, and was subsequently transferred to the Rangpu district of Bengal after its permanent location in Assam, consisted mainly of 'Hindustanis and Gurkhas with a sprinkling of Manipuris and natives of the province'.[30] Likewise, the Sylhet Local Battalion – afterwards the Sylhet Light Infantry – with headquarters at Sylhet, entrusted with the defence of the Surma valley (Barak valley), which was raised in 1824, recruited chiefly Manipuris who had left their own country and settled in Sylhet and Cachar during the internal troubles and frequent Burmese invasions of the first quarter of the last century. Two companies of this regiment were stationed at Silchar, and at a later date, it also occupied Cherrapunji.[31] In similar fashion, the Sebundary regiment with 'Gauhati as headquarter . . . was composed mainly of Rabhas, Kacharis and other kindred tribes'.[32]

Even when this tradition ended, the Cachar Levy, which ultimately was to become the Assam Rifles, a name formally given to the unit only in 1917 after the end of World War I in recognition of the service it provided to the war effort,[33] still served as the feeder unit for the various Gurkha Rifles regiments. By this arrangement, experienced and outstanding recruits of the Cachar Levy, known by different names at different stages of its development, but mostly as the Assam Military Police (AMP), continued to graduate to be soldiers of the Gurkha Rifles. Such transfers obviously would have been considered as a jump in service hierarchy by the recruits, for it would have amounted to moving up from a mere militia body to a regular service in the British Indian Army. At one stage, the recruiting bases of the AMP shifted to among the traditional Nepali martial communities, Gurungs and Magars.[34] However, when about 1887, the Gurkha Rifles began their own independent recruitment drives from among these Nepali communities, the British Government put a ban on the AMP recruiting from among the Gurungs and Magars, thinking this would deplete the recruitment pool of the Gurkha Rifles. It was then that the recruitment bases of the militia shifted to other Nepali communities, such as the Rai, Moormi and Limbu from the Darjeeling area, as well as from among other martial tribes, such as the Jarua, Shan and Cachari.[35]

During World War I, the military police predecessor of the Assam Rifles was in a serious crisis. This was on one count because of the call by the Government of India to supply drafts for the Gurkha Rifles to fight the war in Europe. This seriously weakened the force, having sent almost all its experienced soldiers to the Gurkha Regiments. 'A.M.P by 1916 were supplying drafts to Goorkha Regiments at an average of 200 men a month until the end of 1917.'[36] At about this time, there was a widespread rebellion by the Kukis, which spread from the hills of Manipur right across the Lushai Hills (Mizoram) and the Chin Hills in Burma, in defiance of the government's move to raise a labour force of war porters from among these tribes to be sent to the war fronts in Europe. This left the administration to tackle the Kuki uprising with a military police force of largely new, inexperienced recruits, making the task all the more difficult, and therefore, the inordinate time taken in suppressing the rebellion.[37]

After the war, apart from the AMP being officially given the title 'Assam Rifles', in 1924, each of the five original units of the force, depending on which Gurkha Regiment each provided drafts for, was permanently affiliated with the particular Gurkha Regiment.[38] Under this scheme, the affiliations were as below:

1st Assam Rifles, A.R. (Lushai Hills Battalion) is affiliated with the 2nd Group, 2nd and 9th Gurkha Regiment, G.R.
2nd A.R. (Lakhimpur Battalion) is affiliated with the 5th Group, 7th and 10th G.R.
3rd A.R. (Naga Hills Battalion) is affiliated with the 1st Group, 1st and 4th G.R.
4th A.R. (Manipur Battalion) is affiliated with the 4th Group, 5th and 6th G.R.
5th A.R. (Darrang Battalion) is affiliated with the 3rd Group, 3rd and 8th G.R.[39]

The last named, 5th A.R., was disbanded in 1932 to make the force leaner and meaner, but re-raised on 1 April 1942 to meet the demands of World War II. 'It was to act as training battalion and also to shoulder operational responsibility on the Northern (Indo-Tibet) border.'[40]

It is interesting that the history of Assam Rifles runs virtually parallel to the history of the Northeast. Many of the major hill towns developed around where Assam Rifles headquarters were set up, although this could also be explained by the fact that the Assam Rifles headquarters were initially set up wherever the British administration decided would be their administrative headquarters, and these were always strategically vantage points – in most cases, the biggest villages in the area.

After the British left India in 1947, independent India inherited the Assam Rifles, as it did all or most other institutions of the British administration. It is interesting to note here why India ended up inheriting almost intact an administrative legacy from its former colonisers, unlike some other former colonies, which opted different routes to decolonisation. A. G. Noorani briefly explains the legal point surrounding the circumstances, which culminated in such an outcome, saying the very wording of the Indian Independence Act, 1947, declaring the end of British paramountcy in India (and Pakistan), spelled this out. He contrasts this with the route to independence that Republic of Ireland and Burma took at the end of British paramountcy: 'The leaders of India and Pakistan accepted transfers of power from British hands and devolution on India and Pakistan of treaties which the British rulers had concluded. They were estopped from contesting that position. They consciously did not follow the Irish model.'[41]

This was also the route taken by Canada and Australia. In the case of the establishment of the Republic of Ireland, the decision of the Irish leaders was radically different:

> The British Parliament enacted the Government of Ireland Act, 1920 to establish separate parliaments for Northern Ireland and the rest of the country. Irish Nationalists used its machinery to elect a House of Commons, just as India's leaders used the Constituent Assembly elected under the Cabinet Mission's Plan of 16 May 1946. The Irish called this House Dail Eireann. Britain and Ireland signed a Treaty on 6 December 1921 on the establishment of the Irish Free State. The British Parliament enacted the Irish Free State Constitution act, 1922. To this day Ireland holds that the State's power is derived directly from its people who elected the Dail Eireann, and not from the British Parliament.[42]

For India and Pakistan, it was a transfer of power. The Irish allowed the transfer of power to happen, but once this was done, abandoned the earlier power structure and built a new one of their own making. Burma provides the third route. Here, the British simply relinquished power and left Burma

to fend for itself: 'The Burma Independence Act, 1947 provided simply that "on the appointed day, Burma shall become an independent country" (Section 1). Power was relinquished; it was not transferred.'[43]
Like all other major institutions in India, such as the legislature, judiciary, executive and the army, the Assam Rifles is also very much the same paramilitary organisation the British built, and its purpose too remains very much the same – to ensure internal security. If, in the British days, the objective was to subdue hill tribes and protect British revenue interests in the plains, today, its main responsibility is to fight insurgency and to establish area dominance in insurgency-prone areas. The force, though today more military than the police, coming as it does under the operational command of the Indian Army, has still retained some of its founding credos and principles. Its motto, loudly displayed everywhere any unit of the forces is present, 'Friends of the Hill People', encapsulates this succinctly. In the past, unlike the army, which maintains a distance from the civil population to the maximum extent possible, the Assam Rifles, in keeping with its origin as a civil militia, has been known for fraternising with the civilian population, but also gathering intelligence as a way of sizing them up and keeping them under check, therefore in its own way, being in control of these insurgency-prone areas.

Oinam and paramilitary

However, the flaw of this approach, especially in tackling ethnic insurgency in a democratic state, has been exposed time and again, the most serious being at a Poumai Naga village called Oinam in the Senapati district of Manipur. The human costs of these lapses were also truly agonising. On 9 July 1987, on a day the camp was sparsely guarded and nearly deserted, it was overrun by guerrillas of the Naga underground organisation, National Socialist Council of Nagaland (NSCN).[44] The NSCN also carried away a huge amount of arms and ammunitions from the camp. The retaliation of the Assam Rifles was brutal, to say the least, and it was the villages around the area they had been fraternising all the while which bore the brunt of this vengeful and murderous violence.

Describing life in Oinam village in the years after the establishment of an Assam Rifles post, well-known human rights worker and Supreme Court lawyer Nandita Haksar, who fought a four-year-long court case against the Assam Rifles to bring justice to the devastated villagers after the carnage, writes in her book *The Judgment That Never Came: Army Rule in North*

East India, co-authored with her partner in human rights activism and life, Sebastian M Hongray:

> Down the years Oinam expanded and many houses came up nearer the Post. But they were not perceived as a threat by the Assam Rifles who were allowed to bring their families to the Post. They built a canteen and a Volley Ball court inside the Post. Soon the people of Oinam and the Assam Rifles challenged each other to football and volleyball matches. Afterwards they enjoyed a cup of tea together. Many soldiers attended the local church and were invited into homes to enjoy the warmth of Naga hospitality. On some occasions a Naga leader could be heard singing a ghazal along with the Assam Rifles officers around a blazing fire.[45]

Describing again the atmosphere on the day of the fateful attack, the authors write:

> Life at the Oinam Assam Rifles Post on July 9, 1987 was as relaxed as it had been for many years. On that fateful day only two Junior Commissioned Officers (JCOs) were present at the Post; there were no senior officers. There were also around 40 soldiers apart from the non-combatants such as the cooks, the canteen-in-charge, and seven families of the Assam Rifles.[46]

The authors' account continues that it was a normal relaxed day – farmers were looking forward to some respite after the completion of rice transplantation, the village elders were eager for the festive season of *Saleni pa*, the sacred feast, and in another corner, a young school teacher, Th. Stephen, was taking his classes, but eager for the day to conclude so he could return home to attend to his indisposed wife at his village, Ngamju, a seven-mile walk down the hill from Oinam. And then, all of a sudden, the attack came, describe Nandita and Hongray. But, 'at the Assam Rifles Post the relaxed atmosphere was shattered by the sound of gunshots. An officer of the Naga army ordered everyone to get into the dining room and as everyone scurried in the door was locked from outside. There were three Assam Rifles soldiers guarding the Quarter Guard and they fired but they did not have a chance. Soon eight soldiers and one JCO lay dead. Three others were severely injured and lay bleeding'.[47]

Stephen, the school teacher, would also be sucked into the violent developments by default. He too heard the shots, and before long, the NSCN men came and took away the older boys from his school to be their porters to carry away and hide the arms looted from the Assam Rifles post. 'There were 150 pieces of arms and more than 125 thousand rounds of ammunitions to be carried.'⁴⁸ The brutal retaliation of the Assam Rifles was beyond imagination. It returned with reinforcement and began a campaign of unprecedented carnage to avenge the attack as well as to recover the lost weapons under an operation codenamed 'Operation Bluebird'. For almost four months, Oinam and the surrounding villages literally lived in hell. At the end of the four months, the Assam Rifles claimed most of the weapons lost were recovered, but the price was also disproportionately heavy. In all, 14 villagers were killed, many more injured, more than 100 houses razed to the ground, and because the villagers were confined to their village, there was a huge failure of crops.⁴⁹

It was a vital lesson for everyone – the Assam Rifles, as well as the villagers. A new distance between the forces and villagers, both physical and psychological, was also inevitable. Jungles were cleared around the Oinam Assam Rifles post, homes which had come too close were pushed back, the fraternising spirit cooled, and when it revived, it was only as part of the larger official military–civic programmes, and therefore, the soul was missing. Understandably, it was also reported that in the aftermath of the Assam Rifles operation, recruitment of young men and women to the underground NSCN took an appreciable leap from Oinam and the surrounding area.

For months, and indeed years, after the Oinam village incident, the debate raged both in the official circles as well as among the civil society as to who was the more guilty party in the case. Here was a situation in which a paramilitary organisation had fraternised too closely with a population in a zone of civil unrest, and because of it, paid a heavy price. The official argument was that the devastating attack at the Oinam Assam Rifles post could not have been possible had it not been for the support of the villagers. There was not a hint of intelligence passed on to the security men of the presence of the militants in their villages and the militants' intent of attacking the post. The argument also goes that after the attack, the villagers would have helped the militants in transporting what was estimated to be nearly a ton of weapons and ammunitions from the post to various hideouts of the militants in the jungles for there was no way the militants themselves could have accomplished this feat. Could all these have been merely a case of a population caught in the crossfire, and that the villagers did what they did out of bullying coercion? It is probable that coercion and the fear of reprisal might have been a factor, but could these have been the only factors?

Beyond the charges of the establishment, a far deeper question remains to be addressed. Does the part played by these villages in the militant raid on the Assam Rifles post mean the villagers were complicit in the NSCN attack? This answer can never be in black and white. To attempt to do so would be to betray a total lack of understanding of the sinews and fibres that make an insurrection, and more specifically, the Naga insurrection – which all who have studied the phenomenon of insurgency in the Northeast would agree is the most fundamental and, therefore, enduring. Insurgency in the context of the Northeast is a radical movement of the people, and in the case of the Nagas, at least for a long time, was the most total of all. Within this understanding, while the insurgents themselves become what Frantz Fanon called the 'mailed fist',[50] the larger causes and energies that drive these insurrections are shared by the people among whom the rebellions have erupted. The 'mailed fist' is merely a delivery system for these shared angers and aspirations of the people. In their unadulterated sense, these insurgencies are truly a people's war. This is how Nandita and Sebastian acknowledge this:

> For the Assam Rifles the villagers were all insurgents; for us they were merely Naga villagers who had become victims of a brutal counter-insurgency operation.
>
> Now, looking back over the events, more than twenty years later one question still begs to be answered: what was the source of the tremendous courage of the villagers who refused to betray the Naga insurgents? Why did the village elders and school teachers prefer to be tortured to death rather than tell where the insurgents were hiding?
>
> The people did not look upon themselves as mere victims. They were aware of their deep roots in history. And this was the source of their remarkable courage in the face of the cruelty and violence of the Indian State.
>
> They knew that the military repression was aimed not so much at the recovery of the stolen arms but at wiping out their history as a people. And they were not ever going to allow that to happen.[51]

What is indicated is the need for a more nuanced understanding of the complexities of insurgency, and with it, the suitability as well as the propriety of the use of the military in tackling an ethnic insurrection. It may be helpful in this regard to briefly consider the larger question of unrests among ethnic and indigenous populations as such, the universality of which has made even the United Nations take note and make an effort to redefine the notion of human rights so as to incorporate the indigenous world and its outlook. A failure at coming to grip with this understanding has added a different dimension to the various conflicts in the Northeast region. The prolonged use of the military in tackling insurgency in the region under a controversial AFSPA is a case in point.

The AFSPA is a legal mechanism to have the Indian Army operate not against external aggression, as is the normal duty of any army in the world, but in situations of civil insurrection. The Act is applicable to the seven Northeastern states of Arunachal Pradesh, Assam, Manipur, Meghalaya, Mizoram, Nagaland and Tripura, and the state of Jammu and Kashmir, and becomes operational if any of these states, or regions within the states, have been declared as disturbed. In the years since its inception, the AFSPA has come up for strong criticism from various human rights watch bodies, including the UNHCR, not only because it gives the army sweeping powers in its policing duties, but also because army personnel acting under its jurisdiction are given legal immunity from being prosecuted under ordinary law for excesses they may have committed.[52]

A panoramic sketch of the nature and reasons for the militarisation of the Northeast in the postcolonial era will be necessary to ensure the entirety of the picture is placed in the proper perspective. This is so because the tendency has been, especially among civil rights campaigners, to do a headcount of military against civil population to create graphic pictures of what they would then interpret as evidence of state oppression on the pretext of fighting civil unrest. This is only a partial truth, for there can be no denying that militarisation of the region is not just insurgency-related, or an inherited legacy of British colonialism only. A relook at the region's political geography should make it absolutely clear why, other than for the need to fight insurgency, there is such a disproportionate presence of the military in the Northeast.

Arms race and militarisation

In 1947, at the time of its independence, India believed its only immediate worry was a hostile Pakistan, and in the context of the Northeast, East Pakistan. The threat of aggression from East Pakistan was not too grave, but it must be remembered when the Radcliffe Line was being drawn to partition the country, the Assam unit of the Muslim League was campaigning hard to have Assam awarded to Pakistan, and this would naturally have been a cause for worry for India even though Assam ultimately remained with

India. This alarm, however, would soon be overtaken by another much greater perceived looming danger in the north, when in 1950, China's Red Army entered and claimed sovereignty over Tibet. Then, 12 years later, in 1962, India would suffer a humiliating defeat in a short but brutal border skirmish with China.

But even before all these developments, the other cataclysmic event – World War II – devastated the region, especially Manipur and Nagaland. Indeed, for these frontier states, their World War II experiences were a dramatic opening to the modern world, as much as they represented unimaginable trauma. They had been exposed to the British colonial army much earlier and some of them had also seen action during World War I in various European theatres of the war, either as soldiers of the Assam Rifles recruited into the Gurkha Rifles, or else as volunteers directly enlisted into the Labour Corps, but these were nothing compared to the scale of violence they witnessed in their own home grounds, suddenly transformed into a very intensely fought front of World War II. The world knew very little and still knows very little of the Imphal–Kohima front during World War II, but in April 2013, a decision by vote in a contest by the British National Army Museum to identify 'Britain's Greatest Battle' ever voted this battlefront as the most significant of all the battles Britain has fought in its entire history, just ahead of D-Day and Waterloo, in that order.[53]

The battles of Imphal and Kohima saw the British and Indian forces, under the overall command of Lieutenant-General William Slim, repel the Japanese invasion of India and helped turn the tide of the war in the Far East.

The scale and sweep of modern warfare, the destructive capacities of weapons employed, the sizes of troops, all so suddenly introduced in the region, were, simply unprecedented and beyond the ordinary imagination of the people on whose grounds two most powerful alien armies in the world of the time were engaged in a do-or-die struggle for possession of their lands. The figures of casualties suffered by the two armies stand as convincing alibi of the shock and awe the locals would have gone through. The Japanese bombing of Imphal began in May 1942, but the main infantry battle of Imphal lasted from 8 March to 3 July 1944, and in it, the British employed four infantry divisions, one armoured brigade and one parachute brigade, and the Japanese engaged three infantry divisions and one tank regiment. The casualties of killed and wounded on the British side was 17,500 and on the Japanese side, they were 53,879.[54]

In the battle of Kohima, the British had one infantry brigade of about 1,500 men fit for duty before they were reinforced by two infantry divisions, one 'Chindit' Brigade and one motor brigade. The Japanese brought one infantry division of about 12,000 to 15,000 fighting fit troops. The casualty figure of the dead and wounded is estimated at 4,064 for the British and 5,764 for the Japanese.[55] Although civilian casualties in terms of direct deaths caused was not too heavy, the war, nonetheless, and expectedly, resulted in extreme trauma and misery for the people. In the short run, there were the all-round uncertainties, with people at very short notices having to evacuate homes in towns and wherever else there were military concentrations, to take shelter in safer villages in the peripheral regions, therefore forcing unsafe drinking water and living conditions on them, causing outbreaks of killer cholera and typhoid epidemics and so on. In the longer run, there were also the harms caused by disruptions in education, civil amenities and overall trauma of witnessing and experiencing violence.[56]

No proper study has ever been done on the extent of post-traumatic stress disorder the populations were left burdened with after the war, nor has there been any substantial effort to explore in art or science if there are any connections between the violence witnessed then with the violence the two states are plagued by even today. Even if the psychological impacts were not too heavy, there were other consequences. The war also obviously left behind arms and ammunition dumps, especially by the vanquished Japanese Army in their desperate retreat. It is anybody's guess these would have augmented the fire power of many early generations of insurgent guerrillas.

The fact that World War II entered India from Manipur and Nagaland, though stopped at this point, also is a loud testimony to how important this route is strategically – therefore, another reason to ensure its militarisation. It is also for the same reasons that two Asian Highways, AH-1 and AH-2, cut through Manipur today. This strategic importance was immediately recognised by the British administrators in the nineteenth century. In Alexander Mackenzie's words, 'the Manipur Valley forms the great highway between the British Provinces of Assam and Cachar on the one side, and the Kubo Valley, which now belongs to Burma, on the other'.[57] Thankfully, for India, its eastern neighbour, Burma (now Myanmar) is far from hostile. Much before the arrival of the British, this was also an ancient trade route linking the region with the rest of South-east Asia and further on. Today, there is a much hyped, though little seen, Look East Policy of the Government of India to reopen this trade route again to integrate the economy of the Northeast to that of the prosperous Association of South-East Asian Nations (ASEAN) region.

As we have seen, not long after the dust from the World War II experience settled, another traumatic event, the Partition of India, followed – this was, in turn, to be followed by the invasion of Tibet by the People's Liberation Army of China in 1950. Tibet suddenly transformed from a neutral country, culturally and religiously bonded to India, to a wing of a rival power. Though not immediately a threat then, it was only a matter of time before it did become one. Tensions over the boundary between India and China also arose almost immediately, as China made it plain it did not recognise the McMahon Line in the Northeast sector or India's claimed boundary in the Ladakh sector of Kashmir. This friction between the two giant neighbours was never allowed to be defused until border skirmishes gave way to a short, but full-scale war. Under the circumstance, it was a foregone conclusion that militarisation would be the destiny of the Northeast for the foreseeable future.

It is next to impossible to acquire, and understandably not permitted as well to make public assessments of classified information on military deployment, but from open sources on the internet and unclassified information made available to the media by the government and the military, today, it is public knowledge that almost the entire Eastern Command of the Indian Army is focused on the Northeast. In addition, India has announced it will be raising a mountain brigade in the near future, to be deployed in the Northeast along the McMahon Line. This will be part of a total of four divisions to be brought into the Northeast region in a five-year expansion plan, bringing up troop strength by 90,000, over and above the 120,000 already stationed in the region.[58] India has also announced the deployment of the Brahmos supersonic cruise missile, with a flight range of 290 km, and has now tested the Agni V missile, capable of hitting any Chinese city. This is besides two squadrons of Sukhoi 30MKI fighter planes with a base at Tezpur in Assam.[59]

The military modernisation and build-up is even larger on the other side of the McMahon Line in the Tibetan Autonomous Region of China. This includes the replacement of 'China's old liquid fuelled, nuclear capable CSS-3 intermediate range ballistic missile, intercontinental missiles such as the DF-31 and DF-31A with range of 5,500 km to 8,000 km, 13 Border Defence Regiments amounting to around 300,000 PLA troops, upgrading of airfields etc. There are also an additional six of China's elite Rapid Reaction Force, RRF divisions stationed in Chengdu, which can be airlifted to the Indian border within 48 hours'.[60] Almost as a parallel offensive on the political front, China has been increasingly employing aggressive rhetoric and stance on its claim to Arunachal Pradesh.[61]

It would be naive to believe militarisation resulting out of this friction between India and China can be simply wished away. Such an outcome can only come after a comprehensive settlement has been reached on the border issue and the border tension between the two countries defused conclusively. For this to happen, there are larger issues of politics involved, not the least the Tibetan question, which is unlikely to die just as yet, and India is very much entwined and implicated in this by default as the Tibetan Government in Exile under the leadership of the 14th Dalai Lama is situated on its soil.

This larger issue of rivalry between India and China, however, is not the focus of this book, and the brief foray into the subject is just to distinguish between the two reasons for militarisation happening in the Northeast, of which the one just described would fall within what can be considered as legitimate security concerns and measures of any country. After all, the role of any army is essentially to ensure security of its land and people from perceived threats of external aggressions. And such a perception is a reality on either side of the border at this moment, though in recent times, growing trade relations between the two countries have established a growing network of interrelations at the individual and institutional levels, thereby beginning to provide hope and vision of a time in the future when scenarios of military conflicts have been rendered improbable, if not redundant.

Internal security

Militarisation happens at another level for a different reason as well, as mentioned earlier. For whatever its compulsions, India has also been using its military might in situations of civil unrests in the Northeast and Kashmir for a prolonged period, and unlike the first scenario, it is this one that has come up for severe scrutiny within the country as well as internationally. To enable the use of the military in civil policing duties, India has enacted an infamous, extraordinary law, the Armed Forces Special Powers Act (Assam and Manipur) 1958, later to be amended to become Armed Forces (Special Powers) Act. The necessity for such an Act was first felt in the then Naga Hills district of Assam, when the Naga National Council (NNC), under the leadership of Angami Zapu Phizo, after their peaceful campaigns – including by a Naga plebiscite in 1951 and the boycott of independent India's first election in 1952 – to secure sovereignty for the Nagas from the newly born Indian republic, took to arms in the mid-1950s. In 1972, the Act was amended to make it applicable to all the other new Northeast states created out of the former British province of Assam, as well as to Tripura and Manipur.

A rough idea of how and how much of this second form of militarisation of the Northeast region was widespread is available from the account of Neville Maxwell, a British-Australian journalist, to whom the classified Henderson Brooks-Prem Bhagat Report on India's disastrous 1962 war with China was leaked. Maxwell writes in his book *India's China War* that 'the Army's peacetime deployment reflected a balance between the possibility of war with Pakistan and the requirements of internal security, almost as much a consideration with Indian military planners as it had been with their British predecessors'.[62]

He continues, 'these dispositions continued until 1956, and the Army was more or less static in size as well as equipment. The rebellion of the Naga tribes in 1956 necessitated a progressive build-up of forces in the north-east, and by end of the 1950s a division was tied down in guerrilla fighting in the Naga hills'.[63] He also says that unlike West Pakistan, East Pakistan presented no strategic threat. However, as the 'demands of the Naga campaign increased, so more units of the Indian Army were siphoned across from Punjab to the north-east. New units were formed to sustain the Punjab force's strength, and consequently the Army began slowly to grow again'.[64]

He also writes of how the army formations were actually changed, and a new formation XXXIII Corps, with headquarters (HQ) in Shillong, was introduced.[65] The XXXIII Corps itself would ultimately be sidelined with the hasty formation of another corps, the IV Corps, to facilitate the takeover of the crucial front marked by the McMahon Line, by Gen. B. M. Kaul and push away his detractors and sceptics of India's forward policy along the McMahon Line, without actually shaking up the existing established hierarchy, therefore avoiding possible unrests.[66]

Maxwell has also publicly released what he claims are 100 pages of the document on his website on 18 March 2014, curiously on the eve of the Indian parliamentary elections scheduled the next month, in April 2014. The released section of what is claimed to be the Henderson Brooks report does corroborate closely Maxwell's description of the politics that went into the Indian Army's preparation for its 1962 forward policy, codenamed 'Operation Leghorn', aimed at evicting Chinese troops from the Thag La ridge.[67] Details of such and other internal politics in the army at the time, however, is not the primary concern of this book. I will, instead, return to a discussion of the army's deployment to fight civil unrest and the human rights situations this gives rise to.

AFSPA and human rights

As noted earlier, the AFSPA gives soldiers, even of the rank of a non-commissioned officer, the power to 'use force to the extent of causing death' on mere suspicion. The soldier can also 'enter or destroy shelters without warrant', again only on suspicion that these structures were, or could be, used by insurgents as hideouts. But most dangerous of all, the AFSPA gives sweeping legal immunity to soldiers accused of excesses during operations under the Act.

On the face of it, a soldier accused of committing atrocities under the Act can be prosecuted, but to do so, a special prosecution sanction has to be first had from the Union Home Ministry. The emptiness of such a supposed legal avenue available to victims will be sworn by numerous victims, just as a 7 February 2012 report in *The Hindu* indicated. The report said that in all, 42 requests by the Jammu and Kashmir police to the Union Home Ministry in the last four years (of the publication of this *The Hindu* news) to initiate legal proceedings against army soldiers were flatly rejected. 'Thirty-one of these cases in which sanction was denied relate to rape, culpable homicide or murder. The others involve a wide variety of crimes, ranging from criminal trespass to illegal confinement. In not a single case, *The Hindu* found, had sanction been granted.'[68]

This is a demonstration of how impervious this legal shield is, and therefore, how frustrating and hopeless it is for victims seeking justice in such cases. I will, however, not go into the details of what atrocities have resulted under the AFSPA. There are too many well-documented cases, thanks to a surfeit of human rights NGOs, and few or no soldier ever has been punished for them. Suffice it to say there is a woman called Irom Sharmila – 40 in 2014, who has been on a hunger strike for over 14 years and still continuing – who is trying to have the AFSPA repealed, after troops, angered by an ambush attempt on a convoy, went berserk in her neighbourhood at Malom in an Imphal outskirt, killing 10 people, including an elderly lady and a young child, at a nearby bus stand and injuring scores more in a week-long rampage in nearby villages, more than 50 of whom had to be hospitalised. She has been all along interned in solitary confinement at a special jail ward of the Jawaharlal Nehru Hospital, Imphal.

Furthermore, the United Nations Human Rights Commission (UNHRC) on several occasions has, in no uncertain terms, said the AFSPA has no role in a democracy and that India must repeal it. The latest of these UN pleas was by Christof Hyns, the UN Special Rapporteur on Extrajudicial, Summary or Arbitrary Execution, during his fact-finding mission to India in 2012.[69]

Earlier, the UN had also called for an explanation from the Indian government on why the AFSPA should not attract censure for racial discrimination in a Committee on Eradication of Racial Discrimination (CERD) case, for the Act is applicable only in certain regions of 'non-mainstream' India, namely, the Northeast and Kashmir.[70] An answer is still awaited despite several reminders. The AFSPA was promulgated in the Northeast from 1958 and it was extended to Kashmir in 1990. It is pertinent to note that in central India, where a tribal Leftist rebellion, popularly referred to as Maoist rebellion, is raging, one which even a former prime minister of India, Manmohan Singh, had termed as the greatest threat to India's integrity since its independence, the AFSPA is not invoked.

The AFSPA is, undoubtedly, a grotesque response by any democratic standard to a civil situation. The Act has contravened the universal understanding of rectitude which is even more fundamental than the notion of law or the legal definition of rights.[71] Laws can be bad, as the AFSPA obviously is in the opinion of many, and soldiers, even those who commit excesses under it, are playing by rule of law. Bad laws, therefore, are ones that do not inspire a sense of rectitude or 'rightness'.

This distinction between 'rights' and 'rightness', the 'law' and 'rectitude' is poignantly brought out by celebrated theatre director from Manipur, Ratan Thiyam's in his play 'The Blind Age',[72] in which he imagines what might have been after the Mahabharata War of the Hindu epic, in which five Pandava brothers kill their 100 Kourava cousins in the name of upholding goodness. While it may be well within the moral limits of religion for the virtuous Pandavas to destroy their wrongdoer cousins, there was something simply not 'right' about the devastating war that destroyed so much so totally. The magnitude and scale of the physical as well as spiritual destruction simply dwarfed any justification of the war, even if religion and its moral codes sanctioned it. It provoked the feeling that the definition of virtue would have to be qualified by the consequences of its defence too.

To be ethical, then, the play seemed to be saying, is to be able to see this 'rightness' of action and deed not just through the prism of any defined religion or legal frames, but through a filter fashioned from the realisation of the common human predicament. It will also not be easy to hit this 'right' decision for it is a moving target. The only way to arrive at this truth will have to be through relentless, sometimes agonising, self-questioning, as indeed the characters in Thiyam's play are made to go through.

The script is obviously inspired by the discourse between Krishna and Arjuna in the *Bhagavad Gita*, a small section of the Mahabharata which Amartya Sen in *The Argumentative Indian* summarises as 'a tussle between two contrary moral positions – Krishna's emphasis on doing one's duty, on one side, and Arjuna's focus on avoiding bad consequences (and generating good ones), on the other'.[73] Thiyam seems to be taking Arjuna's vantage, as indeed many, including Sen, feel is not easy to ignore despite losing out to Krishna's sermonising advice, for 'the tragic desolation that the post-combat and post-carnage land – largely the Indo-Gangetic plain – seems to face towards the end of the Mahabharata can even be seen as something of a vindication of Arjuna's profound doubts. Arjuna's contrary arguments are not really vanquished, no matter what the message of the Bhagavad gita is meant to be'.[74]

Away from the arts, two lectures, one by Prof. Ashis Nandy at the Jama Millia Hamdard University, New Delhi, in 2006, and another by Prof. Charles Douglas Lummis, in Imphal, in 2005, arrived at very much the same conclusion. Both used the same information from a study which said the twentieth century was the most violent century in human history, and during its course, over a 100 million people died of state violence. The century saw two world wars, two atom bombs, the Holocaust, devastating revolutions, genocides, ethnic cleansing campaigns and the list goes on. Prof. Nandy's lecture was on the structure of politics and power in India, and Prof. Lummis' was on the nature and character of the nation state.

The nation state was once optimistically thought to be the culmination of human social organisation. Prof. Lummis recalled Max Weber's definition of the nation state as the repository of all powers and the paramount institution, which holds monopoly over 'legitimate violence', implying also it has another extraordinary right – the Right to Belligerence or to declare war. The violence vested in the nation state, both as an instrument for internal administration as well as in wars with other nation states, then, is to be considered legitimate, for this violence is deemed to be for the good of the larger national community. But it is precisely this 'legitimate violence' vested in the state that caused the deaths of 100 million people.

The question in the end is, again, how legitimate is this 'legitimate violence' if it can cause such a magnitude of devastation?[75] After the devastations of World War II, including, not the least, the Holocaust, the urgency for an answer to this question manifested in the birth of a collective conscience of the international community to check the unlimited powers of the nation state. Of great significance in this regard are the series of resolutions of the Geneva Conventions of 1949, a body of rules to protect victims of war, and earlier The Hague Conventions of 1899 and 1907, which framed rules to moderate the brutality of war. The UN's Universal Declaration of Human Rights, part of this same attempt at answering this question, was thus conceived as a charter of rights to protect the individual from state excesses.

This distinction between law and rectitude, however, is not without complications. This is especially so in assessments and reportage of cases of violent conflicts between state and non-state combatants. Human rights and journalists covering these conflicts will be well aware of this, for often, they too would have faced the allegation of partisanship to the non-state[76] players and that they only report atrocities by state players as human rights violations and not so when the same atrocities are committed by the non-state players.

The defence against this charge from the standpoint of international law is interesting. That state atrocities against the non-state amount to human rights violation and not the other way around is the mandate of the UN charter by which human rights is defined. It is not as if the framers of the human rights charter were not aware of this limitation of the set of rights they drew up, and this is why the nomenclature they chose is 'Universal Declaration of Human Rights' and not 'Declaration of Universal Human Rights'.[77] There is, or can be, nothing as Universal Human Rights though the growing debate on non-derogable international customary laws, peremptory laws and *jus cogen*, especially in the wake of the gaining momentum of the movement for the inclusion of the indigenous peoples' vision of rights into the Universal Charter of Human Rights, are evidence of the need for the evolution of what may be considered as more 'universal human rights'. Legal justice and moral justice must get as close to each other as possible, but it is imaginable how this would not have been easy, if not impossible, for the original framers of the human rights charter to think of a complete congruence.

Acknowledgement of this distance between 'rights' and 'rectitude' is, however, vital, for, then, the effort to bridge it would not be given up. It indeed has not been given up. The introduction of additional protocols to the Geneva Conventions of 1949 is evidence of this. Protocol II is particularly significant to this argument for it calls for a new additional set of rules to govern 'non-international conflicts', in other words, conflicts resulting out of radical internal dissents within a nation state. The Geneva Conventions originally dealt with the consequences of wars between nation states, but this proved inadequate 'as 80 percent of the victims of armed conflicts since 1945 have been victims of non-international conflicts and that non-international conflicts are often fought with more cruelty than international conflicts. The aim of the present Protocol (Protocol II) is to extend the essential rules of the law of armed conflicts to internal wars'.[78]

But this protocol ran into trouble for the 'fear that the Protocol might affect State sovereignty, prevent governments from effectively maintaining law and order within their borders and that it might be invoked to justify outside intervention led to the decision of the Diplomatic Conference at its fourth session to shorten and simplify the Protocol. Instead of the 47 Articles proposed by the ICRC the Conference adopted only 28. The essential substance of the draft was, however, maintained'. However, 'the provisions on the activity of impartial humanitarian organisations were adopted in a less binding form than originally foreseen'.[79]

Even after the thrust of this protocol drawn up by the International Committee for Red Cross (ICRC) had been softened, most countries with serious internal dissents within their territories refrained from signing or ratifying it. Predictably, India is one of them, and in the words of well-known jurist and columnist, A.G. Noorani, in an article in the *Economic and Political Weekly*, India ratified the Geneva Conventions of 1949, but like many other countries, 'it steadfastly refuses to ratify the Protocols'.[80] This is another big hurdle before the effort to bridge the gap between human rights and rectitude. Under the circumstance, human rights workers and journalists cannot be blamed for reporting only state atrocities as human rights violation and not those of the non-state combatants.

The Indian state's dilemma, as indeed most other states facing problems of secessionist insurgencies, in ratifying this protocol is, if they did so, non-state armed combatants would become acknowledged as putative or else aspiring states and their conflict with the state, thus, would have gained some status of war. Therefore, although ratification would have put these non-state combatants under the purview of international humanitarian norms of conducts of warfare, the states they fight against would much rather have these conflicts described as mere internal matters of law and order breaches, to be tackled by their own national laws with no need to invoke international warfare norms.

The 1997 Supreme Court ruling in the *Naga People's Movement for Human Rights versus the Union of India*, presided over by Justice J.S. Verma, which upheld the state's contention that the AFSPA was constitutional, reflected precisely this dilemma. In a nutshell, it ruled that there was no war. Clause 6 says, 'The Central Act cannot be regarded as a colourable legislation or a fraud on the Constitution. It is not a measure intended to achieve the same result as contemplated by a Proclamation of Emergency under Article 352 or a proclamation under Article 356 of the Constitution',[81] therefore implying that the occasions which demanded the invocation of the AFSPA were matters of internal discords of law and order breaches. Yet, these internal discords are grave enough to justify the use of the state's machine of war. Clause 12 says, 'The provision contained in Sections 130 and 131 Cr.P.C. cannot be treated as comparable and adequate to deal with the situation requiring the use of armed forces in aid of civil power as envisaged by the Central Act'.[82]

To return to another lecture by Prof. Lummis, the second one he gave in Imphal, in which he talked of an innate resistance to violence in every normal human being. Prof. Lummis, who is also an ex-soldier, said it is extremely difficult for someone who is not a pathological killer to lift a weapon, take aim at a stranger and pull the trigger. One of the most important trainings a soldier has to undergo is to overcome this innate resistance against killing another. This is done through rigorous, sometimes mindless drills, cultivating blind adherence to authority and a brainwashing regime that the men the soldier is expected to kill are evil, despicable, or else, are sub-humans. Even after such training, it is still not easy, and soldiers often suffer from Post-Traumatic Stress Disorder (PTSD), after having gone through the experience of violence, which involves killing.[83]

The AFSPA, therefore, is an aberration and ugly blemish on Indian democracy. While it is expected of the Indian state to meet violent challenges, it is a demonstration of the weakness of the liberal imagination in the country that no democratic response to replace the AFSPA has come about in the more than six decades the AFSPA has been in operation. This is despite the consensus among rights-conscious liberal civil society in the country that AFSPA has outlived its utility, the liberal dilemma as to what must replace the Act continues.[84]

There have been several attempts on the part of the union government to make amends, and these include, first and foremost, the probe report of a 5-member committee it set up on 19 November 2004, headed by (retired) Supreme Court Justice Jeevan Reddy. The committee's findings and recommendations were ready six months later, on 6 June 2005. The Union government, obviously under pressure from military lobbies against any dilution of the Act, however, has never made the committee's recommendations public, though the English daily *The Hindu* used its wide resources and enterprise to get hold of a copy of the document and webcast it verbatim.[85] In essence, the committee asks for the incorporation of the AFSPA into civil law under the Unlawful Activities Prevention Act, 1967, purging, among others, the legal immunity clause of the AFSPA.

This was followed by the second Administrative Reforms Commission, constituted by the Govt. of India, Ministry of Personnel on 31 August 2005, under the chairmanship of Veerapa Moily, which too recommended virtually what the Jeevan Reddy Committee did, saying the 'discriminatory Armed Forces (Special Powers) Act, 1958 should be abolished and Unlawful Activities (Prevention) Act 1967 must take its place'.[86] Another three-member commission, headed by Santosh Hegde, a retired Supreme Court judge, appointed by the Supreme Court in January 2013, in response to a public interest litigation seeking investigation into 1,528 cases of alleged extrajudicial executions committed in the state of Manipur between 1978 and 2010, after confirming many of these cases, in its recommendation again said virtually what the Jeevan Reddy Committee had prescribed in its 2005 report. 'The commission echoed a statement made by the Jeevan Reddy Committee, a committee formed to review the AFSPA in 2005, which said that the law had become a symbol of oppression, an object of hate and an instrument of discrimination and high-handedness.'[87]

Even Justice J.S. Verma, who, in his earlier ruling in 1997, upheld the constitutionality of the AFSPA, showed a shift in stance and while heading a three-member committee to look into existing laws on rape in the country in the wake of the brutal rape and murder of a 23-year-old woman in Delhi on 16 December 2012, recommended an amendment of the AFSPA, especially when it pertained to rape. He even went to the extent of saying, 'there is an imminent need to review the continuance of AFSPA and AFSPA-like legal protocols in internal conflict areas as soon as possible. This is necessary for determining the propriety of resorting to this legislation in the area(s) concerned'.[88] Despite all these shows of concern at every level of the society, a liberal answer to radical internal dissent capable of replacing draconian, undemocratic measures such as the AFSPA still remains elusive.

This reluctance or inability of the establishment to take the bold decision of removing or else recasting the AFSPA to make it tune up to universally accepted norms of democracy may be a national pathology that is embedded far deeper in the national psychology than is apparent. This pathology may be, as eminent jurist and author Fali Nariman suggested in a paper he read in the Fourth International Conference on Federalism in New Delhi, 5–7 November 2007, a modified version of which has been published in his 2013 book, *The State of the Nation*, a case of the agonising and endemic memory of India's birth in 1947 still refusing to be completely exorcised.[89] The trauma of Partition and the fear of further Balkanisation marked India's early years as a modern nation. India, at the time, faced the challenge of taming more than 560 princely states, many of which were unwilling to join India. India's republican Constitution, the draft of which became ready by 1949 to be finally adopted on 26 January 1950 to make India a Republic, was written during these most uncertain times.

Quite expectedly, this nagging sense of insecurity would have found its reflection in the Constitution of the nation. Nariman points out a number of these, the foremost being Article 3 of the Constitution, which gives the centre the power to merge, break up, change name or even abolish a state altogether without the consent of the state. This Article clearly is a stern message to the nonconforming princely states, that their identity – and indeed, existence – is dependent on the pleasure of the central government. It is also the textual refutation of Article 1 of the same constitution, which embodies the guarantee of the federal spirit that 'India, that is Bharat, shall be a Union of States'.[90]

The constitutional office of the governor of the states is another, especially when read together with the powers conferred to him under Article 356. Under the Article, upon the governor's report that the state government cannot function in accordance with the provisions of the Constitution, the central government can step in and take over administration of the state in what is popularly known as 'President's Rule'. This emergency measure, as the whole nation knows well, is prone to misuse, and the fact that it had been invoked more than 120 times till date should testify to this.[91] The central government's control of the governor is unambiguously specified in the Constitution. Though appointed for a five-year term, the governor owes his or her tenure of office solely to the centre, for under Article 156, he remains in office at the pleasure of the president. Again, although under Article 163, 'he is to act in accordance with the advice state's Council of Ministers, he is also the eyes and ears of Centre – the Centre's representative in the state to determine whether or not the government (in the state) can or cannot function in accordance with the provisions of the Constitution'.[92]

The AFSPA, it must be said, is another product of the same insecure mindset of the Indian Republic's early years. Six and a half decades after India became a republic, India has transformed almost completely from what it was then. Under the circumstance, just as Nariman suggests, it is time to put these demons from the past away. Since an overhaul of the Constitution will neither be practical nor desirable, many of these articles that reflect the mindset of the old insecure past of the nation should be, as Nariman imagines, there only in theory, but never to be put in practice again.[93]

Notes

1 Charles Douglas Lummis, Rajni Kothari chair at the CSDS 2005–06, in a lecture in Imphal, on 28 November 2006. There, however, have been others such as Steven Pinker (*Better Angels of Our Nature*) and Joshua Goldstein (*Winning the War on War*) who advanced the view that the

HISTORY OF MILITARISATION

modern age is much less violent than the past eras. See also http://www.theatlantic.com/international/archive/2014/04/the-slaughter-bench-of-history/360534/ (accessed on 19 November 2014).

2 See Glifford Geertz, *Negara, The Theatre State in Nineteenth-Century Bali* (Princeton University Press, 1980).
3 Edward A. Gait, *A History of Assam* (Thacker Spink & Co. P. Ltd., Calcutta, 1933), p. 388.
4 Ibid.
5 Alastair Lamb, *Asian Frontiers: Studies in a Continuing Problem* (Pall Mall Press, 1968), p. 146.
6 See Wikipedia for summary, http://en.wikipedia.org/wiki/British_rule_in_Burma (accessed on 27 November 2013).
7 Holdich T.H., *Lord Curzon, on Frontiers, 1907*, review http://www.jstor.org/stable/1776809 (accessed on 31 March 2014).
8 See Wikipedia web encyclopedia for more details, http://en.wikipedia.org/wiki/North-East_Frontier_Agency (accessed on 31 March 2014).
9 Ibid.
10 Nari Rushtomji, *Enchanted Frontiers, Sikkim, Bhutan and India's North-Eastern Borderlands* (Oxford University Press, 1971), p. 116.
11 Ibid.
12 See N. Lokendra's monograph, Manipur *During World War II (1942–45): Socio-Economic Changes and Local Responses* (Manipur State Archives).
13 For details, see *Plant Cultures, exploring plants & people* http://www.kew.org/plant-cultures/plants/tea_history_assam_tea.html (accessed on 3 March 2013). Also, Wikipedia web encyclopedia, https://en.wikipedia.org/wiki/Robert_Bruce_(tea_planter) (accessed on 3 March 2013).
14 Col L.W. Shakespear, *History of Assam Rifles*, 1929 (reprinted by Firma KLM Private Ltd, on behalf of Tribal Research Institute, Government of Mizoram, 1977), p. 3.
15 Gait, *A History of Assam*, p. 405.
16 Col L.W. Shakespear, *History of Assam Rifles*, p. 3.
17 Ibid., p. 4.
18 Ibid., p. 121.
19 Ibid., p. 5.
20 Ibid.
21 Sikdar, S, *Tribalism vs Colonialism: British Capitalist Intervention and Transformation of Primitive Economy of Arunachal Pradesh in Nineteenth Century*, Social Scientist (as quoted in Jelle J.P. Wouters, *Keeping the Hill Tribes at Bay: A Critique from India's Northeast of James C. Scott's Paradigm of State Evasion*; European Bulletin of Himalayan Research 39:41–65 (2012)).
22 Devi, L, *Ahom-Tribal Relations: A Political Study*, Gauhati Cotton College, 1968 (as quoted in Jelle J.P. Wouters, *Keeping the Hill Tribes at Bay: A Critique from India's Northeast of James C. Scott's Paradigm of State Evasion*; European Bulletin of Himalayan Research 39:41–65 (2012)).
23 Col L.W. Shakespear, *History of Assam Rifles*, p. 6. See also Gait, *A History of Assam*, p. 353.
24 Ibid., p. 8.
25 Ibid.

26 Ibid., p. 9.
27 See Georgio Agamben, *State of Exception* (University of Chicago Press, 2005).
28 Col L.W. Shakespear, *History of Assam Rifles*, p. 8. See also Gait, *A History of Assam*, p. 363.
29 Shakespear, *History of Assam Rifles*, p. 8.
30 Gait, *A History of Assam*, p. 343.
31 Ibid., p. 353.
32 Ibid., p. 352.
33 Shakespear, *History of Assam Rifles*, p. 246.
34 For details, see ibid., pp. 6–7.
35 Ibid., p. 243.
36 Ibid., p. 245.
37 Ibid.
38 Ibid.
See also, *Guardians of the North East, The Assam Rifles 1835–2002* (Directorate General Assam Rifles, Laitumkhrah Shillong-11, in association with Lancer Publishers & Distributors, 2003).
39 Shakespear, *History of Assam Rifles*, p. 19.
40 See, *Guardians of the North East, The Assam Rifles 1835–2002*.
41 A.G. Noorani, *India-China Boundary Problem, 1846–1947*, p. 5.
42 Ibid., p. 6.
43 Ibid.
44 The NSCN has split since then, and one of the factions, the NSCN(IM) has changed the 'Nagaland' in NSCN to 'Nagalim', signifying a greater Nagaland, not just the Indian state of Nagaland.
45 Nandita Haksar, *The Judgment That Never Came: Army Rule in North East India* (Chicken Neck, an imprint of bibliophile South Asia, New Delhi, 2011), p. 21.
46 Ibid., p. 23.
47 Ibid., p. 25.
48 Ibid., p. 26.
49 *The Times of India*, April 27, 1989.
50 See Frantz Fanon, *The Wretched of the Earth* (Penguin Books reprint 1990).
51 Nandita Haksar and Sebastian M Hongray, *The Judgment That Never Came*, pp. 15–16.
52 Full text of the AFSPA is available here: http://www.satp.org/satporgtp/countries/india/document/actandordinances/armed_forces_special_power_act_1958.htm (accessed on 4 March 2014).
53 http://www.telegraph.co.uk/history/10008053/Second-World-War-clashes-named-as-Greatest-British-Battle.html (accessed on 23 May 2013).
54 Louis Allen, *Burma: The Longest War*, p. 638, quoted in http://en.wikipedia.org/wiki/Battle_of_Imphal (accessed on 3 March 2014).
55 Ibid., p. 643, as quoted in http://en.wikipedia.org/wiki/Battle_of_Kohima (accessed on 3 March 2014).
56 See N. Lokendra's monograph, *Manipur During World War II (1942–45): Socio-Economic Changes and Local Responses* (Manipur State Archives).

57 Alexander Mackenzie, *History of the Relations of the Government with the Hill Tribes of the North-East Frontier of Bengal* (Reproduced by Mittal Publications, 1999), p. 149.
58 Namrata Goswami, *IDSA Occasion Paper No. 29, China's Territorial Claim on Arunachal Pradesh: Alternative Scenario 2032*, pp. 8–10.
59 Ibid., p. 10.
60 Ibid., pp. 7–8.
61 Ibid., pp. 15–17.
62 Neville Maxwell, *India's China War* (Jaico Publishing House, 1970), p. 181.
63 Ibid., p. 182.
64 Ibid.
65 Ibid.
66 Ibid., pp. 323–4.
67 Ibid., pp. 303–4.
68 Praveen Swami, *The Hindu*, 7 February 2012.
69 http://www.un.org/apps/news/story.asp?NewsID=41676&Cr=india&Cr1#.UyCrwbtWFdg (accessed on 23 April 2013).
70 http://www.forestpeoples.org/sites/fpp/files/publication/2010/09/indiacerdfollowupjan08eng.pdf (accessed on 23 April 2013).
71 Pradip Phanjoubam in a paper presented at a seminar on 'Law and Democracy in India', organised by the Indian Institute of Advanced Study in collaboration with School of Advanced Study, University of London and South Asian Studies Council, Yale University, during 20–22 June 2012.
72 Ratan Thiyam's Chorus Repertory Theatre production, Blind Age, 2005.
73 Amartya Sen, *The Argumentative Indian* (Penguin Books, 2005), pp. 3–4.
74 Ibid. p. 5.
75 Imphal Free Press, report of lecture by Prof. Charles Douglas Lummis, on '*Nation State's Right to Legitimate Violence*', 28 November 2005.
76 I use 'non-state' here to mean insurgent challengers of the state in the hope of forming their own state. This is distinct from the use of the term to mean pre-modern societies among whom the state has not as yet evolved, as I will be doing in the next chapter in the discussion of James Scott's notion of Zomia.
77 Imphal Free Press, Douglas Lummis, Imphal lecture, 2005.
78 Official ICRC website, http://www.icrc.org/eng/resources/documents/misc/additional-protocols-1977.htm (accessed on 16 June, 2012).
79 Ibid.
80 A.G. Noorani, *India and the Geneva Conventions Protocol*, Economic and Political Weekly, April 4, 1998.
81 The text of the operative part of the judgment is available at: http://www.upr-info.org/IMG/pdf/COHR_IND_UPR_S1_2008anx_Annex_XXIII_Supreme_Court_ruling_on_AFSPA.pdf.
82 Ibid.
83 Imphal Free Press, report of Prof. Charles Douglas Lummis' lecture on *State's Right to Belligerence* in Imphal, 29 November 2005.

84 Pradip Phanjoubam, *AFSPA: A Demonstration of the Poverty of Liberal Imagination* (IDSA Monograph Series No.7 November 2012), pp. 31–7.
85 The full report available at *The Hindu* website, http://www.hindu.com/nic/afa/ (accessed on 16 June 2012) and at http://notorture.ahrchk.net/profile/india/ArmedForcesAct1958.pdf (accessed on 16 June 2012).
86 http://en.wikipedia.org/wiki/Second_Administrative_Reform_Commission (accessed on 16 June 2012).
87 Amnesty International report, available at http://www.amnesty.org/en/library/asset/ASA20/042/2013/en/d47290df-5a65-42ec-ac49-de305f299229/asa200422013en.html (accessed on 21 March 2013).
88 *The Times of India*, 24 January 2013, http://timesofindia.indiatimes.com/india/Justice-Verma-panel-suggests-amendments-to-AFSPA/articleshow/18157655.cms (accessed on 21 March 2013).
89 Fali S. Nariman, *The State of the Nation*, pp. 219–36. An earlier version of the same essay is available at: http://www.findindianlawyer.co.in/articles/THE%20FEDERAL%20WAY%20FORWARD.htm.
90 First Article of the Indian Constitution, quoted in Fali Nariman, *The State of the Nation*, p. 223.
91 Nariman, *The State of the Nation*, p. 225.
92 Ibid.
93 Ibid., p. 235.

3

EASTERN FRONTIER OF NORTHEAST INDIA

State and non-State

Of all the frontiers of Northeast India, the border with Myanmar in the east has seen the least controversy. This is partly because both Myanmar and India were till as late as 1937 part of British India. In that year, the British government created a separate Burma Office, distinct from the India Office, as per the Government of India Act 1935, although the two continued to share the same secretary of state and the same building.[1] Moreover, much of the region where this boundary ran was still untouched by State consciousness,[2] inhabited on either side by tribal communities, till then living in splendid isolations and among whom the seeds of the modern State had still not been sown. Here, more than anywhere else in India, would James C. Scott's theory of State evading non-State populations, living in a world that Willem van Schendel termed 'Zomia',[3] be relevant. Briefly, Zomia refers to the massif of mainland South-east Asia that has historically been beyond the control of governments based in the population centres of the lowland valley States. One of the biggest challenges of writing about the Northeast region, and in particular, of the three eastern states, Nagaland, Manipur and Mizoram, has always been of determining the territories of State and non-State, and consequently, of history and no-history, of documented records and memory, of historical facts and everyday facts.

The important question at the very start of such a project would also be the legendary one, 'what is history?' The answer would provide valuable insights into the dynamics of ethnic conflict, and indeed, these three states have been the theatres of some of the most violent and enduring internal wars, in which sometimes, various ethnic communities are pitted against the Indian State, and at other times, against each other. This chapter will scan through some of the typical conflict scenarios as well as the broad patterns they fall into, and how these conflicts are, directly and indirectly, a consequence of new statehood aspirations of previously non-State ethnic populations coming into friction with established States, either of other ethnic groups favoured by geography, or else, of the modern State, once represented by the British colonial administrations and now by the postcolonial Indian State.

History as story of states

In addressing some of these problems, contemporary writers are somewhat fortunate, for there is already a considerable amount of literature by past scholars on the subject. E. H. Carr, for instance, has left behind for enquirers some very useful starting points for tackling this problem. In an essay titled 'The Historian and His Facts' in his book, *What Is History?*[4] he illustrates this dilemma as well as its resolution by pointing out how Julius Caesar's army crossing the insignificant stream Rubicon in the year 49 BC qualifies as a 'historical fact', while the everyday fact of millions of farmers, shepherds and other ordinary people, who in the course of their daily lives would have also crossed the same stream almost on a routine basis, cannot be considered so. Clearly, stories and events that have a bearing on the State tend to fall within the category of 'historical fact', and those which have no direct relevance to the making or unmaking of the State tend to be ignored by history. The bias history has for State-bearing people over non-State-bearing people should be explained by this. The recognition of the indigenous peoples' movement by the United Nations (UN), and the UN declaration of the 46-article Rights of the Indigenous Peoples, followed by the General Assembly's adoption of the declaration on 13 September 2007, is, among others, an earnest effort to tackle this issue of the absent voice of history with regards the non-State-bearing peoples. Articles 11 to 14 of the declaration in particular address this concern.[5] But today, with the onset of supra-State institutions evolving, particularly after the advent of the global market, which are increasingly encroaching into domains once considered exclusively of the State, even the logic of writing history is beginning to be redefined.

Consider this. 27 September is the birthday of Google. This day is also the birthday of well-known and respected Indian freedom fighter Bhagat Singh, though some claim 28 September to be his birthday. For all the years after Indian independence, Bhagat Singh's birthday was what the Indian media remembered on 27 September, with the union government's Directorate of Advertising and Visual Publicity (DAVP) issuing large eulogising display advertisements ahead of the day, reminding the nation of the day's significance in the Indian independence movement and nation-building. But by the turn of the twenty-first century, amidst the excitement of changes brought about by the liberalisation of the Indian economy and its consequent growing integration with the global market, all major Indian news channels and newspapers began enthusiastically remembering Google, carrying features on this phenomenon of the digital age for days, and in the process, virtually marginalised the memory of Bhagat Singh to the periphery of the media's, and therefore, the public's consciousness.[6] Obviously, the paradigms of history writing are yet getting set for another revolution. If history is the story of the State, as Carr suggested, then history telling must also have to change with the transformation the nature of modern States is going through.

This shift in outlook was also in a different way predicted by Francis Fukuyama in his provocatively titled book, *The End of History and the Last Man*. Fukuyama's argument is that the modern times may have witnessed not just the end of the Cold War, but the end of history as such – that is, the end of mankind's ideological evolution, and with it, the universalisation of Western liberal democracy as the final form of human government.[7] Misinterpretations were to be expected and Fukuyama's clarification that he did not mean the end of 'events', but of 'history' is almost the distinction Carr made of 'facts' and 'historical facts'. There have been strong criticisms of Fukuyama's assumption that capitalism has triumphed once and for all, and the battle for ideology is over, but this debate does not concern this chapter – which is history is the story of States and State-making, and events which contribute to this story qualify to be 'historical', not otherwise. On a similar note, Ramachandra Guha too implies Indian history ended in 1947. The grand themes of national liberation that was the narrative threat of modern Indian history came to an abrupt conclusion at this point, and from there on, it has been largely 'events' that have followed.[8] One thing is certain, for modern chroniclers of the postcolonial Indian State, history writing is a very different challenge altogether. The extended logic from this traditional equation between history and State, one which has come to be pushed to absurd limits in the ethnic conflict scenario in the Northeast, is that history is the alibi of the State. There is, therefore, a contest for unique histories, and with it, nationhood, among all State-aspiring ethnic groups. In the complex maze of ethnic frictions in the Northeast today, then, one underlying cause for the frictions is the multiple and often mutually exclusive projects of construction and contest for unique historical spaces.[9]

Let me not, however, lose the narrative direction by going too deep into the account of the complex and multiple fracture of the Northeast region on ethnic lines just as yet. I will, however, return and delve into this subject a little more in detail later in this chapter. For the moment, I want to sketch a broad picture of a very prominently visible ethnic fault line, one which has, in recent times, attracted the attention of many scholars of repute. I refer here to the hill–valley tension which these scholars, most prominently James C. Scott, identified as a consistent pattern throughout the South-east Asian massif.[10]

Hill–valley friction

This hill–valley divide has also always been very much a feature in the relationship between Assam's two major river valleys, the Brahmaputra valley and the Barak valley, and the surrounding hills, so much so that in 1972, the state of Assam, a direct inheritance of the British province of Assam, had to be bifurcated further to give its major hills districts autonomous statehood under the Indian Constitution. Thus, came into existence Meghalaya, Mizoram and Arunachal Pradesh. Earlier, in 1963, in the wake of a violent Naga movement for sovereignty, and in the hope this would amount to a permanent settlement of the Naga problem, Assam's Naga Hills district was clubbed with the Mon and Tuensang frontier and made into a separate, full-fledged Indian state – Nagaland. Tripura and Manipur, and now, Sikkim, the other three of the eight Northeast states, were always separate principalities.

The other hill–valley divide scenario, and one which is very pertinent to this chapter, is the friction between the Imphal valley and the surrounding hills in Manipur. Here, more than in Assam is a more direct blueprint of Scott's theory of the rise of Paddy States in a constant tug-of-war with State-evading, non-State mountain populations. The conflict scenario today, however, is more complex than during the pristine pre-colonial world. With the arrival of colonial administration and the subsequent intervention of the modern State, Scott's Zomia has transformed and acquired new characteristics. From a State-evading population, the hills are now, more often than not, a State-aspiring one, setting up new equations of conflict with existing States within whose political geography they invariably always find themselves in.

There have been many flashpoints of ethnic frictions in this hill–valley antagonism in the recent past in the Northeast, in particular Assam and Manipur. I will take the example of one such confrontation in May 2010 in Manipur to illustrate this point of how easily any trouble gets to be interpreted in terms of conflict vocabularies extremely circumscribed by this polarisation. In the midst of escalating tension in the state over the revival of the Autonomous District Councils (ADCs) in the hill districts and campaigns for elections to these ADCs, which powerful Naga civil bodies, including All Naga Students Association, Manipur (ANSAM) and United Naga Council (UNC), opposed vehemently, the leader of National Socialist Council of Nagalim (Isak-Muivah faction) (NSCN(IM)), Thuingaleng Muivah, wanted to visit his village Somdal in Ukhrul district of Manipur, but the Manipur government, sensing motives more than just a home visit, disallowed his entry into the state. On 6 May, a confrontation at Mao Gate, the entry point to Manipur from Nagaland along the Imphal–Dimapur highway, between supporters of the Naga rebel leader and Manipur police, resulted in two fatalities.[11] Needless to say, the episode left Manipur mauled both emotionally and physically. It undoubtedly left the different communities in the state as well as observers wondering if there was even an ember of hope left by which the hill–valley relationship could be salvaged. Years after the dust from the episode has settled, the bitter aftertaste has not washed away completely.

But even if a parting of ways between the state's hills and valley were to be considered as an option, it would not be easy because of the enmeshed nature of geography, both physical and human. By human geography, I mean the physical space needed to ensure a realistic sense of security of a community. I have discussed this sense of security in quite some detail in the introductory chapter on how geography determines conflicts. The contention is disregarding this consideration is a sure recipe for deadly conflicts. This geography is not just about the immediate physical space anybody occupies. It is, instead, about a sense of control of the vital arteries that feed and sustain a social organism, or civilisation as it were. The frequent resorts in recent times of blockading the mountain routes to the Imphal valley, whatever their immediate justifications, for instance, would have given everybody a sense of what this geography of conflict is about. If a parting of ways between the hills and valley has to happen, these geographies of security of all communities would have to be addressed adequately and taken care of, without leaving anybody sized up, mutilated and made helpless. This is not a question of pity or mercy on the part of any one party either, but of sound judgement designed to avoid deadly conflicts in the future.

This tragic episode in Manipur is illustrative, so let me elaborate a little more. What then was the sequence of events that led to the Mao Gate incident? First, the immediate manifestation of trouble began with the Government of Manipur declaring elections to six ADCs. This then hardened after the government refused to allow Thuingaleng Muivah, leader of the NSCN(IM), to enter Manipur to visit his village, Somdal in Ukhrul district.

The ADCs are local self-governance bodies evolved as a parallel of the Panchayati Raj as the latter is not welcomed by the hill communities. They came into being in 1973 as per the Manipur (Hill Area) Autonomous District Council Act 1971 of the Government of Manipur, when Manipur was still a Union Territory. The Act, hence, is of union government vintage.

However, since 1989, the district councils became defunct because of agitations in the hill districts that disallowed elections to the ADCs, demanding that they be replaced by ADCs under the 6th Schedule of the Indian Constitution, which would give these councils a measure of legislative and judicial powers as per tribal customary laws. This was never to be for a number of reasons, hence the hills have remained without the benefit of any statutory grassroots local self-governance mechanism all the while. More than two decades later, the government decided to reinstate the ADCs, but the 1971 Act had, in the meantime, undergone an amendment in 2008.

Very broadly, this amendment seeks to transfer some of the traditional powers of the village chieftainship to the elected district councils of tribal leaders. This is what the ANSAM and UNC objected to, and demanded the amendment be scrapped before the ADC elections were held. The government disagreed, saying the hard-won election process should not be delayed, but verbally promised necessary rectifications to the ADC Act can be made after the district councils have been formed. On this point of disagreement, the ANSAM and UNC imposed an economic blockade, which lasted 68 days, beginning from the midnight of 11–12 April 2010.

In the midst of this trouble, on 29 April, the union government informed the Manipur government by a crash wireless message that Thuingaleng Muivah, the general secretary of the NSCN(IM), would be visiting his village Somdal in Manipur on 3 May. Muivah was also to address two public rallies, one at Ukhrul on 8 May and another at Senapati on 10 May. Perhaps it is a coincidence that Muivah who has never expressed a desire to visit his village for 44 years at the time, even though on many occasions he had camped next door in the NSCN(IM) headquarters in Hebron close to Nagaland's commercial capital, Dimapur, wanted to enter Manipur at this juncture. However, the situation being such, it was also understandable for the Manipur government to presume that the economic blockade over the ADC elections and Muivah's intended visit were part of a design. The Manipur government decided to block Muivah's entry. This decision led to the unfortunate Mao Gate incident, in which two Naga students were killed in clashes with the state police forces, and scores of others injured.

Soon enough, the fight also began to acquire an ethnic hue. The ADC elections as well as the blocking of Muivah's visit began, thus, to be portrayed as Meitei (valley dwellers who form the majority population in the state) aggression against the Nagas. This is, to some extent, understandable for while the Meiteis were somewhat indifferent to the ADC issue, the blocking of Muivah, a man who has been a prime campaigner for Greater Nagaland to be formed by merging territories within Manipur, Assam, Arunachal Pradesh and Myanmar, which the Nagas consider as their ancestral territories, with the present state of Nagaland, received strong support from the valley community.

However, contrary to what was projected, the police force at Mao Gate that blocked Muivah's entry was not a Meitei force. Manipur follows a 33 per cent job reservation for schedule tribes. This would have roughly ensured the police force at Mao Gate on that day had at least 33 per cent non-Meiteis. The operation's overall commander and his second-in-charge on the day of the confrontation were both from the hill communities too. It is also untrue that the ADC elections were being forced on the hills with valley interest in mind. All hill affairs, including the amendments to the ADC Act, in Manipur are looked after by the Hill Area Committee (HAC), formed by all 20 hill MLAs of the Manipur State Legislative Assembly. The Manipur Legislative Assembly is 60 strong, 20 reserved seats and 40 general. The HAC functions like a mini assembly within the Manipur Assembly.

The question remains, why the hill–valley binary so easily comes to the fore, even where this should not have been the case? The answer, perhaps, has a lot to do with the troubled nature of what Scott calls formerly non-State peoples waking up to the new reality of the State, and acquiring their own nationalist aspirations. The State and the nation are two different notions. The nation is an imagined community, and it is this imagining which binds together people into political identities[12]. But for this 'imagined community' to have a tangible sustainable architecture, it must have a State as its backbone. The State, in this sense, is a political mechanism invariably involving a centralised bureaucracy or government, with a definite hierarchy of functionaries and institutions to run its political and economic administrations optimally. When this twin projects of National Imagining and State Formation not only succeed, but become congruent, a nation state results. It is also true that just as the State can fail, so can the imagining that makes a nation. Thus, if the former non-State populations' new aspirations for establishing their independent States have remained fruitless, the failure of many established States is in the area of their imagining of a composite national identity. Manipur's problem has been that the imagining of the Manipuri identity has not been able to accommodate, in letter and spirit, all communities domiciled in the state. But Manipur is not alone. This same failure can be said of so many others – the imagining of the Assamese identity, for instance. On a larger canvas, the problem communities from the Northeast have in identifying with the larger Indian identity, or being fully accepted by 'mainstream' Indians as Indians, is also the same issue of a failure of the imagined national community.

There are also a few interesting deductions to be made in both the processes of nation formation and State formation, and there can be few other places more interesting than the Northeast region to make these observations. One of these deductions is that a national community formation would normally precede State formation. Another is that in the process of social evolution, people have existed outside of any national imagining, and thereby, lived outside of the understanding of the State as well. This condition of apolitical organisation of society is indeed an attribute of many, if not most, indigenous populations, at least before the advent of modern times. In other words, both the birth of the national imagining and State formation happened at different times for different peoples, and the evolution of these conditions depends largely on the status of the economy.[13] At its crux, this theory says the State is a mechanism for managing surplus economy, implying that subsistent hunting-gathering or primitive non-productive tribal economies are hardly conditions for the evolution of the State or national consciousness.

The third interesting observation is that just as history is an account of States and State making, States also generally tend to recognise other States only, either as friends or enemies. This is also why non-State communities seldom figure in any known accounts of history. While everybody has a past, the past is not always history technically. Similarly, all facts are not historical facts, as Carr noted. This should explain why in the written royal chronicles available in the region, with all their limitations and biases, only established kingdoms figured substantially. In the 1819 devastating invasion by the Ava (Burma), mentions seldom were found of communities other than those belonging to established States such as Ahom, Manipur, Jantia and Cachari kingdoms and so on, and how these principalities were devastated. It is as if beyond these few feudal principalities of the time, the rest of the map of the region were historical blank spaces. States fight or make friends with States for the most part.

This was also evident in the case of the Nagas. The British took cognisance of the Angamis as a force to reckon with only when Angami villages, such as Khonoma, Kohima, Jotsoma, Mezoma and so on, started forming a confederation and showed signs of State formation in the first half of the nineteenth century. The first expedition of the British into the Naga Hills was in 1839.[14] The problem also is about how treaties and formal agreements can be entered into with non-States, which do not, by definition, have any centralised authority structures that spread beyond small village communities. As in the case of the Angamis, the British also became concerned by the hint of State formation under the leadership of Jadonang and Gaidinliu among the Zeliangrong Nagas during the 1931–33 messianic rebellion led by these two well-known leaders.[15]

The fact that these non-State spaces never occurred in these historical accounts do not necessarily mean they were always independent. In most cases, they were just presumed to be part of one State or another, just as the British presumed territories beyond their Inner Line, though un-administered by them, belonged to them. The changes of suzerainty over the then non-political space of Kabaw valley between Manipur and Ava kingdoms should serve as another illustration of this.[16] The fact is, until the political organisation of these non-State spaces began centralising to acquire attributes of a State, there was nothing much for a State to conquer. When certain villages were proving to be troublesome, they were dealt with separately as independent villages, as the Ahom kings in Assam did by evolving a system called 'Posa' to have cultivators pay a certain percentage of their crops' yields in certain areas to different village chiefs to keep them appeased.[17]

But this notwithstanding, there is still immense bitterness among the hill tribes, including the Nagas, of perceived discrimination by the valley-dwelling Hindu Meiteis. This has a background. The Meiteis are ethnically and linguistically very close to the hill tribes, but after they converted to Hinduism in the early eighteenth century, they imported a caste system in which the hill tribes were treated as unclean, leaving deep hurt and resentment among the hillmen. Quite ironically, Pamheiba, who later changed his name to Garib Newaz, one of the most powerful kings of Manipur who ascended the throne in 1714, and waged successful wars against Ava (Burma) during 1725 and 1749, contributing to the downfall of the Tungoo dynasty in Burma,[18] and who not only converted to Hinduism, but also made it the State religion of his kingdom, was of part Naga descent.[19] He outlawed the original Meitei religion, Sanamahi, and in order to complete the obliteration of the religion, religious books in Meitei script, called the 'Puya', which recorded cultural norms and tantric rites besides making prophesies and so on, were made bonfire of in 1729. He also paved the way for replacement of the Meitei script with the Bengali script. The religion survives to this day, so also the script, which is now being officially revived. The impunity of Pamheiba's cavalry raids into Burma would be avenged in a devastating way by Burma in later years. The first of several punitive expeditions against several outlying kingdoms which harassed previous rulers of the country, taken out by the founder of Burma's powerful Konbaung Dynasty, Alaungpaya, was on Manipur during 1758–59, and the king himself took part in it.[20] Alaungpaya's army devastated and depopulated Manipur though the king himself had to return midway on account of news of aggressions on his kingdom by the Mon kingdom in the south in his absence.[21]

The homeland and the state

There are yet other issues feeding the hill–valley binary in Manipur. The resistance to the ADC election is also on ground that this would lead to compromise of tribal lands. In the land tenure system of a modern State, all land within the territorial boundary of the State belong to the State. Individual landowners are only tenants leasing little plots of lands their homes or farms sit on from the State with certain rights of ownership over them, but this ownership is not absolute. The State can, if it considers necessary, acquire the land back from its tenants by the exercise of the principle of eminent domain of modern jurisprudence.

Obviously, different States would have different land laws, but they would be variations of this basic principle. The modern system is pretty clear-cut and there is hardly likely to be any dispute that cannot be settled by just the plain application of the law. It is when we enter the world of customary indigenous laws that things get a little nebulous. Manipur, as also most other Northeast states, has both these notions of landownership coexisting. The valley has embraced the modern; the hills have stuck to the customary.

While there are mechanisms for settling disputes within each of the systems, this is not so easy when the two are pitted against each other. The difficult question again is, in case a separation of the two geographies becomes absolutely necessary, what would be the criterion that defines notions such as 'ancestral land'? Would it be in terms of actual physical occupation of a particular tract of land for a particular length of time? In this case, the majority of the land in the Manipur hills would be physically unoccupied, and if modern law were to be applied, these would be government land. Or, would it be defined in terms of occurrences in myths and legends of the communities? In this case too, much of these tracts of land, lakes and mountains would occur in the ancient myths of many different communities. This being the case, notions of homelands of indigenous communities overlap, sometimes totally, and there is no way justice can be done by seeking to divide them using instruments of the modern land tenure mechanisms. The

Kuki–Naga feuds in the 1990s, and indeed, the 'Naga integration–Manipur integrity' tensions now over the demand of Greater Nagaland, are tragedies that have resulted or are waiting to result out of this insistence on dividing what are fundamentally indivisible, and therefore, have to be shared.

This is a rough sketch of the eastern frontier of the Northeast region. Though incomplete, it should give an idea of the background against which a national boundary evolved here. Since delineated and demarcated boundaries are very much a Western notion, it would be to the purpose to take a look at what the British found when they entered the region, and what strategies they used to mark the territory they newly acquired in ways they knew and were comfortable with. To do this, a closer study of what is a frontier from this vantage would be interesting, and Lord Curzon's Romanes lecture of 1907 on Frontiers, two years after he retired as viceroy of India, should provide valuable insights into the subject.[22] He reiterates in the lecture that 'in Asiatic countries it would be true to say that demarcation has never taken place except under European pressure and by the intervention of European agents'.[23]

Curzon's frontier

Obviously Curzon's views on frontiers cannot be presumed to be the British official policy statement on the matter, but as a knowledgeable, influential administrator with a long and illustrious career looking after the frontiers of the British Empire, and an explorer of repute in his younger days, these views would certainly conform to the general Western outlook of his time, particularly those of the British. From the perspective of this chapter, the most interesting part in this rather long lecture is in what Curzon describes as artificial frontiers, as opposed to the more obvious, ancient and common, natural ones, formed by the sea, mountains, deserts, marshes and forests and so on. Of the artificial ones, again, it is the category he calls buffers that is most intriguing. These range from simple agreements on 'no man's land' strips of land between neighbouring States to extremely sophisticated political and administrative arrangement between two rival States to keep another in between them as neutral. The Tibet case would rank as one of the most sophisticated. A 1907 treaty between Russia and Britain sought Tibet to be kept under the suzerainty of a lesser neighbour, China, but out of any direct influence of either Russia or Britain.

The same Agreement contains a further novelty in international diplomacy, in the shape of a neutralizing pledge about Tibet made by two Powers, one of which is contiguous while the other has no territorial contact whatever with that country. Tibet is not a buffer State between Great Britain and Russia; the sequel of the recent expedition has merely been to make it again what it had latterly ceased to be, namely, a Mark or Frontier Protectorate of the Chinese Empire.[24]

The 'buffer State is an expedient more or less artificial, according to the degree of stability which its government and institutions may enjoy, constructed in order to keep apart the Frontiers of converging Powers'.[25] In the same lecture, Curzon also talks of the tendency of frontiers to grow outwards, reflecting the urge for colonies to expand. How, 'of all the diplomatic forms of frictions which have latterly been described, it may be observed that the uniform tendency is for the weaker to crystallize into the harder shape. Spheres of Interest tend to become Spheres of Influence; temporary leases to become perpetual; Spheres of Influence to develop into Protectorates; Protectorates to be the forerunners of complete incorporation'.[26] To this, he adds: 'The process is not so immoral as it might at first sight appear; it is in reality an endeavour, sanctioned by general usage, to introduce formality and decorum into proceedings which, unless thus regulated and diffused, might endanger the peace of nations or too violently shock the conscience of the world'.[27]

This pattern of colonial expansion also marked the British penetration of the Northeast region. Here, however, it was not always expanding by annexation of established States, but also of non-State spaces, and therefore, the peculiarity of the evolution of this frontier. No other mechanism is a louder articulation of this frontier policy, and indeed, the ingenuity of the British government in frontier administration, than the Inner Line system, which came into existence by the Bengal Eastern Frontier Regulation of 1873. The Inner Line was, in many ways, the British administration's answer to tackling the non-State spaces they encountered in the Northeast region. However, as the administration made it plain, 'this line does not necessarily indicate the territorial frontier but only the limits of the administered area . . . it does not in any way decide the sovereignty of the territory beyond'.[28]

Inner Line

It is interesting that the Inner Line Regulation was the first law promulgated in Assam. This was done 'under the authority conferred by the

Statute 33 Vict., Chapter 3, which gives to the executive Government of India a power of summary legislation for backward tracts. Such laws are called Regulations to distinguish them from the Acts, or laws passed after discussion in the legislature'.[29] This implies, from the time Assam came under the British in 1826 till the time of the promulgation of the Inner Line Regulation in 1873, Assam was governed under no particular law. The Inner Line then is also, as Richard Keatinge, the first chief commissioner of Assam who assumed office on 7 February 1874 and given the task of demarcating the line, discovered, not just about giving a 'territorial frame to capital', but 'more deeply, it was also supposed to demarcate the Hills from the plains, the nomadic from the sedentary, the jungle from the arable – in short, the tribal areas from the Assam proper'.[30]

> what lay enclosed by the Inner Line was not only a territorial exterior of the theatre of capital – it was also a temporal outside of the historical pace of development and progress. Though encountered on the numerous plateaus of everyday life, the communities forced to stay beyond the Line were seen as belonging to a different time regime – where the time of the law did not apply; where slavery, headhunting, and nomadism could be allowed to exist. The Inner Line was expected to enact a sharp split between what were understood as the contending worlds of capital and the pre-capital, of the modern and the primitive.[31]

What was it that made it necessary for the British to draw this? When the British took over Assam from the Ahoms, because there was never anything as a demarcated boundary, the outer limits of the Ahom kingdom were not certain, but the hills surrounding the Assam valley were. Though loosely controlled, they fell within the Ahom domain through tributary relationships with the hill tribes; therefore, the British presumed they had inherited them from the Ahoms. It must be kept in mind that 1873 was the time tea gardens were expanding rapidly and speculators in tea were hungering for more land. Together with them, timber, rubber and coal merchants were entering Assam in a big way. These speculators invariably were routinely encroaching into the hills, and thereby, coming to be in friction with the hill tribes. The government was increasingly under pressure from these businesses, especially tea planters, to extend its administration into the hills so that they could get the protection of the law, and to this purpose, 'getting it entangled in several legal disputes'.[32] The Inner Line finally happened because the government increasingly realised that 'because of its lack of control over the communication between the non-rent-paying populations and the speculators the government was losing out on substantial amount of revenue'.[33]

The administration had a more sanitised explanation:

> The unrestricted intercourse which formerly existed between British subjects in Assam and the wild tribes living across the frontier frequently led to quarrels and sometimes, in serious disturbances . . . The opening of tea gardens beyond the border-line also at times involved the Government in troublesome disputes with the frontier tribes in their vicinity.[34]

One thing among others is clear. The need for the Inner Line became urgent because of the new economic activities that came along with the colonial administration, driven as it was by revenue concerns. This should also make enquirers into this chapter of the history of the region curious as to what the relations between the hill tribes and the Ahom rulers were before the advent of the British colonial administration. A growing volume of scholarship now exists on this subject, driven especially by a renewed awakening of academic curiosity in the region's hill–valley, State–non-State relationships. Much of the credit for this fresh interest must go to James Scott's provocative book, *The Art of Not Being Governed: An Anarchic History of Upland Southeast Asia*.

Zomia and posa

Scott describes Zomia as 'a new name for virtually all the lands at altitudes above roughly three hundred meters all the way from the Central Highlands of Vietnam to northeastern India and traversing five Southeast Asian nations (Vietnam, Cambodia, Laos, Thailand, and Burma) and four provinces of China (Yunnan, Guizhou, Guangxi, and parts of Sichuan). It is an expanse of 2.5 million square kilometres containing about one hundred million minority peoples of truly bewildering ethnic and linguistic variety'.[35]

Scott forwards a peculiar and controversial theory of the relationship between valley States nurtured by surpluses produced in their fertile river valleys and inhabitants of the hills that surround these valley States, or paddy States. Very briefly, in Scott's postulation, the paddy States and the non-State hill tribes are always positioned antagonistically. This is because the paddy States are always in short supply of manpower to run their increasingly diversifying economies, and therefore, it is characteristic of them to fill the shortage by raiding the hills, or neighbouring paddy States, to capture populations. 'As manpower machines capturing and absorbing population, they also, in the same fashion, disgorged state-fleeing populations to the hills and created their own "barbarian" frontier'.[36]

In Scott's scheme, the hill tribes are State evaders, receding to the most inhospitable mountaintops and out of the reach of the paddy States. They not only flee the paddy States, but are, by nature, so abhorrent of the State that they would consciously avoid State-like characteristics developing among them. In Scott's own words: 'My thesis is simple, suggestive, and controversial. Zomia is the largest remaining region of the world whose peoples have not yet been fully incorporated into nation-states. Its days are numbered'.[37] Scott disagrees with the popular interpretation that the backwardness and statelessness of Zomia is on account of their being left behind in the development process. On the contrary, they are in the condition of where they are by choice. They are 'state-repelling societies – or even anti-state societies'.[38] In other words, the backwardness of Zomia is backwardness by choice.

While Scott's thesis, insofar as it creates a lucid and interesting backdrop for further enquiry and understanding of the social dynamics that govern life in Zomia, has been much appreciated, the extent and insistence with which he pushes what he sees as irreconcilable and antagonistic relationship between the valley States and non-State hill tribes has seen stiff challenges from other scholars. I will restrict my focus only on works of some scholars demonstrating how Scott's thesis applies or fails, using the Northeast as alibi. Some of these works predate Scott's, but they nonetheless indicate how their observations either are explained or go against Scott's theory.

In the pre-colonial days, scholars agree the Ahom administration did exercise authority over the hill tribes and maintained it through a tributary system, but it was not always so straightforward. This is only to be expected, for just as the colonial administration was also to discover, the problem was about the State managing non-State spaces. The problem was the same, but the approaches and mechanisms employed to achieve a solution were different, often radically. The Ahom did not resort to anything close to drawing an Inner Line to separate the two spaces. Instead, they managed it their own way, sometimes taking out punitive expeditions to recalcitrant villages and extracting reparations, but for most of the time, wary of the effort, time and expense, buying peace by allowing those hill chiefs who were traditionally aggressive to levy an annual tribute of a percentage of crop yields from nearby villages in the adjoining plains by a system which came to be known as 'Posa'. The Ahom rulers, thus, remained the overlords of the hills and the plains, but in the more immediate domains of these hill chiefs, they were allowed a certain degree of local suzerainty over villages in the foothills for the promise of sparing these villages violent raids, lootings and slave-taking. Edward Gait has this description of the Posa system:

> The same weakness of the central administration which had led to the abandonment of the above Duars resulted further east in the acknowledgment of the right of certain small tribes of independent Bhutias, and of the Aka and Dafla hillmen, to levy posa, or tribute, in certain villages along the foot of their hills. The Hazarikahowa Akas were thus permitted to levy from each house 'one portion of a female dress, one bundle of cotton thread and one cotton handkerchief,' and the right of the other tribes were similarly defined. The inconvenience of permitting these savages to descend annually upon the cultivated lands, for the purpose of collecting their dues, was very soon felt . . . [39]

The existence of the Posa system is one testimony that unlike what Scott presumed, the relationship between the valley States and the hillmen in Zomia was not always one of hunter–prey in which the former is the hunter and the latter the prey. The equation, as in Assam, has always been much more complex in most of the Northeast region. Gait also gives an account of the population movement, which also did not conform to Scott's theory of the hillmen as self-marginalised people, 'runaway, fugitive, maroon communities who have, over the course of two millennia, been fleeing the oppressions of state-making projects in the valleys'.[40] Gait wrote of how as 'the Bhutias in the north, so also the Khasis, in the south of Kamrup, had gradually established themselves in the plains; and the Ahom viceroy of Gauhati, finding that he was unable to oust them, had contended himself with receiving a formal acknowledgment of the Ahom supremacy'.[41]

This is, however, not to discount altogether that one of the inherent characteristics of the valley States in Zomia is they raid non-States as well as neighbouring valley States to capture people to fill the manpower shortages in their kingdoms, but that this characteristic was not a rule which can be generalised across the entire canvas. Raids and capture of people were a feature of these States indeed, and the testimony of this is borne by villages of descendants of captive Meiteis around Mandalay, the old capital of Burma, even today. Most of these captives are artisans, court astrologers and people in various other commerce and arts activities.[42] These captives, once settled in the lands of their captors, though not citizens, can even enjoy a higher status in society than original citizens, depending on the skills they bring along.[43] There were other accounts of such captures of populations:

> Nothing could have been more wretched than the state of Assam when the valley was first occupied by our troops. Thirty thousand Assamese had been carried off as slaves by the Burmese. Many thousands had lost their lives, and large tracts of country been laid desolate by the wars, famines, and pestilences which for nearly half a century had afflicted the province.[44]

After the British annexed Assam, the Posa system lived on, though unlike the Ahom, who legitimised the administrative mechanism, the British had no vocabulary for it except to call it blackmail.[45] Though not brought within the legal administrative frame, the British nonetheless allowed it to conveniently continue, disguising it with a thin coat of self-defined moral legitimacy, claiming that in the hands of the new administration, this payment has been made conditional, and therefore, ceased to be blackmail. 'The essential difference between "blackmail" and the annual allowances paid to the Abors is this: that in the one case the forbearance of the savage tribe is made by them conditional on payment of the stipulated allowance, and in the other the payment of the allowance is made by us conditional on the good conduct of the tribe. One is initiated in an aggressive spirit, the other in a spirit of conciliation'.[46]

Posa was also deliberately allowed to evolve as 'a very complex and critical strategy of the British Indian state in its north-eastern frontier. Far from being a dying trait of a meaningless medieval practice, posa in the nineteenth and twentieth centuries was a dynamic register of shifting relationships between the contending elements of an unofficial biography of capital. Seizing on the traces of the customary rights of some of the non-state space communities recognized by the Tungkhungia kings, the colonial state over the years built an intriguing network of control and constraint beyond its formal jurisdictional limits'.[47]

The British soon would rearrange the Posa to good administrative effect to ultimately turn the table against the 'blackmailing' hill chiefs by 'monetising, regularization, hierarchization, and authenticization'.[48] This rendered, first and foremost, the 'transborder communities vulnerable to the forces of inflation and market'[49] as the valuation and determination of Posa, till then paid in crop yield, would remain fixed, regardless of market fluctuations.

Gait gives an account of what the Posa sums fixed were: 'a sum of Rs. 1,740 is paid annually to the Bhutias of Char Duar; Rs. 146 to the The Bengia Bhutias; Rs. 700 to the Akas; Rs. 4,130 to the Daflas; and Rs. 1,118 to the Miris'.[50] Gait's list of Posa recipients, however, is not exhaustive, for there is also evidence that the Ahoms made similar arrangements with some Naga tribes as well, 'to secure the adhesion of the Nagas, like those of the northern tribes, King Pratap Singha (1603–41) granted the chiefs and communities specified areas, commonly known as khats, to supply their requirement of grain and other necessaries'.[51] The British arrangement of fixing time, place and a definite method of receiving the Posa also put the Posa receiving communities at the mercy of the bureaucracy's red tapes, as well as gave them the sense of being subordinate to the administration:

> An acute sense of embarrassment runs through the vast colonial archive on posa. Usually defended as a necessary mechanism for procuring 'peace', posa was often criticized as an obstacle to 'improvement'. A number of officials repeatedly argued that nothing corrupted the 'idle, happy-go-lucky people' more than easy money.[52]

The argument is that Posa was retarding the development of Posa receiving communities. 'The fact that the Mishmis, who were not posa receivers, started to work on the roads, or sought employment in cutting canes and clearing jungles in large numbers since 1890 led many frontier officials to argue that discontinuing posa would teach the Abors and the Daflas to appreciate the superior value of labour and thus enhance development'.[53] The irony is apparent and bitter. The British administration allowed the Posa tradition of the Ahom king to continue, initially in order to buy peace and avoid the extra expenses and administrative burden of having to extend its law into the wild hills, and then later, to arm twist these hill communities into submission. In course of time, what was initially a reluctant concession to an inherited tradition of annual ransom paid to 'blackmailing' by marauding tribes from the wild hills ultimately proved to be a cynical, though effective, administrative mechanism. It was not only about corrupting the 'blackmailers' by encouraging indolence, thereby retarding development among them, but also having the predator and prey change places so that blackmailers of yore ended up as the blackmailed. 'Posa was indeed a form of blackmail: the posa-receiving communities were made responsible for their own acts as also of the communities staying on farther lands. It was the singular mechanism through which the population outside the limits of the British law could be held by the state in ransom'.[54]

Reflecting on the nature and ultimate fate of the Posa system in pre-colonial Assam, its passage from a customary annual ritual that established a peculiar bondage between the State and non-State who rubbed shoulders at the time to, ultimately, a hardnosed, often sinister, machination of the modern colonial State to subvert and bring to subordination the non-State spaces and peoples, it is difficult not to be tempted to see parallels in the manner the modern Indian State also deals with troublesome communities in the Northeast. Although it is not in the scope of this chapter or this book to explore too deep into the compulsions as well as thoughts that went into these current policies, or into their rewards and prices, the nature of peace agreements and accords in general that the government has signed so far, or are in the process of doing so, with various ethnic insurgencies in the region, does seem to offer a vision or spectre of a continuity of the same policy approach of how the colonial State once dealt with the non-State actors. All the ingredients of the old policies, beginning from appeasement in the name of buying peace, and then slowly but surely leading the process on to what has been described as 'monetising, regularization, hierarchization, and authenticization' and regimentation, continue to be repeated almost with ritualistic faithfulness. The strategy is legitimate to the extent that it is driven by the State's desire for peace. But the problem, as this little historical sketch of the Inner Line and the Posa system has shown, is purchased peace always comes with a very dear social price.

The answer to the vexed question obviously is not in purchased peace, but one which is won. Maybe there is a lesson in the manner the Ahom kings dealt with the problem. Their solution, as we have seen, was not by drawing any rigid segregating lines between the hills and the plains, the law and no-law, revenue and no revenue areas, but by acknowledging and understanding the issue not in any legalist and administrative terms alone, but as an existential predicament in which all players have to face and live together, in the spirit of mutual accommodation, adjustment and respect of each other's compulsions, limitations and conveniences.[55]

For a better understanding of the reasons for the raids by hill tribes, I will return briefly to the earlier discussion of James C. Scott's theory, and analyse how river valleys, because of their agricultural surplus, are generally where State formation first happen.

Some of Scott's lectures on the subject prior to the publication of his influential book, such as the one he gave at the London School of Economics on 22 May 2008, are provocatively titled 'Why Civilisations Can't Climb Hills: A Political History of Statelessness in Southeast Asia'.[56] That the valley States and their surrounding hills took different trajectories of development and social organisation, there can be little to dispute. These differences are visible even today and, indeed, constitute some of the major causes of much of the contemporary problems of the Northeast. What has been most challenged in Scott's theory is his assertion that the hill communities are State evaders and that this is evident even in their preference of shift cultivation, choice of difficult mountaintop as sites for their villages, and so on. In the picture of Zomia he evokes, the Zomians are given no individual agency at all. The picture is one of a cat and mouse situation in which instinct determines the hillman is perpetually on the run, with the valley man perpetually after him. There is little difference to be made by people to people bondages, personality of individuals, quality of leaderships and so on in this equation between the Zomian hills and valleys.

Myths, legends, histories both written and oral, however, say otherwise. Indeed, as Bengt G. Karlsson of Stockholm University observes in a paper,[57] there is a deafening absence of Zomian voices in Scott's account of Zomia. The hill–valley relationship was quite obviously far more complex than envision by Scott: 'The Ahom cultivated different relations with different hill tribes. Hence, framing Ahom-hill tribes' relations in terms of a single, progressive narrative would involve grave over-simplifications. Nor were hill tribes themselves placid in this process; the Ahom incorporated some in the ranks of their army, but there were also instances in which a hill tribe sought the support of the Ahom army to intervene in an inter-tribal conflict'.[58]

So then, what explains the raids by hill tribes on the plains in Assam? Taking the cue from Mackenzie's description of the condition the British found Assam in when they took over, that the place was 'surrounded north, east, and south by numerous savage and warlike tribes whom the decaying authority of the Assam dynasty had failed of late years to control, and whom the disturbed condition of the province had incited to encroachment. Many of them advanced claims to rights more or less definite over lands lying in the plains; others claimed tributary payments from the villages, below their hills, or the services of paiks said to have been assigned them by the Assam authorities',[59] another critic of Scott's book, Jelle J. P. Wouters, observes that 'this suggests that early state projects – with their potential agricultural surplus, concentrated manpower, and the overall amenity of life believed to prevail there – made a strong impression on those living in the less productive uplands. For them, state resources became an object of aspiration, if not, at times, an essential supplement to cover their basic needs', and 'that the plains provided too essential a resource for those living in the relatively "barren" hills to ignore'.[60] The hill tribes then raided the more resource bountiful plains out of necessity determined by geography and economy 'because the uplands were less productive than the more fertile plains, plundering may have been their last resort'.[61] Also implied in this interpretation is, rather than being compulsive State evaders, the hill tribes also were given to State envy, and the economic security that the State provides for its citizens.

This then was the hill–valley relationship that the Ahoms and the communities in the mountain hinterlands of the Assam valley arrived at in their own ways, long before the advent of modern colonial administration, and the success of this conflict resolution, it can be argued, is what is epitomised by the tradition of Posa. Understandably, its genesis would have also involved coercions and frictions before finally each party resigned to the inevitability of geographical destiny and came to terms with each other's needs and compulsions, and encoded it as a shared custom. It is quite imaginable and understandable that 'the policy of Ahom rulers towards these tribes varied from time to time according to the exigencies of the political situation'.[62]

The British then arrived and not only gave this custom a different interpretation, but also refashioned it to suit their own administrative needs. The Inner Line drawn to segregate the two spaces is just one outcome of this new interpretation. The British, however, left enough room for revising and redrawing the Line to suit their needs.

> Well until the second decade of the twentieth century, the Line was repeatedly redrawn in order to variously accommodate the expansive compulsions of plantation capital, the recognition of imperfection in survey maps, the security anxiety of the state, and the adaptive practices of internally differentiated local communities. If new tea or coal tracts were found or valuable forest areas were reported to exist beyond the Line, small insertions in the Government Gazette casually declared unblushing extensions of the Inner Line to include those areas.[63]

Gait also gives us this account: 'There was also formerly an Inner Line on the Lushai marches, but it has been allowed to fall into desuetude since our occupation of the Lushai hills'.[64] Segregating the hills from the plains by this hard, though malleable, administrative Line by the British administration, it is obvious from these accounts, had little interest of the local communities. But this administrative decision had the longer-term fallout of accentuating the alienation of the hills from the plains. Thus, Wouter in his essay concludes: 'From this point of view, the hills took on their identity as remote places peopled by insulated tribes only after the colonial annexation of the Assam plains, which isolated and essentialised hill dwellers in unprecedented ways'.[65] Sanjib Baruah similarly observes on the matter of the British view that the hills and plains were different entities, that 'This new perception led to a policy of strict boundary maintenance that was superimposed on a complex world of interrelationships . . . the colonial policy of segregation, combined with economic and cultural changes in the hills and the plains that took place during the colonial period, profoundly affected the new projects of peoplehood that emerged in the region'.[66]

Although with local variations, but remarkably similar in approach and outlook, this same colonial policy would be replicated in other theatres in the Zomian political geography where hills and valleys, State and non-State, revenue and no-revenue areas found themselves juxtaposed, and thereby, sharing a common existential destiny as in Assam. Manipur is another example of such a conflict theatre.

Eastern buffers

The Inner Line was obviously not the limit of British India territory in the Northeast region as the British saw it. The name Inner Line, however, itself implies an Outer Line. But was there ever a tangible, demarcated Outer Line? It does not seem so, and this Outer Line – it seems, at best – was notional, though some scholars – not the least, Alastair Lamb – insist there was, and that this line ran not only parallel to, but also almost exactly where the Inner Line was. At some sectors, Lamb argues, the Inner Line and the Outer Line were the same.[67] Officially, however, this does not seem to be the case. Unlike the Inner Line, which was created by the Bengal Eastern Frontier Regulation of 1873, there is no record of any Regulation or Act that created the so-claimed Outer Line. It is likely then the Outer Line existed vaguely in the official circuits, but at the unofficial level, largely as a result of confusing the Inner Line as Outer Line by government functionaries at the operational level. I will go a little deeper into this controversy in the next chapter for this controversy is not pointless. Based on the claim of the existence of an Outer Line, or else, confusing the Inner Line as the Outer Line in the north, Arunachal Pradesh has been in the eye of a storm with China claiming it.

For now, I will return to the question more relevant to the present discussion: where then was the outer limit of British India's frontier beyond the Inner Line? I will tackle the eastern border first. Alexander Mackenzie, lieutenant governor of Bengal when Assam was still a part of the British province of Bengal, provides a glimpse into the answer.[68] Very broadly, the policy outlook was to keep both the then non-State spaces on either flanks of the small kingdom of Manipur – to the north, the Naga Hills, and to the south, the Lushai Hills, as well as Manipur itself – as a buffer zone. Although there were pressures from tea planters and other businesses for the government to either abolish the Inner Line, or else, to extend the government's direct control beyond the Inner Line, so they could benefit from the protection of the law while prospecting and expanding their interests in the hills, the government remained reluctant to do so. One of the main reasons for this was the poor revenue prospects from these hills. For instance, on a suggestion by Nowgong authorities in 1839 of making the Naga Hills 'a substantive district under a separate officer',[69] the objection was, from this proposed district, 'the whole return would have been only Rs. 3,000 yearly, against an expenditure of over Rs. 16,000'.[70] The scheme was, therefore, not approved. Similar considerations also held the British administration back from immediately occupying the Lushai hills. As for the small kingdom of Manipur in between these two un-administered hill tracts, which the British helped liberate from the occupying forces of Burma in 1826, they had a different use.

To understand the mind of the colonial authorities in their consideration of these frontier territories, it would be helpful to refer back once again to Lord Curzon's Romanes lecture. As in the picture of frontier administration sketched by Curzon, after their entry into the Northeast, the British obviously wanted to follow a policy of 'frontier of active responsibility', defined as a condition of administration whereby 'over many of these tribes we exercise no jurisdiction, and only the minimum of control; into the territories of some we have not so far not even penetrated; but they are on the British side of the dividing line, and cannot be tampered with by any external Power'.[71] He also talks of how, in his own time in India, he had pursued a policy of encouraging the communities in these buffer territories 'to find in their self-interest and employment as Frontier Militia a guarantee both for the security of our inner or administrative borders and also for the tranquillity of the border zone itself'.[72]

Before we return to the actual policies and practices of these parameters by the British administration in their dealing with the territories beyond the Inner Line, one more question should be interesting, and indeed, prerequisite to an explanation of all these policies. If these territories were to serve as buffers, who were the British buffering themselves from? Burma had not only been conclusively defeated in the First Anglo–Burmese War, but also, in many ways, had become a de facto subordinate State After the Treaty of Yandabo of 1826, the British quite visibly exercised a hegemonic relations with the Burmese, making the latter concede to its whims, annexing its western provinces of Arakan and Tenasserim to British India, altering boundaries at will, including in 1881, when it set up a boundary commission to realign the boundary between Manipur and Burma and going ahead with it even when the Burmese refused to be part of the commission. If Burma at the time was still considered a threat to British territory, it was, by no means, a major one. Applying Curzon's brief summary of this scenario, Burma itself appears part of a buffer against another European power, the French.

Outlining the policy of protectorates of the Indian Empire, he says the first concern is to surround 'its acquisitions with a belt of Native States with whom alliances were concluded and treaties made'. Such a policy in the Northeast resulted in a chain of protectorates, including Nepal, Sikkim and Bhutan and 'on the extreme north-east the annexation of Upper Burma has brought to us the heritage of a fringe of protected States known as the Upper Shan States'.[73] Beyond the protectorates of the Shan States and the State of Siam, lay the 'Spheres of Interest' of another great European power, France.[74] This policy was being pursued with equal earnest by France in the east of the British Empire and Russia in the north-west of it, Curzon also notes. It is also known how, beginning from the signing of the Treaty of Yandabo, bit by bit, the whole of Burma would ultimately be annexed to British India through wars which were, in essence, excuses forced on an unwilling adversary to cede territories. As many are of the opinion, British rule in Burma can actually be said to extend from 1824, when the British forces effectively defeated the Burmese in Assam and then in Manipur, to 1948, when Burma became independent after the end of British paramountcy.[75]

On the Northeast frontier too, just as Curzon described the British Empire's north-western frontier in Afghanistan, the British frontier policy was also marked by a need to create a multi-buffered frontier. The first layer of the buffer would be the territories between the Inner Line and the imagined Outer Line that would form the boundary between British territory and that of Burma; after this would be the State of Burma itself; then come the protectorates of Shan States and the State of Siam before the French spheres of interest is encountered in Indo-China and Yunnan. It is of extreme relevance here that one of the pretexts of the Third Burmese War in 1885, by which the British waged war on Burma and annexed the rest of whatever remained independent of the country, was that the latter was getting too close to the French. It would also be of interest here to recall how Curzon described the layered buffer on the Afghanistan frontier more lucidly: 'The result in the case of the Indian Empire is probably without precedent, for it gives to Great Britain not a single or double but a threefold Frontier, (1) the administrative border of British India, (2) the Durand Line, or Frontier of active protection, (3) the Afghan border, which is the outer or advanced strategical Frontier'.[76]

What then was the nature of the Northeast's eastern frontier? To answer this, I will need to go a little deeper into the British outlook towards its eastern buffer territories lying between its Inner Line in Assam and Burma. I will not extend this brief discussion to the more southerly frontiers of Tripura, Chittagong Hills Tract and Meghalaya, though they too shared much of the concerns and policies of the British, for the chief reason that they were embedded within British India territory already from the time of the Treaty of Yandabo and, therefore, remained internal issues of the British administration. They would, however, be touched upon in other chapters.

Mizoram, Manipur, Nagaland

The region that now constitutes the three states of Mizoram, Manipur and Nagaland, with Manipur placed right in between the other two, for reasons quite obvious – in particular, of geography – were always treated as different segments of a single frontier of concern by the British administration. Equally understandably, the pasts of the peoples of this sub-region were also very intricately intertwined, not just in relatively recent historical times, but also in their myths and legends. In a classic illustration of James Scott's panoramic sketch of Zomia, the small but very fertile Imphal river valley nurtured a paddy State. The Naga Hills and the Lushai Hills, which flank Manipur to the north and south, were non-State by this definition. Alexander Mackenzie's assessment of this frontier from the British standpoint is revealing. He describes how Manipur was used in shaping the British relations with the Naga Hills and the Lushai Hills of Assam, for Manipur 'though independent, is at the same time a protected State, and has played and continues to play a prominent part in the politics of the North-East Frontier'.[77]

According to British estimates of the time, 'Manipur is a little territory lying on our North-East Frontier between Cachar and Burma. The population is about 75,000, and the aggregate money revenue is about Rs. 21,000 per annum, in addition to a considerable amount of land revenue, which is paid in kind . . . The region is rich but undeveloped'.[78] This account also mentions that 'the early history of Manipur was barbarous in the extreme. It was not only marked by constant raids of the Manipuris into Burma, and of Burmese into Manipur, but by internal wars of the most savage and revolting type, in which sons murdered fathers and brothers murdered brothers, without a single trait of heroism to relieve the dark scene of blood and treachery'.[79] Obviously, the reference is to the succession wars to the Manipur throne, the reality of which needs no reminder. The account further notes that a form of 'slavery' called 'Laloop', by which every adult subject of the king was obliged to give free compulsory service of 10 days in 40 days to the State, existed as an institution. It also says 'the hill tribes, consisting of numerous Naga and Kookie clans, also live in frequent feud'.[80]

These observations provide valuable insights into the social structures, mores and institutions of the then kingdom of Manipur. Succession norms of the monarchy were obviously still not fine-tuned or institutionalised strongly enough, therefore the perpetual fratricidal wars for control of the throne among the royals. As Scott predicted, this paddy State too was in short supply of manpower, therefore the Laloop system is an ingenious device by which available manpower was optimised. Under this system, it was mandatory for every adult in whatever profession to contribute 10 days of 40 days of free service to the King, and these services are often military duties. Those who rendered Laloop service to the King, however, were exempted from paying taxes.[81] It is, therefore, also a form of tax. For a small State perpetually on a warpath with a more powerful neighbour, Burma, each taking turns to raid the other, this ingenuity in manpower organisation must have been a survival need.

In the same breath, the report sketches how the hills were, at the time, still beyond ordinary law. The British intent of keeping this belt of hill tracts as its first layer of buffer was always quite transparent. A memo by none other than the governor general of British India at the time, Lord William Bentinck, on 25 March 1833 outlined this policy intent quite unambiguously.[82] Bentinck was quick to identify the important role that existing established States in the region – those of Tripura, Cachar and Manipur – would have to play. Manipur, in particular, was most vitally positioned in this theatre. Bentinck's note reveals how closely the British administration had been gathering revenue as well as military intelligence of principalities and communities in the region. In the note, giving an account of what Manipur's military strength might be, how many firearms its army might be possessing and what the status of fighting morale and discipline they could be in, he concludes that it might not be the army that can withstand an invasion from Burma or other superior forces, and floats the idea of placing a small garrison of British troops in the kingdom. This, he wrote, would probably be welcomed by the people, as they would see it as a measure for their protection.[83] It was in this spirit that the British signed two treaties with Manipur in 1833 and 1834. The 1833 treaty, apart from defining boundaries between British territories in Assam and Manipur, also made Manipur pledge that in the event of any war between the British and the Burmese, Manipur would assist the British. In another clause, the treaty also bound the Manipur king to come to the assistance of the British Government 'with a portion of his troops in anything happening on the Eastern Frontier of the British Territories'.[84] This clause made Manipur an anticipatory party to any adventures and expeditions of the British in both the Naga Hills as well as in the Lushai Hills. The 1834 treaty transferred the Kabaw valley, which had been awarded to Manipur by the Treaty of Yandabo, to Burma and a boundary line, which came to be known as the Pemberton Line, was drawn between Manipur and Burma, along the western edge of the Kabaw valley.

The 1833 treaty, which bound Manipur to assist the British, would come to be used to the fullest in the years leading to the latter's ultimate subjugation of the tribes both of the Naga Hills and the Lushai Hills. The Manipur Army, which, by the time, came to have a good number of Kukis, would be called into service to assist the British in numerous expeditions, punitive as well as exploratory into the hills, the details of which are beyond the scope of this book to recount. The increasing induction of Kukis in the Manipur Army again is a vindication of Scott's prediction that the Zomian paddy States, because of the increasing diversification of occupations as their economy got more sophisticated, were always short of manpower and looked to other denizens of Zomia to fill these shortages.

Naga Hills

The British, as a matter of policy, would have left these hill tribes living beyond their Inner Line alone, had it not been for the rise in the raids the latter made into the plains of Assam, where a thriving tea industry was rapidly expanding its gardens, often encroaching into territories that the tribes considered theirs traditionally. Both among the Lushais as well as the Angami Nagas, there was also, as the British soon discovered once they started penetrating into these hills, a slave-taking and trading tradition, which made them raid the plains to take captives. If this is so, this is another area where Scott's postulate needs revision. The raids for corvee labour were not always by the paddy States on the State evaders, but the other way around as well.

But despite enlisting Manipur as a partner in their projects of subjugating hill tribes, in many of the reports of British officials, a suspicion of Manipur secretly making alliances with factions of warring tribes, or else, ones opposed to the British, thereby playing their own politics, are quite open. In the Naga Hills, for instance, although the British sought Manipur's assistance in subduing the Nagas, they were also always wary that the Manipuris had their own design on the Naga Hills. Time after time, in political proceedings of the British administration, the matter of the partisan nature of their ally in dealing with various Naga issues came up. A discussion after a Naga raid at a Shan outpost in December 1844, for instance, brought up the charge that 'Manipuri troops had at this time again been actually helping one Naga clan to attack and destroy another. It seems impossible to get Manipur to carry out honestly the orders of the Government'.[85] After another series of Naga raids in December 1849, the matter of 'Manipur . . . fomenting disturbance by underhand intrigue' came up in another political proceeding.[86]

Manipur was again accused of aiding the Angami village of Konemah (as spelled in British report), hostile to the British, in the latter's feud with British-friendly Mozemah village in 1851. After capturing the stockade of Konemah, a report by a British officer said it would be safe to withdraw their troops if not for 'the Manipuris, of whose secret aid to the hostile Nagas he entertained no doubt, could be restrained from aiding them further'.[87] The matter was taken very seriously by the British government. It even merited a very strong caution from the governor general, Lord Dalhousie, in his minute of 20 February 1851. The governor general did not mince words or hide his rage:

> With respect to the share the State of Manipur has borne in these transactions, I must observe, that the reasoning by which Major Jenkins is led to assume that Manipur has been abetting the Nagas is loose in the extreme.
>
> If however, better proof of the fact be shown, and the complicity of Manipur either recently or hereafter shall be satisfactorily established, there can be no difficulty in dealing with it.
>
> In such case it would be expedient to remind the Rajah of Manipur that the existence of his State depends on a word from the Government of India; that it will not suffer his subjects openly or secretly, to aid and abet the designs of the enemies of this

Government; and that if he does not at once control his subjects and prevent their recurrence to any unfriendly acts, the word on which the existence of his State depends will be spoken, and its existence will be put an end to.[88]

The authenticity of these reports of a secret alliance between certain Angami villages and the Manipur Rajah is not known, though stories abound both in Nagaland and Manipur even today that this was true. Such stories are there of the climactic confrontation between the British and the Angamis in October 1879, when Angami tribesmen of various villages, led by Konemah (Khonoma), laid siege to the British headquarters in Kohima. When all seemed lost for the British post after a week of siege and attacks, the news that 2,000 soldiers of Manipur were approaching Kohima broke the siege. Colonel James Johnstone with a strong detachment of Manipuri troops, on 17 October, 'marched in unopposed, and the siege was at an end'.[89]

The famous Battle of Khonoma followed, the outcome of which marked the beginning of the complete dominance of the Naga Hills by the British. Rumours of a tacit understanding between the Angamis and the Manipur Rajah in this case too, if at all, have never been proven, but nonetheless exist. But even if the rumours have a basis, and there indeed were secret fraternal bondages established between the two parties, it would be only understandable. After all, they were neighbouring communities who, despite all their differences, have lived and accommodated each other in the same region for as long as their living memories. They would very well have found ways of coexistence while accommodating their differences, just as the Posa symbolised such a relationship in Assam.

The Lushai Hills

The script is quite similar in the Lushai Hills, south of Manipur. Just as colonial historians recorded, these hills were inhabited by a number of kindred but bitterly warring tribes, each ousting and pushing the other northwards. They would not only raid each other in the hills beyond the Inner Line, but often also into the administered territory of the British government in the Assam plains within the Inner Line, besides the fringes of Cachar, Manipur and Tripura. With an expanding tea industry in the Assam plains, this became a cause for concern for the British. As noted already, to the extent possible, as in the case of the Naga Hills, the British tried to follow a policy of no intervention, and instead, tried to have Manipur and Cachar control these tribes. The Cachari kingdom at the time was extremely weak, and as in the case of the Nagas, their king, Tularam, pleaded helplessness, so much of the responsibility fell on Manipur.[90]

The tribesmen continued their devastating periodic raids in the tea gardens in Cachar, but things went out of hand in 1871, when, beginning 23 January, a Lushai party under chief Sookpilal[91] made a series of murderous raids, and one of these was at the Alexandrapore tea garden in Cachar, destroying its factory, killing the planter living there, Mr Winchester, and wounding many and carrying away captives, including six-year-old Mary Winchester, daughter of the murdered planter. The raids happened even as a civil officer in Cachar with very moderate views, J. Ware Edgar, was reportedly in the raider's village to negotiate boundaries and terms for peace.[92]

The event occasioned a major punitive expedition into the Lushai Hills from 9 December 1871 to 24 February 1872, in which, again, Manipur's service was requisitioned. Several villages were severely punished until the responsible chiefs were subdued. The captors surrendered Mary Winchester in December itself, but the operations continued and were called off only upon 'submission of the tribes being now complete'.[93] The operations, from the point of view of the British, 'were decidedly successful'.[94] Indeed, what the siege of Kohima and the Battle of Khonoma in 1879 was for the Naga Hills, the Lushai Expedition of 1871–72 was for the Lushai Hills.

What happened on the Manipur side is of interest. The peculiar relationship between the British authorities and its protectorate state of Manipur is once again brought to the fore by an incident during this expedition, and some more, which I will scan briefly. As in the case of Manipur's relationship with the Naga tribes in the north, here too, this alliance was marked by an implicit suspicion by the British of the kingdom's own politics and relationships with the various hill tribes that might go against British interests. According to Mackenzie's account, during the Lushai Expedition of 1871, the Manipur king supplied a contingent of about 2,000 men accompanied by Manipur's two majors at the time, Thangal and Balaram, who acted under the order of Major-General W. F. Nuthall, the then officiating political agent in Manipur.[95] Quite obviously, a good percentage of these soldiers would have been Kukis, as by then, the Manipur king's soldiery constituted a good percentage of Kukis, as also another incident, which I will recount later will demonstrate.

General Nuthall was 'to occupy the extended line of posts along the southern boundary of Manipur' to block off the Lushais while Brigadier-General Bourcheir was executing the punitive operations in the

Lushai Hills through Cachar. This ostensibly was also to test the fidelity of the Kamhows or Sooties[96] to the British and see if they would extend help in the operations against the Lushais. After the operations, when the Manipur troops were returning, 'they fell in with a party of Kamhows under their chief named Kokatung, who were carrying away 957 captives from two Lushai villages'.[97] The Manipur troops took into custody the Kamhow captors and their chief, Kokatung, and imprisoned them. They also took the captive Lushais to Manipur and settled them there as free subjects. In the political proceedings that followed the Lushai Expedition, the Kamhow incident was described as 'treacherous' by the operation commander, Brigadier-General Bourcheir and Mr Edgar, the liberal civil officer from Cachar, who also took part in the expedition; after all, the Kamhows were helping the British in fighting the Lushais. General Nuthall, though not around when the arrest of the Kamhow fighters were made as he and his party had gone a little ahead, however, defended the action of the two Manipur majors, saying the Kamhows have been committing raids on the Manipur king's distant villages in past years. Despite the unsavoury incident, the Kamhows made peace with the Manipur Rajah two years later in 1873. Their chief, Kokatung, would die in Manipur prison, but all the rest of their captured clansmen, including Kokatung's son, would be released.[98]

Details of the account of the Lushai Expedition by the same civil officer, Edgar, from Cachar provide more insights into the various layers of underlying frictions that caused conflict in the region at the time. On the Lushai raids, which led to the extreme resorts on the part of the British, he wrote: 'The raids could have been averted if we had been less ignorant of the Lushais and taken more trouble to find out their grievances', noting that the 'Lushais, like the Nagas in the north, looked upon the extension of the tea-gardens as encroachments upon tracts which they claimed as their own'.[99]

In another lengthy note after a reconciliatory trek through the Lushai Hills, after the dust of the Lushai Expedition had settled, he wrote that despite all the raids and retributive expeditions which had happened, a deeper mutual affinity and respect between the communities were still not lost and he also realised 'from the statements of the Lushais who came to see me at the end of the rain, that the eastern people still looked upon Manipur with some of the feeling with which Colonel McCulloch had tried to inspire them'. The memo also notes 'in the same way whenever I spoke about Vonolel or any of his sons, except Deowte, I was told that they sent Muntries and presents into Manipur, and that they wished to be the Rajah's people'. Among Edgar's recommendations is: 'If the Rajah of Manipur were to fix a boundary for the Lushais and to tell them that it would be respected only as long as they behaved well, he would have no small security for their future good conduct. The effect of this would be still greater if the Political Agent were to go over some of this boundary with the Lushais, and if the Rajah were to give them a sunnud counter-signed by him'. He continues with his reconciliatory note that 'the Lushais would probably meet the Political Agent with presents, some for the Rajah and some for himself. The Rajah might be encouraged to make some return presents, and the Political Agent might be allowed to give something of small value on the part of our Government'.[100]

There are many more instances to demonstrate the suspicion British officials always had of possible secret friendships of and understandings the Manipur Rajah may have established with various hill tribes to the south. There were also many expeditions to control raiding tribes, including one in 1857, in which the young Maharaja Chandrakirti, then in his mid-twenties joined, which ended disastrously even before the expedition commenced, when his troops broke up in panic and fled. Many more expeditions, both punitive as well as exploratory, independently conducted as well in assistance of the British, followed under more experienced commands. A particular one in 1871 was interesting.

Violent tribal raids among each other as well as clan feuds were common features of the Indo-Burma region from very early times, but after the award of Kabaw valley to Burma in 1834 and the subsequent drawing of a boundary along the western edge of the valley and the eastern slope of the 'Murring hills' – an imaginary line which came to be known as the Pemberton Line after the name of the British officer, Captain R. Boileau Pemberton, who drew it – these feuds often acquired an international dimension as many of the feuding clans found themselves on either side of the boundary. This made law-keeping next to impossible as the tribes would slip in or out across the international boundary.

An episode will illustrate this point. In the 1871 incident, a party of Balaram, Major of Manipur, who had just been raised to the rank of Ayapoorel Major (Manipur Foreign Minister)[101], had gone to the Burma border area with a few soldiers to acquaint himself with his new responsibility. While on this trip, his men had a dispute with a border village, where they halted for a night, and the villagers rose and killed 12 of his men. This led to the Ayapoorel to make a punitive expedition accompanied by '150 Manipuri sepoys and 700 Hill Kookies . . . They assembled at Khongal Thannah, from whence they proceeded and destroyed the offending village, killing nine men, and then returned to the Thannah'.[102]

However, when the party returned to base, it was found that the Burmese had lodged a complaint with Manipur that the Kookies soldiers with the Ayapoorel Major had, during the night, raided Nampee, falling within the territory of Samjok, a Shan kingdom on the Burmese side of the border and a tributary state of Burma. The Ayapoorel, however, stood by his soldiers and said such an attack would not have been possible for his party returned to Kongal Thannah on 1 February after their mission was accomplished, and the attack on Nampee was said to have been on the night of 2 February. Though 'none of the Kongjais were seen between the Kongal Thannah and Nampee, they were accused because the Burmese considered that no other party could have committed the raid'.[103]

The then political agent, Dr R. Brown, who was out of station in Cachar at the time, upon his return, recommended to the Maharaja the suspension of the Ayapoorel for this offence, pending an inquiry. The young Maharaja Chandrakirti, however, said such a rash action before a proper enquiry to ascertain guilt would be unfair. An enquiry was set up in which Dr Brown alleged the king threw up hurdles before the enquiry. In the course of the enquiry, however, Dr Brown, along with the Ayapoorel Major, visited Nampee in the Samjok kingdom. There, they found no evidence of the claimed attack, and even the king of Samjok avoided meeting Dr Brown's team on the plea of indifferent health of his mother. The Ayapoorel's name was thus cleared.[104]

Apart from betraying their inherent distrust of the kingdom's functionaries and the relationships they established with the hill tribes, the incident was also to make the British realise the extra burden now of habitual skirmishes of border tribes assuming the dimension of bilateral international issues. This matter became even more urgent with the rise in prominence and aggressiveness of Chasad Kookies in the border area. They began terrorising Lahoopa Naga (Tangkhul) villages in Angoching ranges in Burmese territory as well as more Tangkhul villages within Manipur jurisdiction. The Kookies were armed with guns, allegedly supplied by the Samjok king, and therefore, were no match for the other villages. The Chasad Kookies began their major attacks around 1878, and things were threatening to go out of hand. Col. James Johnstone had taken over as the political agent in Manipur and he too was not very happy in the way Manipur dealt with the Chasad problem. Some incidents will highlight the cause for this dissatisfaction.

On December 1878, six Manipuri sepoys at Kongal Thannah were overpowered and taken into custody 'by a party of 30 Chasad Kookies and six Kubo men' and were in their custody for 26 days, but were not subject to any indignity. The sepoys were then brought to Yangapokpee Thannah and handed over to the subedar in charge, along with their weapons and a letter to Tangal (Thangal) Major, the charismatic commander of the Manipur Army, who would be made general in time, that the sepoys were arrested because they strayed into Burmese territory.[105]

The Chasad Kookies' rampage in the border continued, especially on Naga villages, razing Chingsao, Chattik, Chowhoom Khoonao and then, Chowhoom Khoolel, and the Kookies were assisted by Shan soldiers of the Samjok king, ostensibly in the hope that these villages would want to sever ties with Manipur and seek to be subjects of the Samjok king, a tributary kingdom of Mandalay.[106] Colonel Johnstone was convinced Chasad fell within Manipur territory by the Pemberton Line, and had the Manipur government send a punitive expedition, led by Thangal Major and Balaram Major to chastise the Chasad Kookies. The political agent was again greatly disappointed at the manner the expedition was managed: 'The Chasad were allowed under pretence of negotiations, to leave their village in a body, and finally nothing was done', except to burn some houses. The Burmese too did little or nothing to help.

The suspicion of complicity aside, these developments led Colonel Johnstone to begin to feel the need for boundary realignment so that the uncertainty of jurisdiction along the border ended and Manipur did not have to enter Burmese territory on these punitive expeditions. The chief commissioner of Assam at the time, C.A. Elliott, concurred: 'Manipur, as a protected State, is prohibited from seeking forcible remedies in the shape of reprisals, and it is only to the interference of the British Government that she can look either for satisfaction or protection'.[107]

1881 boundary commission

A boundary commission was finally set up in 1881 to rectify the flaws of the 1834 Pemberton Line with Colonel Johnstone as Boundary Commissioner and R. Phayre, C.S. of the British Burma Commission, as his assistant. The Maharaja of Manipur deputed his Ayapoorel to the Commission. The Burmese government, however, refused to participate, so did the Sumjok Rajah on the plea he was not authorised by Mandalay. Nonetheless, on 10 January 1882, the mission was completed.

> It was found that the imaginary boundary known as Pemberton's line had been incorrectly drawn on the map, for it neither agreed

with the actual condition of things, nor did it carry out the terms of the Treaty of 1834: for, instead of following the eastern slopes of the Yomadoung or Malain Hills, and curving round the head of the valley, it cut off from Burma and handed over to Manipur a large portion of the Kubo Valley. The Commission, however, laid down a boundary which agrees as nearly as possible with the terms of the Treaty, while it gives a fair and clearly-marked frontier. The boundary thus fixed follows the base of the eastern slopes of the Malain range, crosses the River Namia a few hundred yards south of Kangal Thanna, thence turns east to the Talain River, follows that river upward to its source, and then proceeds down the Napanga River to where it passes through a gorge in Kusom range. From thence it runs northward along the crest of that range. The point where the boundary intersects the Namia River and touches the Talain River have been marked with pillars, and a road has been cut connecting these two points.[108]

This boundary was not ratified by the Burmese government, but brought the desired result. 'Some of the Chasad villages situated on the frontier formerly debated have moved westwards and peaceably settled down as quiet subjects of Manipur, and thus removed the possibility as to whether they belong to Burmese or Manipur territory'.[109] Not long after, in 1885, the whole of Burma would be annexed and incorporated into British India, recasting the urgency of this border. Manipur's service would be called for again during the British campaign to annex Burma, this time to rescue European employees of the Bombay Burmah Corporation from Kendat in the Chindwin valley. James Johnstone and the Ayapoorel on 19 December marched to Burma with a force of 50 men of Johnstone's 'own escort of the 4th Bengal Native Infantry, and some 300 or 400 Manipuris'.[110] They reached Kendat on Christmas and, after a brief engagement with Burmese forces, accomplished their mission.[111] In 1891, Manipur too would be taken over by the British, further reducing the significance of the boundary. Still another British political agent, Lt. Col. H. St. P. Maxwell, made minor changes to the line in 1896 and erected 38 boundary pillars along it.

The Burma–Manipur boundary was hence the only treaty-backed boundary in Northeast India's eastern frontier in the colonial era. Though without the benefit of treaties, other sectors of the boundary with Burma were also determined, but the entire boundary was ratified only in 1967 by the Boundary Agreement between the Government of the Republic of

India and the Government of the Union of Burma, signed at Rangoon on 10 March 1967.[112]

> In 1837, the Paktai Range was accepted as the boundary between Assam and Burma, being delimited without benefit of a treaty after British annexation of Assam, Cachar, and Jaintia. In 1834, the Manipur-Chin Hills boundary was demarcated, and in 1896 Col. Maxwell re-demarcated the Pemberton-Johnstone area, placing thirty-eight pillars on the ground. These are referred to by number in the 1967 agreement. The Lushai Hills – Chin Hills boundary was demarcated in 1901 with minor alterations in 1921 and 1922.[113]

The Government of India Act 1935 envisaged the separation of Burma from India and this came into effect in April 1947. The boundary between India and Burma that the colonial government described at the time was: 'all territories which were immediately before the commencement of Part II of this Act comprised in India, being territories lying to the east of Bengal, the State of Manipur, Assam, and tribal areas connected with Assam'.[114]

After World War II, when both Burma and India gained their independence from the British, no Burma–India boundary was specified in the Independence Acts. Resolution of the border was thus left to the newly independent governments, and such a resolution was achieved by the 10 March 1967 Rangoon Treaty.[115]

In these curious interactions in the Zomian space shared by the paddy state of Manipur and the non-State Naga Hills and Lushai Hills of the time under the watchful eyes of the colonial authorities was thus demonstrated what Curzon meant by a buffer. It is a sphere of influence which is 'less developed form than a Protectorate, but it is more developed than a Sphere of Interest. It implies a stage at which no exterior Power but one may assert itself in the territory so described, but in which the degree of responsibility assumed by the latter may vary greatly with the needs or temptations of the case. The native Government is as a rule left undisturbed; indeed its unabated sovereignty is sometimes specifically reaffirmed'.[116]

Other than the administrative outlook of the British in the Northeast, I have also tried to show the response of local administrators to the same situations before the arrival of the British. The Posa system of the Ahom as a reconciliation strategy evolved through shared experience of strengths and limitations of the hill communities and the kingdoms in the valleys was one of these. In the relationships between Manipur, Naga Hills and Lushai Hills too, though their articulations were muted under the hegemonic supervision of the British colonial authorities, despite their overt feuds, the undercurrents of another essential bondage established through aeons of sharing the same living space and resultant acknowledgement of the inevitability of continuing to live as neighbours were also unmistakable.

It may be a coincidence, but the two commanders of the Manipur Army, Thangal Major and Balaram Major, left legends and myths that have lived long after they are gone. Balaram, who died in 1889, two years before Manipur lost its independence, was generally assigned the responsibility of looking after the southern hills. Described as coolheaded and firm, he became extremely close to the southern tribes, and indeed today, the Kukis claim he and his Sougaijam clan were Kukis by kinship originally. Though there was no watertight division of responsibilities between the two, Thangal, the more charismatic and well-known of the two, described as bold though often rash, generally looked after the northern hills. He lived on to fight for his kingdom's independence against the British in 1891 and, after defeat, was hanged to death along with Jubaraj Tikendrajit and others for waging war against the Empire, while some more princes in the rebel camp were exiled to Andaman and Nicobar Islands, then known notoriously as Kala Pani. Thangal too is claimed today by the Thangal Nagas as one of their own flesh and blood. Whatever the veracity of these claims, they do unmistakably tell of a different story of human bondages between the different communities of this Zomian landscape before the dawn of the modern among them.

Notes

1 http://en.wikipedia.org/wiki/Burma_Office (accessed on 3 March, 2014).
2 I use the term 'State' with upper case 'S' to signify its usage indicating a sovereign political organisation, and with a lower case 's' to signify its usage in the sense of a province of India.
3 http://en.wikipedia.org/wiki/Zomia_(geography) (accessed on March 3, 2014).
4 E. H. Carr, *What Is History, The George Macaulay Trevelyan lectures delivered in the University of Cambridge January – March 1961* (Penguin Books, 1961).
5 See http://www.un.org/esa/socdev/unpfii/documents/DRIPS_en.pdf (accessed on 3 September 2015).
6 After the nationalist Bharatiya Janata Party took over power in New Delhi in 2014, this trend has somewhat been, with a conscious effort, reversed.
7 See Francis Fukuyama, *The End of History and the Last Man* (Penguin Books, 1992).
8 See Ramachandra Guha, *India after Gandhi: History of the World's Largest Democracy* (Picador, 2008).

9 Among the preconditions of the Naga militant group, National Socialist Council of Nagalim, led by Isak Swu and Thuingaleng Muivah, NSCN(IM), for peace talks with the Government of India, for instance, is the latter's recognition of the 'unique' history of the Nagas.
10 See James C. Scott, *Art of Not Being Governed*.
11 The description of this episode and its analysis are a summary of the author's article in *Economic and Political Weekly* immediately in the wake of the trouble, titled *The Homeland and the State: The Meiteis and the Nagas in Manipur*, Economic and Political Weekly, June 26, 2010 Vol XLV Nos 26 and 27.
12 See Benedict Anderson, *Imagined Communities: Reflections on the Origin and Spread of Nationalism* (Verso, 1983).
13 See Friedrich Engel, *Evolution of Family Private Property and State*.
14 See, Col. L.W. Shakespear, *History of Assam Rifles*.
15 See Prof. Gangmumei Kamei, *Jadonang a Mystic Naga Rebel*.
16 See, D. G. E. Hall, *A History of South East Asia*, pp. 359–62, G. E. Harvey, *History of Burma* and p. 283, Edward Gait, *A History of Assam*, p. 321, for an account of the frequency and manner in which the Kabaw Valley changed hands between Manipur and Ava kingdoms.
17 See Bodhisattva Kar, *When Was the Postcolonial? A History of Policing Impossible Lines*, in *Beyond Counter-insurgency: Breaking the Impasse in Northeast India* (ed.) Sanjib Baruah, pp. 49–77.
18 D. G. E. Hall, *A History of South East Asia* (Macmillan London, 1964), pp. 262–3.
19 Gait, *A History of Assam*, p. 321.
20 D. G. E. Hall, *A History of South East Asia*, pp. 385–7; see also G. E. Harvey, *History of Burma, from the Earliest Time to 10 March 1824, the Beginning of the English Conquest* (Frank Cass & Co, 1967), pp. 238–9 and 208–12.
21 D.G.E. Hall, *A History of South East Asia*, p. 387.
22 Lord Curzon of Kedleston, *Romanes Lecture 1907*, https://www.dur.ac.uk/resources/ibru/resources/links/curzon.pdf (accessed 4 March, 2014).
23 Ibid.
24 Ibid.
25 Ibid.
26 Curzon, *Frontiers*, 1907.
27 Ibid.
28 Gait, *A History of Assam*, p. 387.
29 Ibid., p. 387.
30 Bodhisattva Kar, *When Was the Postcolonial? A History of Policing Impossible Lines*, occurring in *Beyond Counter-insurgency: Breaking the Impasse in Northeast India*, Sanjib Baruah (ed.) (Oxford University Press, 2009), p. 52.
31 Ibid.
32 Ibid., p. 54.
33 Ibid.
34 Gait, *A History of Assam*, p. 386.
35 James C. Scott, *Art of Not Being Governed: An Anarchist History of Upland Southeast Asia* (Orient Blackswan, 2009), p. ix.

36 Ibid., p. 129.
37 Ibid., p. ix.
38 Ibid., p. 128.
39 Gait, *A History of Assam*, pp. 364–5.
40 James C. Scott, *Art of Not Being Governed*, p.ix.
41 Gait, *A History of Assam*, p. 365.
42 G. E. Harvey, *History of Burma*, p. 239.
43 Bryce Beemer (Sr. Fullbright Scholar), *Slave Taking Tradition in South East Asia*, lecture delivered at the Manipur University, 2010.
44 Alexander Mackenzie, *History of the Relations of the Government with the Hill Tribes of the North-East frontier of Bengal* (reprinted by Mittal Publication 1999, as *The North-East Frontier of India*), p. 7.
45 Ibid., p 54. See also Bodhisattva Kar, *When was the Postcolonial?* Sanjib Baruah (ed.), p. 63.
46 Alexander Mackenzie, *History of the Relations*, p. 54.
47 Bodhisattva Kar, *When Was the Postcolonial?*, p. 63.
48 Ibid., p. 67.
49 Ibid.
50 Gait, *A History of Assam*, p. 365.
51 Barpujari H. K., *Problem of the Hill Tribes: North-East Frontier, 1873–1962 Vol-III* (Spectrum Publication, Guwahati), p. 7.
52 Bodhisattva Kar, *When Was the Postcolonial?*, p. 68.
53 Annual Report upon Native States and Frontier Tribes of Assam (as quoted in Ibid., p. 69).
54 Ibid., p. 70.
55 See Richard Falk, *The Rights of Peoples (In Particular Indigenous Peoples)*, James Crawford (ed.), *The Rights of Peoples* for discussion on such reconciliations.
56 The London School of Economics lecture is available on last access on 27 February 2014 at http://www.lse.ac.uk/newsAndMedia/videoAndAudio/channels/publicLecturesAndEvents/player.aspx?id=164 (accessed on 10 May 2013).
57 Bengt G. Karlsson, *Ethnicity in Northeast India through the Lens of James Scott* (Asian Ethnology Volume 72, Number 2, 2013).
58 Luthra P. N., *North-East Frontier Agency tribes: impact of Ahom and British policy*, Economic and Political Weekly 6(23): 1143–49, 1971 (as quoted in Jelle J. P. Wouters, 'Keeping the Hill Tribes at Bay: A Critique from India's Northeast of James C. Scott's Paradigm of State Evasion', *European Bulletin of Himalayan Research* 39, pp. 41–65 (2012)).
59 Alexander Mackenzie, *History of the Relations*, p. 7.
60 Jelle J. P. Wouters, Keeping the Hill Tribes at Bay: A Critique from India's Northeast of James C. Scott's Paradigm of State Evasion, *European Bulletin of Himalayan Research* 39, pp. 41–65 (2012).
61 Devi L., *Ahom-Tribal Relations: A Political Study*, 1968 (as quoted in Wouters, *Keeping the Hill Tribes at Bay*, pp. 41–65 (2012)).
62 Barpujari, H. K., *Problem of the Hill Tribes: North-East Frontiers, 1873–196*, p. 7.
63 Bodhisattva Kar, *When Was the Postcolonial? In Beyond Counter-insurgency: Breaking the Impasse in Northeast India*, Sanjib Baruah (ed.), p. 55.
64 Gait, *A History of Assam*, p. 387.

65 Jelle J. P. Wouters, *Keeping the Hill Tribes at Bay*, pp. 41–65 (2012).
66 Sanjib Baruah, *India Against Itself: Assam and the Politics of Nationality*, pp. 29–30.
67 See Alastair Lamb, *The McMahon Line, A Study in the Relations Between India, China and Tibet 1904 to 1914* (Routledge & Kegal Paul, 1966).
68 See Alexander Mackenzie, *History of the Relations of the Government with the Hill Tribes of the North-East frontier of Bengal (Reproduced by Mittal Publications, 1999).*
69 Political Proceedings, 14 August 1839, Nos. 107–109, as quoted in Alexander Mackenzie, *History of the Relations*, p. 105.
70 Ibid.
71 Curzon, Frontier, *Romanes Lecture, 1907*.
72 Ibid.
73 Ibid.
74 Ibid.
75 http://en.wikipedia.org/wiki/British_rule_in_Burma.
76 Curzon, *Romanes lecture 1907*.
77 Alexander Mackenzie, *History of the Relations of the Government*, p. 149.
78 Ibid.
79 Ibid.
80 Ibid., p. 150.
81 Komdam Singh Lisam, *Encyclopedia of Manipur*, p. 218.
82 Alexander Mackenzie, *History of the Relations of the Government with the Hill Tribes of the North-East Frontier of Bengal*, p. 151.
83 Ibid.
84 Aitchison's Treaties, Vol-1, p. 123 (reproduced in Ibid., p. 151).
85 Political Proceedings, 23 May 1846, Nos. 30–31, as quoted in Alexander Mackenzie, *History of the Relations of the Government*, p. 108.
85 Political Proceedings, 22 December 1849, No. 102, as quoted in Ibid., p. 111.
86 Alexander Mackenzie, *History of the Relations of the Government*, p. 113.
87 Governor General, Lord Dalhousie's Minute of 20 February 1851 (as reproduced in Alexander Mackenzie, *History of the Relations of the Government)*, pp. 113–15.
88 Alexander Mackenzie, *History of the Relations of the Government*, p. 136.
89 See Alexander Mackenzie, *History of the Relations of the Government . . .*
90 I have used spellings of the names and places, to the extent unavoidable, as they are entered in British records and reproduced in Ibid.
91 Alexander Mackenzie, *History of the Relations of the Government . . .*, p. 305.
92 Ibid., p. 316 (A blow-by-blow account of this major expedition is on pp. 312–16).
93 Ibid.
94 Political Proceedings (India), August 1872, No. 70 (as quoted in Ibid., p. 166).
95 Alexander Mackenzie, *History of the Relations of the Government*.
96 The spellings are as in British records. The Kamhows are Chin tribes from the Tiddim area of the Manipur–Burma border, and as Kuki scholars in

Manipur point out, and are close cousins of the Guite tribe of the Chin-Kuki family who are now also settled in Manipur.
97 Political Proceedings (India), August 1872, No. 70 (as quoted in Ibid., p. 166).
98 Ibid., p. 168.
99 FPA, 1872; August, 70 in Nos. 61–113, Edgar to Commissioner of Circuit, Dacca Division, 3 April (as quoted in H. K. Barpujari, *Problems of the Hill Tribes: North-East Region*, pp. 30–31).
100 The full text of J. W. Edgar's note to the Commissioner of Circuit, Dacca Division, No. 548, dated Cachar, 3rd April 1872, is attached as appendix in Alexander Mackenzie, *History of the Relations of the Government*, pp. 437–65.
101 Alexander Mackenzie, *History of the Relations of the Government . . .*, p. 188.
102 Ibid., p. 194.
103 Ibid. Kongjai is the term for Kuki in Manipuri.
104 Ibid., p. 196.
105 Ibid.
106 Ibid., p. 207.
107 Ibid., p. 206; see also James Johnstone, *Manipur and the Naga Hills* (republished Gian Offset 1983), pp. 208–15, for Johnstone's own account.
108 Ibid., p. 210; see also James Johnstone, *Manipur and the Naga Hills*, pp. 233–5.
109 Ibid.
110 Robert Reid, *History of the Frontier Areas Bordering on Assam, from 1883–1942* (republished Bhabani Books, 2013), p. 86; see also James Johnstone, *Manipur and the Naga Hills*, pp. 245–50.
111 Ibid.
112 See Rangoon Agreement and full text of boundary alignment at US State Department's website, http://www.law.fsu.edu/library/collection/limitsinseas/IBS080.pdf.
113 Ibid.
114 Ibid.
115 Ibid.
116 Lord Curzon, *Romanes Lecture 1907*.

4

INNER LINE AS OUTER LINE I
Making of the McMahon Line

When the British took over the administration of Assam in 1826 after repelling the Burmese in the First Anglo–Burmese War, Assam constituted almost the entire Northeast, with the exception of the kingdoms of Tripura and Manipur. Available commentaries and records from the period indicate there were two primary interests of the British in the newly acquired territory of Assam, which was initially made part of the British province of Bengal.

The first is strategic. The British were interested in keeping the region as the first layer of buffer between their established Indian territories and possible hostile neighbours and rival European powers, as we have seen in the previous chapter. That the British thought fit to intervene and stop the Burmese push westwards, beginning 1824, is testimony to this interest. The Burmese kingdom, with its capital at Mandalay, would also come to be ultimately annexed into the British India Empire after the Third Anglo–Burmese War in 1885, and Burma itself would become the next layer of buffer between core British territory and what Lord Curzon called 'spheres of interest'[1] of the rival European power, the French.

The second interest was economic. The region, it was soon to be discovered, is rich in mineral and forest resources. Its potential as a tea-growing area had already become evident. Robert Bruce encountered wild tea growing in the Assam hills in 1823, and in the next few decades, tea gardens rapidly spread through the Brahmaputra and Barak valleys, causing land pressure and frictions between tea planters and local farmers. These lucrative expanding business interests, obviously, had to have security cover. Details of how the British charted out their ways to ensure a level security matching their needs and interests, cost-effectively, have also already been described in the chapter on militarisation of the Northeast.

INNER LINE AS OUTER LINE I

A convenient entry point to start an assessment of the concerns of British administration in the Northeast region would be to briefly refer to the history of the McMahon Line 1914, the northern boundary of the Northeast, and the circumstances of its drawing. One of the consistent themes that run through all boundary-making exercises of the British in their former colonies is the notion of the frontier as distinct from a boundary. Here is how Sir Henry McMahon, the architect of the McMahon Line, described this notion. In his address to the Royal Society of Arts in 1935, he noted that 'a frontier meant a wide tract of borderland which, because of its ruggedness or other difficulties, served as a buffer between two states. A boundary, on the other hand, was a clearly defined line expressed either as a verbal distinction, that is, "delimited", or as a series of physical marks on the ground that is "demarcated". The former thus signified roughly a region, while the latter was a positive and precise statement of the limits of sovereignty'.[2]

The Northeast in British hands began as a frontier, therefore boundaries were ambiguous for a long time, and some of these ambiguities, in particular that of the McMahon Line, tragically still persist. This outlook is evident in the manner in which the British looked at the hill areas beyond the fertile alluvial plains of Assam. This is also again evident in Henry McMahon's effort to create a double-layered Tibet – Inner Tibet and Outer Tibet – the southern overlapping perimeters of which would form the border between Tibet and India, during the Simla Conference of 1913–14. This will come up for a more detailed discussion later in this chapter. There is still more evidence of this frontier approach to the Northeast. For instance, the notion of the 'excluded area' and 'partially excluded area' declared on 3 March 1937, as per the Government of India Act, 1935, amounts to giving an institutional mandate to this outlook. Much earlier, in the administration of the tribal areas of the Northeast, this approach had been around in different avatars. Hence, by the Government of India Act, 1919, the territories that came to be categorised as 'excluded areas' and 'partially excluded areas' were simply called as 'backward tracts' and were left un-administered.

The Bengal Eastern Frontier Regulation 1873 can be said to be a prominent predecessor of these later declarations. The regulation created an Inner Line beyond which no British subject could cross without a permit. However, as if anticipating future misinterpretations, British authorities and commentators of the time repeatedly stated that the Inner Line did not constitute the international border. By implication though, beyond this Inner Line was an Outer Line. However, this ambiguity, expected of any frontier, had to have its share of controversy. Some eminent scholars such as Alastair Lamb claim the Outer Line was not just implied, but existed officially, thereby raising the question of where this Outer Line actually was. This is pertinent, for if this Outer Line did exist officially, it would mean this was where the international boundary was between British India and Tibet. Furthermore, the path of the Outer Line, Lamb contends in a map,[3] is nearly identical to the Inner Line. It runs from the southern base of Bhutan along the foothills of Arunachal Pradesh right up to Nizamghat near Sadiya in the Lohit valley.

Outer Line

The intriguing thing about this claim is, if the Inner Line and the Outer Line are either identical or, else, are set apart by only a few kilometres, it does not make administrative sense. The British India government as well as the British home government denied there ever was an official Outer Line, and that the implied Outer Line was always roughly where the McMahon Line was drawn in 1913–14. Lamb himself notes that 'the India Office, as we have seen, was already in November 1911 implying that the new Outer Line was really the same as the old Outer Line. The Indian Republic is still saying this today'.[4] Tellingly however, while Lamb reproduces a number of maps showing separately the Inner Line and Outer Line, there is not one which has both the lines on the same map. He also acknowledges overlaps of the two in certain sectors: 'The definition of the Inner line in Darrang and Lakhimpur Districts of Assam adjacent to the Himalayan range, which took place in 1875–6, rather tended to obscure the definition of the international boundary, or Outer Line, which was made here at the same time'.[5]

Lamb is so passionate about this theory of the existence of two lines that he would go to the extent of calling those who deny this as 'apologists of the Indian side'.[6] He further writes: 'Of the existence of the Outer Line, however, there can be no real doubt. It has been implied in such instruments as the British agreement with some Abor *gams* . . . It followed the line of the foot of the hills a few miles to the north of what became the course of the Inner Line'.[7] Two administrative boundaries running parallel to each other, one of which is an international one, separated from each by only a few miles and even overlapping in certain sectors seem to defeat the very purposes of these lines, that is, if at all an Outer Line officially existed.

There probably were some inter-governmental exchanges of notes in which an Outer Line was referred to, but these could have been slips borne out of bureaucratic mental lethargy so common in routine and mundane references, and what was actually meant was the Inner Line itself, for unlike the Inner Line, which came into existence by promulgation of the Bengal

Eastern Frontier Regulation 1873, there exists no record of any ordinance or regulation or act by which the Outer Line was created. Since Lamb's old Outer Line runs along the foothills of the Assam hills, this supposed 'international boundary' excludes the present state of Arunachal Pradesh, somewhat giving credence to China's claim of this territory as South Tibet. Lamb claims this old Outer Line was later pushed northwards as a counter to a Chinese Forward Policy in the first decade of the twentieth century, to become the new 'Outer Line', or the McMahon Line.

Nobody, however, disputes or can dispute the existence of the Inner Line, which was created by a definite regulation. The logic for introducing this line, even Lamb admits, is also far from ambiguous: 'It was a device to create a buffer zone, as it were, between the international boundary and regularly administered territory, a tract which marked the transition between the tribal hills and the Assamese plains. By limiting access from the south to this area it was hoped to minimise the risk of trouble with the tribes. At the same time, tribesmen who crossed the international boundary from the north, but remained beyond the Inner Line, still passed under British jurisdiction should the authorities choose to exercise it'.[8]

The official explanation for introducing the line was that 'the unrestricted intercourse which formerly existed between British subjects in Assam and the wild tribes living across the frontier frequently led to quarrels and, sometimes, to serious disturbances. This was especially the case in connection with the traffic in rubber brought down by the hillmen, for which there was great competition. The opening out of tea gardens beyond the border-line also at times involved the Government in troublesome disputes with the frontier tribes in their vicinity'.[9] This line was 'being prescribed merely for the above purpose, it does not in any way decide the sovereignty of the territory beyond. Such a line has been laid down along the northern, eastern and south-eastern borders of the Brahmaputra valley'.[10] These accounts also indicate how the Inner Line was amenable to changes as per the whim of the administration: 'There was also formerly an Inner Line on the Lushai marches, but it has been allowed to fall into desuetude since our occupation of the Lushai hills'.[11] Further, the other important purpose of the Inner Line was to limit the land grab by tea planters into the hills causing frictions between the administration and the hill tribes. 'Planters are not allowed to acquire land beyond the Inner Line, either from the Government or from any local chief or tribe'.[12]

The Bengal Eastern Frontier Regulation, therefore, 'gives power to the Lieutenant Governor (of Bengal and with responsibility for Assam) to prescribe a line, to be called "inner line" in which each and any of the districts affected, beyond which no British subjects of certain classes or foreign residents can pass without a license. The pass or license, when given, may be subject to such conditions as may appear necessary. And rules are laid down regarding trade, the possession of land beyond the line, and other matters, which give the executive Government an effective control. The regulation also provides for the preservation of elephants, and authorizes Government to lay down rules for their capture'.[13]

However, even if the official existence of the Outer Line is doubtful, the very existence of an Inner Line still implies the existence of an imaginary Outer Line as well. The land in between these two lines was described as:

> It should be observed that Tibet is nowhere coterminous, with the settled districts of British India, but with a belt of country which, though geographically part of India, politically is partly a no-man's land inhabited by aboriginal savages, partly the territories of states, independent (Nepal), and subordinate (Bhutan and Sikkim) . . . [14]

It also implied that this imaginary Outer Line was along the watershed of these mountains. If so, then it vindicates the perception that this line was where the McMahon Line was formalised. For indeed, the underlying logic by which the McMahon Line was drawn is the watershed principle of map-making. 'Political relations are now being opened up with the tribes on the Indian side of the watershed – a step which was directly necessitated by the presence of Chinese missions among them, and by the Chinese military expedition to the Pomed country which is immediately north of the Abor country'.[15]

Even Lamb agrees on this point, saying if the old Outer Line that he claims was drawn by the British administration did not initially coincide with the international border demarcated by the McMahon Line, it does not necessary mean that 'the British frontier was also the Tibetan frontier'.[16] In other words, the intervening territory was, for all practical purposes, treated as wild 'no-man's land' till it was claimed officially and, in this case, by the McMahon Line.

Tawang question

If the no man's land explains this ambiguity, the Tawang question also provided a curious case, quite unique in its own way. Its inclusion in India when the McMahon Line was drawn was purely on security considerations, deviating from the usual practice of demarcating boundaries along natural land formations, such as mountain watersheds: 'It may be assumed, therefore, that in the middle of the Simla Conference Britain decided to extend her claims to Tawang on strategic grounds. The McMahon Line was a logical defence barrier and Sino-Tibetan territory should not be allowed to extend too close to the Brahmaputra valley. The Tawang monastery, moreover, was said to control villages south of Se La, so that administration would be easier if the whole area were included in Indian territory'.[17]

Otherwise, the Tawang Tract, which extends 'almost to the very edge of the Assam plains, is inhabited by tribes which, on any realistic scheme of classification, must be more closely related to Tibet than to the Indian lowlands. These are the Monpas, Buddhist, greatly Tibetanised in language and culture, similar to the inhabitants of Eastern Bhutan and, more remotely, to the Himalayan groups as the Lepchas of Sikkim'.[18]

There were also, indeed, British officials in India who were of the opinion that the Tawang should rightly belong to Tibet not just from the irredentist logic, but also from the point of view of administrative ease and benefits. Henry Twynam, who was acting governor of Assam during the absence of Governor Robert Reid during February 1939, took the opportunity to make himself heard. In a letter to Viceroy Lord Linlithgow on 17 March, he wrote that ' . . . from the practical point of view there is no advantage and considerable risk in pressing the matter further with the Tibetan Government'.[19] Twynam even suggests that it would be much more cost-effective for the administration to establish the frontier in the neighbourhood of the Se La pass and the Digien river, instead of India asserting their full rights under the McMahon Agreement to the whole of the Tawang area.[20] This letter was in the light of a discussion in the British administration as to whether an expedition should be sent to Tawang to send out a fresh message that Tawang was on the Indian side of the McMahon Line. Although it was true that Tawang was south of the McMahon Line, the British had allowed the border to remain soft in view of the cultural and ethnic affinities of the tribes on the Indian side of the McMahon Line and the Tibetans, and Tibet was allowed to continue to be the de facto suzerains of Tawang. The dangers of this arrangement was exposed earlier when a botanist, Francis Kingdon-Ward, strayed into Tawang area in 1934–35 without realising it while researching in what he imagined was territory within Assam. Tibet was a soft and friendly country, but China's presence and ultimate control of Tibet was already becoming imminent again. Still, Twynam's suggestions came to be virtually accepted by the

British home government, but the build-up of World War II at the time in Europe relegated the matter to the backburner.

Twynam belongs to the camp in the British administration that even questions the legal validity of the McMahon Line, as the line resulted out of a bilateral exchange of notes between the British and Tibetan representatives at the tripartite Simla Conference of 1913–14 without the knowledge of the Chinese plenipotentiary. The Chinese, in the end, did not ratify the agreement. Karunakar Gupta, a well-known critic of the Indian position on the McMahon Line, describes Twynam as 'a man with much experience on the north-east frontier (he had long served in the Assam cadre of the Indian Civil Service)', and his letter is 'the quintessence of the "moderate" school of thought' on this matter.[21] Opposed to them are the hardliners, led by men such as Olaf Caroe, by then, the foreign secretary of India, and the governor of Assam, Robert Reid. In 1937, upon Reid's suggestion, a small expedition, led by Captain Lightfoot, had been sent to Tawang to impress upon the inhabitants that they belonged to India. This had been protested by Tibetans.[22] Just before Twynam's intervention in 1939, Reid had again suggested another expedition be sent to Tawang to establish British authority there in a personal letter to the viceroy in early 1939. He pictured three alternatives before the British:

> there are three alternatives. The first is to wash our hands of the whole thing in spite of the fact that we told the local people that they were our subjects and not subjects of Tibet. This would save a lot of trouble and expense and, unless there are great changes in the situation in the north, would possibly have no inconvenient consequences for us. But one cannot contemplate with satisfaction a policy of abandoning to their fate those who have been told to regard themselves as dependent upon us.
>
> The second alternative is the permanent occupation of Tawang with consequential expenses. Other things being equal, this is a policy which obviously is the most desirable.
>
> The third alternative is that to which I have referred above, a further visit on a small scale this spring; but it is no use shutting our eyes to the fact that such a visit, if it is to be worthwhile, would have to be repeated periodically.[23]

The fact of the matter is, long after the McMahon Line was drawn, India continued to neglect the Tawang Tract until, as noted earlier, in 1934–35, this lapse was shockingly revealed by a botanist, Francis Kingdon-Ward, who strayed into Monyul, where the Tawang monastery is located. It was this 'escapade' that flustered the official dovecots in New Delhi and awakened them to the harsh realities of a fairly grave situation.[24] It may be of interest to note that as far back as 1928, the then political officer in Balipara had sounded a note of warning: 'Should China gain control of Tibet, the Tawang country is particularly adapted for a secret and early entrance into India'.[25] Kingdon-Ward's words were no different: 'Sooner or later India must stand face to face with an enemy looking over that wall into her garden – or fight to keep her out of the Tsangpo Valley. With Monyul a Tibetan Province, the enemy would already be within her gates'.[26]

World War II and the Japanese threat

By the time World War II broke out, Japan made a sweep of South-east Asia, including Burma, and was knocking on the eastern doors of the Northeast. In the north too, they were threatening to do the same in China. The fear of the British was not just of China ultimately gaining control of Tibet, but of Imperial Japan penetrating it and reaching India. As early as 1942 during the war, the Allied powers were looking for an alternative to the Burma Road, which they had lost control of, to supply General Chiang Kai-Shek's nationalist forces, then putting up a resistance against the Japanese advance. American general Joseph Stilwell was entrusted with this mission, and in his study he 'concluded that the DC-3s flying the "Burma Hump" couldn't carry the needed munitions and equipment often or quickly enough. Moreover, the route over the High Himalaya was unreliable due to weather. A land route was essential, and Tibet was at the centre of the equation'.[27] However, Tibet had different concerns. Not wanting Chinese military presence in Tibetan territory, Lhasa refused the American request made through the Chinese government, for passage of Allied military hardware to the Chinese nationalists through Tibet.[28] The British were then called upon to persuade Lhasa, and the British used the familiar 'carrot and stick' tactics of withholding recognition of Tibetan autonomy to have the Tibetans finally agree, and gave permission for two Americans, 'Ilya Tolstoy, the grandson of the Russian novelist, and Brooke Dolan to enter the rooftop kingdom'.[29] The Tibetans had their own considerations for agreeing to this. They were eager for international recognition of their independence from China and were hopeful the favour extended to the Americans would enlist the latter's support.[30] In the end, however, the proposed road was not built through Tibet for various reasons, including Tibet's unease about Chinese presence, the suspicion of the British that

Americans had more reasons for sending a reconnaissance mission to Tibet than just the road and the Chinese unease about foreign presence in Tibet. Not the least, the Chinese also thought 'it would take too long and have little impact on the war effort'.[31] The Stilwell Road would ultimately be built from Ledo in north-east Assam to Kunming in China via the Kachin territory of Burma.

But leaving aside the Tawang case and returning to the earlier discussion on no man's land, the approach of the British colonial administration to what it calls its un-administered areas was quite familiar in other tribal regions of the Northeast. For instance, an account says 'the hilly tract inhabited by various tribes known to us collectively as Nagas had never been subjugated by the Ahoms, and it was no part of the British policy to absorb it. Pemberton and Jenkins marched across the hills from Manipur to Nowgong, but, as it appeared that the opposition of the tribesmen would throw difficulties in the way of maintaining communications by this route, it was decided to leave them to their own devices'.[32] It was only when the strategy of keeping the tribes contained through neighbouring principalities obligated to the British administration proved unsatisfactory that the British decided to resort to 'repression by our own troops; and between the years 1835 and 1851, ten military expeditions were led into the hills'.[33]

Even after the British established its authority in the Naga Hills, the Nagas were left largely 'to their own devices'. These hills were also to come to be categorised into two broad regions. Where the British established their posts, it came to be known as 'administered area' and the more remote interior dubbed as 'un-administered area'. The colonial administration's familiar strategy of demarcating inner and outer territory as a measure of securing frontiers is again broadly reflected here on this smaller Naga canvas.

Inner and outer Tibet

But this administrative strategy had far-reaching consequences. China's claim that the Indian state of Arunachal Pradesh should rightly belong to them, and therefore, terming the state as disputed territory is testimony to this. The Chinese have persistently asserted: 'that the Inner Line along the foothills, proclaimed in 1873 by the Government of British India as the limit beyond which people were prohibited from going without special permission, really constituted the international boundary. The agreements with the hill tribes who promised "to act up to any orders we may get from the British authorities" and often received annuities conditional on their good behaviour were not accepted by China as sufficient proof of British sovereignty and jurisdiction'.[34]

It is interesting that China, however, did not accept a variant of the same British principle of Inner Line and Outer Line when it came to its application in Tibet at the time of the Simla Conference in 1913–14, when the proposal was made to create an Outer and Inner Tibet. The tripartite Simla Conference during 1913–14 between India, Tibet and China had two objectives. The first and more well-known is the demarcation of a boundary between India and Tibet, which after the line was drawn and agreed upon, came to be known as the McMahon Line. In the other, the British were pushing for the demarcation of a two-layered boundary between Tibet and China. There was to be, thus, an Inner Tibet and an Outer Tibet, along the Mongolian model.

The McMahon Line (ML), shown by a red line on the 1914 map, was an integral part of a longer, more comprehensive line drawn on the convention map to illustrate Article IX thereof; the latter designed to show the borders of Tibet, and the boundary between Outer and Inner Tibet. A blue line on the same one-sheet map marked the boundary between Inner Tibet (nominal Tibetan control, *de facto* Chinese authority) and Outer Tibet (*de facto* Tibetan Control, nominal Chinese authority). The map is initialled by the three plenipotentiaries 'in token of acceptance' on the 27th day of April 1914. Part of the red line showing the India-Tibet boundary in greater detail is etched on a two-sheet map, copies of which were exchanged between the British and Tibetan Plenipotentiaries along with formal letters on 24–5 March. The latter map does not contradict the former; it only shows a part of the whole and in greater detail. The part came to be known as the ML.[35]

China's concern for a long time was the division of Tibet and not so much the McMahon Line. 'The Chinese refusal to accept the McMahon Line as a valid boundary resulted, some years before the outbreak of the Second World War, in Chinese claims to the Assam Himalaya right down to the pre-1914 "Outer Line". The Chinese did not, of course seriously maintain that all this large extent of territory, more than 30,000 square miles, had ever been Chinese, or even Tibetan. They used their claims as symbols of their refusal to accept the fact that since 1912 Tibet had passed from Chinese control and had become to all intents and purpose an independent state'.[36]

In his book, *India-China Border Problem*, noted jurist A.G. Noorani reasons that 'a genuine boundary problem of long standing festered in the western sector. In the eastern sector, the McMahon Line came under a cloud only in 1936 only by a cartographical assertion (by China), not by an official claim. In 1959, a boundary problem assumed the character of a boundary dispute, proper, involving large territorial claims'.[37] He also further suggests in a reconciliatory tone that a give-and-take solution based on real needs is imminently possible, asserting that this 'is a dispute pre-eminently susceptible to a fair solution; for each had its vital non-negotiable interest securely under its control. India had the McMahon Line while China had the Xinjiang-Tibet road across the Aksai Chin in Ladhak'.[38] He claims that 'Zhou En-Lai was all too ready to accept such a solution during his visit to New Delhi in April 1960. He was rebuffed. China proceeded to practice its own brand of unilateralism, sanctifying territorial gains won by armed force'.[39]

Before Noorani, Belgian diplomat W.F. Van Eekelen had a slightly different conclusion. On this particular episode of whether Zhou En-Lai ever made such an offer during this same visit, he says, 'anxious anticipation by Indian observers of the forthcoming meeting between the two premiers centred around two points. Firstly, China's willingness to reach an agreement on the basis of the historical background and the present actual situation gave rise to the suspicion that China was aiming at a bargain to exchange her acceptance of the broad principles of the McMahon Line for Indian concessions on the corner of Ladhak. Although there is reason to believe that China never suggested such a deal in a concrete proposal, her emphasis on the status quo and the line of actual control implied that she was thinking of a compromise along those lines'.[40] But even if there were no official offers made to this effect, 'the same impression was gathered from (Zhou) Chou's press conference before departing when he said that as China was prepared to accommodate the Indian point of view in the eastern sector, India should accommodate China in the west; McMahon Line was completely unacceptable, but he would not cross it. In practice, all that was available to India was a provisional agreement containing a standstill on China's claims in return for conferring legitimacy on the Chinese occupation of Aksai Chin'.[41]

The question remains as to whether there was a disparity between what was officially conveyed to be the Chinese stand and what was told to the media about what this stand implied. The same ambiguity is pronounced in what another top Chinese leader, Deng Xiaoping, told the External Affairs Minister of India of his time, Atal Behari Vajpayee, during the latter's visit to Beijing on 14 February 1979, 'that the eastern sector was of economic value and the area of the biggest dispute'[42] and what he told Krishna Kumar, Chief Editor, *Defence News Service*, on 21 June 1980, that 'according to the line of actual control . . . for instance, in the Eastern sector we can recognize the existing status quo – I mean the so-called McMahon Line . . . but in the western sector, the Indian Government should also recognize the existing status quo . . . I think you can pass this message to Mrs. (Indira) Gandhi'.[43] Whether this ambiguity carries more meaning than plain bargaining strategy, in which the bargainer inflates the price he pays and undervalues what the other gives back in the exchange, will remain a matter of speculation.

Chinese diplomacy

There were other instances of Chinese ambiguity on the border question and its dealing with India on the matter. In 1958, after China took over Tibet and started expanding its road and airfield infrastructures in Tibet, it also began, as noted earlier, making cartographical claims on Arunachal Pradesh. 'When Nehru saw Chinese-drawn maps including Indian territory as part of China in a *China Pictorial* magazine of July 1958, he was incandescent. He wrote to Chou En-lai to remind him of their past conversations about the border issue. Chou reassured him that the Chinese maps were outdated and would be corrected'.[44] This was interpreted in a declassified Central Intelligence Agency (CIA) document as 'This provided the Chinese premier with a means for concealing Peiping's long-range intention of surfacing Chinese claims at some time in the future'.[45] True to this prediction, after China had established a position of strength in Tibet, and also after having completed construction of the Aksai Chin highway connecting Xinjiang and Tibet, 'In a letter dated 23 January 1959 to Nehru, Chou finally admitted that "border disputes do exist between China and India . . . and that now there would be difficulties in changing the old maps" . . . '.[46] Chou also called for 'the two sides to temporarily maintain the status quo, that is to say, each side keep for the time being the border areas at present under its jurisdiction and not to go beyond'.[47]

What is evident is that China's interest in Arunachal Pradesh and the Northeast is not simple clamouring. The place is not just of 'economic value', but also of extreme political significance. Just as Kashmir is the key to the control of the Indus valley, controlling Arunachal Pradesh, from which nearly all of the major tributaries of the Brahmaputra originate, will be key to the future control of the entire Northeast and lower riparian

Bangladesh. It would take China one significant step closer to its ambition of sustaining its current formidable trajectory in its quest to be a global economic and military power, for, in such an eventuality, besides the good fortune geography heaped on the country in terms of a long coastline and useful sea ports in the Pacific Ocean, its hunger for an opening to the Indian Ocean and beyond would have become suddenly much more achievable.

Against this background, a closer look at the making of the McMahon Line would be of interest, and to do this, a closer scrutiny of the British colonial policy in Tibet and the Northeast is vital. From this standpoint, these two regions have to be considered together. The Inner Line, and by implication, the Outer Line in the colonial administration of the Northeast and the proposal for creating an Inner Tibet and Outer Tibet during the Simla Conference of 1913–14, which created the McMahon Line, emanate from the same outlook to frontier administration.

But this outlook of the colonial administration was certainly not on a single track. Towards the end of the nineteenth century and the early decades of the twentieth century, there had emerged two clear and contrasting visions on how the British Empire's frontier issues in India were to be tackled. On one side was the British Government of India, and on the other, the British home government in London. The first was concerned with India-specific security issues. The second, on the contrary, considered these India-specific interests as secondary and often detrimental to what was seen as the larger interest of the British Empire. The India administration, for instance, saw control of Tibet important for the security of India, but the home government saw things differently. This friction is interesting as much as it is important and a more detailed account of it will be dealt with in the next chapter. Nonetheless, it has to be touched upon, even if briefly, here as well for it is the bridge to the next idea of how the Simla Conference of 1913–14 became urgent.

Foremost of those who saw Tibet as important in British India's security was Curzon. While he was viceroy, suspecting that the 13th Dalai Lama was getting too close to Russia for the comfort of British India interest, he commissioned the Younghusband Mission to Lhasa in 1904, and forced a treaty on Tibet, which literally made it a British protectorate. This treaty would be systematically undone by the India Office in the course of the following few years.

Secretary of state for India, Lord John Morley, sitting in the India Office, saw the frontiers, including Tibet and the other Himalayan states, as commercially of little worth, therefore a waste of resources to put too much policy energy into. British India saw beyond commerce and thought of the security consequences of ignoring the region. In these clashes of policy interests, London always prevailed. In what was deemed as the British Empire's larger interest, these India-specific interests were, more often than not, sacrificed. The change of guards in London with the conservative Arthur Balfour government making an exit in 1905 to give way to the liberal Henry Campbell-Bannerman government tilted the debate still farther away from the concerns of the 'frontier men'. When, finally, the Empire dissolved in the mid-twentieth century, India was thus left to bear the burdens of the Empire's deliberate oversights.

However, China's forward policy surge towards 1910 in Tibet and the Himalayan region was a jolt for the British establishment, rudely shaking it out of complacency. This too would come up for a more detailed discussion in the next chapter. But in its wake, the need to determine the status of Tibet, and with it, the northern boundary of the Northeast sector became urgently felt. The Simla Conference of 1913–14 was, in this sense, an effort to undo some of the ill effects of the policy of non-interference in Tibet pushed so aggressively by Morley and others. The felt need at that juncture was to bring Tibet into the contours of Indian security vision again. By then, the British had already tied themselves down considerably with two treaties – with Russia in 1907, and to a lesser extent, by another treaty with China in 1906 – both of which were born directly or indirectly out of the British establishment's Russia anxiety in the heat of the Great Game. Some of dynamics of Great Game between the two imperial powers was touched upon in the first chapter on geography and conflict, whereby the British were left in a dilemma about whether to claim the contiguous flatlands of the Yarkand valley and Aksai Chin for fear that Russia would take possession of them and cut a passage to Tibet.

Had it not been for the Anglo–Russian Convention of 1907, there would have been no need to have China as a party in the Simla Conference of 1913–14. In this alternate scenario, the decision on India's northern boundary with Tibet could probably have been concluded legally by a bilateral Anglo–Tibetan treaty. However, this was not to be as the Anglo–Russian 1907 Convention made it necessary to include China in the exercise. At the time of the Simla Conference, a greatly weakened China after the Republican Revolution, which brought down the Qing (Manchu) Dynasty, had little or no authority over Tibet. In many ways, though China was represented in Simla, the McMahon Line was a bilateral agreement between Tibet and India. It is also for this reason critics have been terming the agreement illegal and invalid.

1907 Anglo–Russian Convention

In the agreement concerning Tibet in the 1907 Anglo–Russian Convention at St. Petersburg, Britain and Russia recognised the suzerainty of China over Tibet, first and foremost. This recognition was essentially pushed by Britain with the purpose of excluding all possibilities of Russia directly establishing relations or concluding treaties with Tibet. In the process, Britain also excluded itself from concluding any direct treaties with Tibet. The second article in the 'Agreement concerning Thibet' in this convention clearly states that 'In conformity with the admitted principle of the suzerainty of China over Thibet, Great Britain and Russia engage not to enter into negotiations with Thibet except through the intermediary of the Chinese Government'.[48] This is directly against the spirit of Curzon's foreign policy with regards to Tibet, who had come to be convinced that the idea of China's suzerainty over Tibet was just fiction.

By the terms of this 1907 treaty, China had to be a party at the Simla Conference, and the doubt over the legitimacy of the McMahon Line on account of China's only partial assent to it was, thus, preordained. Had the Curzon line of thinking prevailed, and the British continued to conduct Tibet business with Tibet without the intermediary of China, thus giving Tibet's de facto sovereignty at the time a de jure status as well, the boundary issue between India and China would probably have been a lot different. But Britain was also apprehensive that such a status accorded to Tibet would not serve its interest in the end. For a sovereign Tibet, then, would have had the legitimate power to enter into treaties with other rival powers of the British as well – a prospect the British had always dreaded.

But these are just counterfactual speculations, and therefore, even in the event of such an alternate predicament, there could have been no guarantee that Tibet would have remained independent of China, for China always considered it a part of the great Chinese nation even at times when its actual control over the region was next to nil, and would likely have still invaded and taken control of it, as it did in 1950. The big difference, however, would have been, in the second scenario, the legitimacy of China's claim that it was only reclaiming and liberating a territory that was always its would have carried little weight in the eyes of international law. This not being the case, when the People's Liberation Army of China entered and overran Tibet in 1950, Tibet's fervent appeal for the matter to be taken up in the United Nations was largely ignored by most nations, including India, Britain and America.

India did try to prevail upon China not to resort to invading Tibet through diplomatic notes. 'The Chinese military campaign against Tibet started on 24 October, 1950 and led to a sharp exchange of notes between Delhi and Peking. The Indian note of 26 October reminded the Chinese Government of their assurances to solve the problem by peaceful means and stated that the invasion could not but be regarded as deplorable and not in the interest of peace'.[49] China had no ear for these appeals, and in its replies to Delhi, it said Tibet affairs were China's domestic problem and that China had 'sovereign rights in Tibet' and charged India with obstructing them.[50] Then, the Lhasa government 'requested India to sponsor her case before the United Nations, but received the reply that the appeal should be sent direct to the UN. Eventually it was El Salvador which filed the request for a debate and submitted a draft-resolution to establish a committee entrusted with a study of appropriate measures that could be taken by the General Assembly against this act of unprovoked aggression'.[51]

The UN General Committee considered the question on 24 November 1950. 'A cablegram from the Tibetan delegation then residing at Kalimpong, was circulated which blamed British persuasion for the signing of a treaty by Tibet "which superimposed on it the nominal (non-interfering) suzerainty of China" though that country was strictly forbidden to meddle in the internal affairs of Tibet'.[52] It further argued that China, by walking out of the Simla Conference, and thereby, not becoming a signatory to the agreement, by default, accorded Tibetan sovereignty de jure status.[53]

The Tibetan cablegram was circulated to the delegations, but there was hardly a worthwhile discussion. The delegations all tamely agreed to wait for the committee to come up with an 'idea of the possibilities of a peaceful settlement' proposed by Britain, and supported by the Indian, Australian and Russian delegates. The discussion was thereafter adjourned sine die.

In Parshotam Mehra's words, 'at the UN in New York, Tibet's efforts to secure international intervention proved still-born. Lip service apart, there was little hard support for Lhasa's cause especially because of New Delhi, and Whithall's lukewarm championship, if not supine submission'.[54] On the Tibet question, nationalist China did not differ much from communist China. On this occasion, the delegate from nationalist China remarked 'that Sino-Tibetan relations had not been cordial for many years but that for seven centuries all Chinese regarded Tibet as part of China'.[55] This fact of nationalist China agreeing with communist China on the Tibet question also had earlier proven to be a major inhibitor before US support for Tibet in its anti-communist campaign worldwide, and indeed, at this UN discussion in question.[56]

McMahon Line urgency

Although the Chinese forward policy of 1910 died in a whimper on account of the Republican Revolution in China, even as its threat began to be felt with alarm in the British establishment, there was no longer any doubt left that India's northern boundary had to be, once and for all, decided and edified beyond any legal uncertainty. This urgent concern ultimately culminated in the holding of the tripartite Simla Conference of 1913-14.

Moreover, the British were feeling the pressure from another direction. As noted earlier, in the Anglo–Russian Convention 1907, the British, in order to keep the Russians out of Tibet, had managed to come up with a formula by which both Russia and Britain would keep their hands off Tibet. But the flaw in this arrangement was soon to become painfully evident long before the Simla Conference was conceived of. The British realised that while they could not exercise any influence in Tibet without violating the 1907 Convention, the Russian could still do so quite effectively, though indirectly.

Russia at the time had great influence on Mongolia with transborder communities such as the Buriat living on either side of the Russia–Mongolia border. Mongolia, in turn, was very close to Tibet physically and spiritually. The 'Tibetan Buddhist Church', as Alastair Lamb calls Tibetan Buddhism, with the Dalai Lama as the head, had extensive following among the various tribes of Mongolia and their close ethnic cousins, the Russian Buriat community in Siberia. Since the 1907 Convention said nothing of Mongolia maintaining relations with Tibet, Russia could, through Mongolia, still exercise influence in Tibet. At some stage, the British even considered to have the 1907 treaty renegotiated or else abrogated, but this abrogation was not to come about till 1921. In a series of revolutions Russia witnessed in the period, the Tsarist regime fell in 1917, followed by a civil war in which Vladimir Lenin's Bolsheviks came out victorious in 1921 to finally establish the Union of Soviet Socialist Republics (USSR) in 1922.[57] The USSR, thereafter, withdrew from most of the treaties concluded by Russia's Tsarist regime.

The vulnerability this flaw brought to the British became urgent, particularly in view of a string of agreements between Russia and Mongolia, first at Urga at the end of 1912, by which Russia pledged to assist Mongolia to preserve her autonomy, and in return, obtained privileges that gave Russia a strong grip, economical and political, over Mongolia. This was followed by another treaty concluded between Russia and China towards the end of 1913, 'embodying the principles involved in the Urga Convention securing to Russia the privileges set forth in the Protocol accompanying the Convention. Chinese suzerainty over Mongolia was acknowledged by Russia, while China agreed to recognize the autonomy of Mongolia, and to retain from colonization or military occupation'.[58] Amidst these, Mongolia and Tibet were rumoured to have reach an agreement in January 1913, by which Mongolia and Tibet agreed to 'afford each other aid against dangers from without and from within'.[59] However, with the power equation in Europe making radical shifts in the build-up to World War I, and Russia having become an ally of Britain by then, offending the Russians at this stage was thought undesirable.

In the preparation for the Simla Conference, the British were aware the Chinese may not be happy about a foreign power negotiating terms on Tibet, for they always considered Tibet as their domain. However, after initial hesitation, the Chinese accepted the invitation to the tripartite talks, just as the British had calculated. The British guessed correctly that 'it was unlikely that the Chinese could ignore the possibility of direct British dealings with the Dalai Lama on the analogy of recent Russian relations with the Mongols. To do so would be to provide an occasion for international recognition of Tibetan independence, which it had long been the object of Chinese policy, under both the Manchus and the Republic, to avoid'.[60]

There was also a suggestion during the preparatory discussions among British policy makers that the talks should not result in a tripartite treaty, again influenced by anticipation of possible Russian objection that British participation in the agreement violates the Anglo–Russian Convention of 1907. Instead, 'the talks should be between the Tibetans and the Chinese . . . and the British role should be limited to the offering of benevolent assistance'.[61] This thought was reflected in an official statement of the president of the Conference, Henry McMahon, proclaiming 'a state of war now exists between the Government of China and the Government of His Holiness the Dalai Lama, whereby . . . [the Anglo-Chinese Convention of 1906] . . . has been rendered of no effect'.[62] The 1906 Convention, which was concluded in keeping with the foreign policy mindset of Morley in the India Office, altered drastically the content of the Lhasa Convention of 1904, signed at the end of the Younghusband Mission. While the Lhasa Convention was signed between Tibetan and British officials without any Chinese representation – therefore, the Chinese opposition to it – the Peking Convention of 1906 was an agreement between Chinese and British officials on Tibet, with no Tibetan representation.

Simla Conference progress

The first meeting of the Simla Conference was held on 6 October 1913. The British delegation consisted of Sir Henry McMahon as plenipotentiary, assisted by Charles Bell as Tibetan adviser and Archibald Rose of the Consular Service, as Chinese adviser. The Tibetan plenipotentiary was Longchen Shatra, and that of the Chinese, Chen I-fan (also sometimes referred to as Ivan Chen). 'Between 6 October 1913, when it began, and 3 July 1914, when it dispersed, the Simla Conference held eight formal sessions. The first two, on 13 October and 18 November; the next three at Delhi on 12 January, 17 February and 11 March 1914; and the last three, again at Simla on 7 and 22 April and 3 July. Negotiations on the boundary between India and Tibet were conducted in Delhi between 17 January and 25 March 1914'.[63]

The idea of partitioning Tibet into Inner Tibet and Outer Tibet on the principle of the Mongolian Declaration occurred to McMahon in the course of the conference, when it became evident the claims by the Tibetan to the territorial extent of Tibet proper and those of the Chinese differed considerably.

> The Tibetan Government claimed all territory in which the population was almost entirely Tibetan. This involved an eastern boundary passing through Tachienlu and a north-eastern boundary passing close to Si-ning in Kansu province in China. Tibet in fact claimed the restoration of those Tibetan districts which China had annexed from time to time.
>
> Far from agreeing to this, the Chinese Government claimed the above districts, and in addition all Tibetan territory which Chao Erh Feng had succeeded in occupying when his power was at its height. They accordingly pressed for a boundary through Gyam-da, only a few days march east of Lhasa.[64]

Chao Erh Feng was the Chinese general in service of the Manchu rulers who had led the military campaign in Tibet during its formidable forward policy in 1910. This episode will be explained in greater detail in the next chapter.

On 27 April 1914, a convention was initialled by the three plenipotentiaries. The chief features of the initialled agreement were:

1. Tibet was divided into two zones, 'Outer Tibet' and 'Inner Tibet'. The former is the part nearer India, including Lhasa, Shigatse and

Chamdo; the latter the part nearer China, including Ba-tang, Li-tang, Tachienlu, and a large portion of eastern Tibet.
2. Chinese suzerainty over the whole of Tibet was recognized, but China engaged not to convert Tibet into a Chinese province.
3. Great Britain engaged not to annex any portion of Tibet.
4. The autonomy of Outer Tibet was recognized. China agreed to abstain from interference in its administration, which was to rest with the Tibetans themselves. She agreed also to abstain from sending troops, stationing civil or military officers (except as in 6. below) or establishing Chinese colonies there. Britain to abstain from all these things throughout the whole of Tibet, but to retain her Trade Agents and their escorts.
5. In Inner Tibet the Central Tibetan government at Lhasa were to retain their existing rights, which included among other things the control of most of the monasteries and the appointment of local chiefs. But China was not forbidden to send troops or officials or to plant colonies there. . . .
6. A Chinese Amban was to be re-established at Lhasa with military escort, limited to three hundred men.
7. The escorts of the British Trade Agencies in Tibet were not to exceed three-fourth of the Chinese escort at Lhasa.
8. The British Agent at Gyantse was authorised to visit Lhasa, in order to settle matters which could not be settled at Gyantse.

The Convention also abolished the Trade Regulations of 1893 and those of 1908. In their place a fresh Trade Treaty was arranged, to govern the commercial relations between India and Outer Tibet . . .

The opportunity was also taken to negotiate the frontier to be established between Tibet and north-eastern India . . . [65]

'Two days after the initialling of the Convention, the Chinese Government disavowed the action of its Representative, and refused to permit him to proceed to full signature. On 6 June the British Minister at Peking informed the Chinese Government that Great Britain and Tibet regarded the Convention as concluded by the act of initialling, and that in default of China's adherence they would sign it independently. In July the Chinese and Tibetan Plenipotentiaries quitted Simla. Two or three weeks later, the Great War broke out and threw Tibetan affairs into the background'.[66] It must be noted here that Chen I-fan did put a condition before he put his initial to the document, that he would be willing to initial the draft and the map, 'but on the clear understanding that to initial and to sign them were two separate actions'.[67] There is, therefore, merit in the argument that his initials would not bind his government.

From the proceedings of the Simla Conference, one thing was clear. The issue of demarcating the boundary between India and Tibet was not the central focus of the discussions. 'The negotiations with China broke down on one point only; namely, the frontier to be established between China and Tibet'.[68] The boundary between India and Tibet in the Northeast sector, the McMahon Line, which was drawn during the conference, became an issue only nearly 20 years later, and developed into a full-blown crisis still later, after China 'invaded' or 'liberated' Tibet in 1950. Even so, developments in Europe on the eve of World War I cost the Simla Conference a lot of the attention it deserved. After World War I broke out, the Tibet issue was relegated to the backburner.

With the exception of the Tawang tract and certain other pockets of land, others such as 'the upper Siang and Siyom valleys, and the Lohit between the Yepak and Kahao, were brought within the territorial limits of the British Indian Empire',[69] and the McMahon Line was drawn, generally in keeping with the watershed principle, identifying the crest of mountain ranges which divides watersheds of rivers flowing into Assam and those flowing into Tibet. 'Unfortunately, the Assam Himalayas do not lend themselves particularly well to a uniform application of the watershed concept of boundary making'.[70] This feature of these mountains was to add to the bitterness of the boundary dispute half a century later, and indeed, the tussle for the control of the Thag La range in the Tawang sector, which was north of the McMahon Line, and therefore, in Tibet, but which India believed was the highest watershed crest, and thereby, by the spirit of the McMahon Line, should belong to India, was how fighting broke out in October 1962 between India and China.[71] Since after the first initialling, the Chinese representative backed out of further discussions, and the McMahon Line was arrived at between the Tibetan and the British plenipotentiaries, the agreement is also often referred as McMahon–Shatra notes by critics of the agreement, underscoring its legal ambiguity.

The Tawang tract was the exception to this watershed rule. This strip, though on the northern crest of the Se La pass, was considered strategically too important for it not to be under Indian control. However, concessions were made to the Tibetans, and Lhasa was to retain its suzerainty over the territory and traditional right to collect taxes explained as 'certain dues now collected by the Tibetan Government . . . from the Monpas and Lopas for articles sold'.[72] The Tibetans agreed to the McMahon Line and the concession of territories they considered their traditional domain, in particular the Tawang Tract, or Monyul territory, as the Tibetans call the region, the domain of the Great Tawang Monastry, the birthplace of the 6th Dalai Lama, in the belief this was part of a larger bargain that 'the British would guarantee a Tibetan boundary with China more to the taste of the Dalai Lama than anything he could hope to secure unaided'.[73]

There were other problems for the British. The acquisition of the Tawang Tract, as indeed the drawing of the McMahon Line itself, may have contravened the Anglo–Russian Convention of 1907. They, therefore, did not publish the McMahon Line in the Aitchison's Treaties until the 1930s, giving rise to other complications. When the map was finally published in 1938, it has been alleged that the then deputy secretary in the British Foreign Department, Olaf Caroe, had modified the original. The allegation goes even further to claim that 'no ratified agreement on the boundary between India and Tibet was in existence'.[74] Parshotam Mehra has these explanations for this long silence on the issue.

> With the World War I on its hands, post 1914 India fought shy of giving shape and form to McMahon's recommendations (one may add in parenthesis, that it was not until after the Raj had been wound up that New Delhi implemented them).
>
> Two, for almost two decades, until the emergence of the Kuomintang as a powerful unifying force, Republican China was in a moribund state. It posed no threat in the Assam Himalayas, it dispatched no uncomfortable probing missions into tribal territory. Understandably, both Whitehall as well as New Delhi – the latter, under the Raj, was politically adjunct of the former – avoided the risk of attracting unwelcome Chinese notice that would have only served to fuel fire of anti-British propaganda, then at white heat. To say that Britain's vital trade, and commercial interests were involved, would be, putting it mildly.[75]

Mehra further explains there were other reasons for the British suddenly deciding to publish the map in the 1930s. One was the death of the 13th Dalai Lama in 1933, leading to political uncertainty in Tibet, with the Chinese making a determined bid to stage a comeback. The second reason was the misadventure of a botanist, Kingdon-Ward in 1934, which has already been discussed, in which he strayed into Monyul, the region where the

Tawang monastery is located. The third reason related to consistent mistakes in the London press that the Inner Line at the base of the Assam's northern mountains was the international boundary, which also added to the urgency.[76]

Further, even though the complication of 1907 Anglo–Russia Convention ended with its abrogation in 1921, the treaty was not published immediately thereafter. This, Mehra attributes to bureaucratic lethargy and amnesia.

Olaf Caroe controversy

Furthermore, the British were of the opinion that 'failure to publish might give the Chinese a handle to argue that no ratified agreement [on the boundary] between India and Tibet was in existence; two, in view of the impending introduction of the Government of India Act 1935, it was necessary to define tribal area in the north-east which were to be placed under the political control of the government of Assam; three, the imminent separation of Burma, which was responsible for part of the ML frontier'.[77]

After weighing the pros and cons, New Delhi decided to re-issue Volume 14. However, some copies of the older version were preserved too, according to Mehra, but according to critics, these survived despite efforts to destroy them. Mehra also goes on to defend the gravest of the charges against Caroe – that he replaced the short factual paragraph about the 1914 convention with a long embellished three-paragraph set. He says that a close scrutiny reveals the meanings of the short original paragraph and those of the newer three paragraphs remain unchanged. The only reason this change had become necessary was that 'the new Aitchison volume contained the text of the 1914 Convention, the McMahon–Shatra exchange of notes on the boundary, as well as the revised (1914) Indo-Tibetan Trade Regulations. Whitehall had ruled that the joint Indo-Tibetan declaration of 3 July was not to be published, its place being taken by an explanatory note. Surely, the additional contents had to be spelt out in terms of a narrative outline that comprehended much more than the earlier version; hence, three paragraphs in place of one'.[78] The only serious flaw, Mehra adds, is that the 1938 version of Volume XIV carried the old dateline.[79]

India takes charge of Tawang

Long after the texts of the Simla Convention were published, on the eve of the Chinese entering Tibet in force in 1950, the status of the Tawang tract, though south of the McMahon Line, was still in some uncertainty.

Nari Rushtomji, who dedicated an entire career as an ICS officer in the Northeast and the kingdom of Sikkim, writes:

> The region that caused us special anxiety was the region of Tawang in the extreme north-west of the Kameng Frontier Division and across the 14,000 foot Se La pass. Although Tawang was undoubtedly south of the McMahon Line and therefore within the territory of India, the Tibetans had, for generations, felt a strong sentimental attachment to the area, partly as the birth-place of the sixth Dalai Lama. The office-bearers of the great Buddhist monastery at Tawang were sometimes selected from among Tibetan lamas of the region and the famous Drepung monastery near Lhasa and the culture of the region had affinities with Tibet as much as with India. Tibetan officers moreover found ample avenues for exploiting the Monpa villagers of Tawang, whom they used to pressurize into disposing of their rice and other produce at ridiculously low prices. The Tibetans were opposed, therefore, to an Indian presence in Tawang.[80]

With Rushtomji at the helm, India decided to clear this political uncertainty and sent in a detachment of Assam Rifles soldiers to Tawang, led by Major Ralengnao (Bob) Khathing, a Tangkul Naga from Manipur, who dutifully accomplished his mission, ending Tibetan administrative presence in the region and replacing it with India's. Rushtomji remarks of his friend with pride and admiration that 'If any officer deserved his Padma Shri, it was this tough, redoubtable Tangkhul Naga from Manipur'.[81]

India only notified the Tibetan government at Lhasa, rather than Peking, of its intention to take over Tawang. China, nonetheless, made no protests. The episode is cited later as an alibi by Neville Maxwell in *India's China War*, that China, although denouncing the Simla Conference and the McMahon Line, was all willing to settle the boundary issue as per the McMahon Line, had India softened its stand on the matter and was prepared to negotiate. 'Although New Delhi now accepted China's sovereignty in Tibet it made diplomatic sense to treat the matter of Tawang as a local question, leaving it to Peking to protest. In the event, the Chinese Government made no comment at all on the Indian move, so far as the record shows. This otherwise puzzling silence can be construed only as China's acquiescence in India's filling out the McMahon Line'.[82]

These words come from someone whose book has been described by reviewers as extremely readable and important, but too 'enthusiastic' to agree with China and equally 'enthusiastic' to disagree with India. Yet, at least on this question, he may have indicated all hope is not lost for the boundary issue between India and China and that it can be settled on mutually agreed terms. Despite all the statements of non-recognition of the McMahon Line, and claims over Arunachal Pradesh, China did not protest at all when India advanced to the McMahon at Tawang and occupied it in 1950. Again, in 1962, after a month-long campaign of aggression into Indian territory, which brought them right to the Assam plains, the Chinese, after unilaterally declaring a ceasefire on November 20, withdrew behind the McMahon Line, leaving India to once again fill up the territory south of the Line. In the Tawang episode of 1950 is perhaps the optimistic indication of a conclusive resolution to the ambiguity over the Inner Line and Outer Line.

Notes

1 Lord Curzon, *Frontiers*.
2 Sir Henry McMahon, 'International Boundaries', *Journal of the Royal Society of Arts*, Vol. 84, 1935 (as quoted by Parshotam Mehra in Essays in Frontier History, India's Land Frontier), p. 86.
3 Alastair Lamb, *The McMahon Line, A Study in Relation Between India, China and Tibet 1904–1914*, Vol. II, p. 293.
4 Ibid., p. 638.
5 Ibid.
6 Ibid.
7 Ibid.
8 Ibid., p. 313.
9 Edward Gait, *A History of Assam*, p. 386.
10 Ibid., p. 387.
11 Ibid.
12 Ibid.
13 Alexander Mackenzie, *History of the Relations of the Government with the Hill Tribes of the North-East Frontier of Bengal*, p. 55.
14 Viceroy's note, Oct. 9, 1913 (as quoted in W.F. Van Eekelen, *Indian Foreign Policy and the Border Dispute with China*, p. 167).
15 Ibid.
16 Alastair Lamb, *The McMahon Line*, Vol. II, p. 314.
17 Alastair Lamb, *The India China Border*, p. 101 (as quoted in W.F. Van Eekelen, *Indian Foreign Policy and the Border Dispute with China*), p. 168.
18 Alastair Lamb, *The McMahon Line*, A Vol-II, p. 295.
19 Karunakar Gupta, *The McMahon Line 1911–45: The British Legacy*, *The China Quarterly* No. 47 Cambridge University Press (Jul–Sept, 1971), p. 538, http://www.jstor.org/stable/652324.
20 Ibid., p. 538.
21 Ibid.

22 Ibid., p. 535.
23 As quoted in Ibid., p. 538.
24 Parshotam Mehra, *Essays in Frontier History, India, China and the Disputed Border*, p. 25.
25 Ibid.
26 Ibid.
27 Lezlee Brown Halper and Setphan Halper, *Tibet: An Unfinished Story* (Hachette India, 2014), p. 29.
28 Ibid., p. 30.
29 Ibid.
30 Ibid.
31 Ibid., p. 33.
32 Edward Gait, *A History of Assam*, p. 366.
33 Ibid., p. 366.
34 Indian official report, p. 203, as quoted in W.F. Van Eekelen in *Indian Foreign Policy and the Border Dispute with China* (Martinus Nijhoff, The Hague, 1964), p. 107.
35 Parshotam Mehra, *Essays on Frontier History, India-China Border*, p. 21.
36 A.G. Noorani in, *India-China Border Problem*, p. 198.
37 Ibid., p. 218.
38 Ibid., p. 229.
39 Ibid.
40 W.F. Van Eekelen, *Indian Foreign Policy and the Border Dispute with China*, p. 97.
41 Ibid., p. 97.
42 A.G. Noorani, *India-China Boundary Dispute*, p. 230.
43 Ibid., p. 231.
44 Lezlee Brown Halper and Stephan Halper, *Tibet: An Unfinished Story*, p. 207.
45 Ibid.
46 Chou's letter of 23 January 1959 (as quoted in Ibid.), p. 227.
47 Ibid.
48 Charles Bell, *Tibet Past and Present*, full text of the agreement reproduced verbatim as Appendix-IX, p. 290.
49 The International Commission of Jurists, The Question of Tibet and the Rule of Law, pp. 132–8 (as quoted in W.F. Van Eekelen, *Indian Foreign Policy and the Border Dispute with China)*, p. 30.
50 R.S. Patel, Foreign Policy of India, p. 269 (as quoted in W.F. Van Eekelen, *Indian Foreign Policy and the Border Dispute with China*, p. 31.
51 W.F. Van Eekelen, *Indian Foreign Policy and the Border Dispute with China*, p. 31.
52 Ibid.
53 Ibid.
54 Parshotam Mehra, *Essays in Frontier History: India, China and the Disputed Border*, p. 238.
55 W.F. Van Eekelen, *Indian Foreign Policy and the Border Dispute with China*, p. 32.
56 See Lezlee Brown Halper and Stephan Halper, *Tibet: An Unfinished Story*.

57 http://en.wikipedia.org/wiki/Russian_Revolution.
58 Charles Bell, *Tibet Past and Present*, p. 150, full text of the Russo-Chinese Agreement, 1913, attached in Appendix XIV in Ibid., pp. 305–6.
59 Ibid., p. 151, the full text of this rumoured treaty is reproduced as Appendix XIII in Ibid., p. 304.
60 Ibid., p. 461.
61 Ibid., p. 467.
62 Ibid., p. 478.
63 D.P. Choudhary, *The North-Eastern Frontier* (as quoted in A.G. Noorani, *India-China Boundary Problem*), p. 185.
64 Charles Bell, *Tibet Past and Present*, p. 157.
65 Ibid., pp. 154, 145. The entire text of the agreement is available at: http://www.tibetjustice.org/materials/treaties/treaties16.html.
66 Ibid., p. 156.
67 Alastair Lamb, *The McMahon Line*, Vol-II, p. 505.
68 Charles Bell, *Tibet Past and Present*, p. 156.
69 Alastair Lamb, *The McMahon Line, A Study in the Relations Between India, China and Tibet*, Vol. II, p. 548.
70 Ibid., p. 533.
71 See Neville Maxwell, *India's China War* (Jaico Publishing House, Bombay, 1970).
72 Alastair Lamb, *The McMahon Line*, p. 548.
73 Ibid., p. 547.
74 Parshotam Mehra, *Essays in Frontier History; India, China, and the Disputed Border*, p. 26.
75 Ibid., p. 25.
76 Ibid.
77 Ibid., p. 26.
78 Ibid., p. 27.
79 Ibid.
80 Nari Rustomji, *Enchanted Frontiers: Sikkim, Bhutan and India's North-Eastern Borderlands* (Oxford University Press, 1971), p. 125.
81 Ibid., p. 127.
82 Neville Maxwell, *India's China War*, p. 73.

5
INNER LINE AS OUTER LINE II
The Empire and its colony

The prevalent tendency in the study of the Northeast has been to look at the region as an island segregated from the rest of the world. Seldom has the region been looked upon as possibly a product of the larger environment within which it exists, which, by the very nature of its political geography, would transcend national boundaries. Often, this outlook is determined by an inherent possessive hubris of a national community wanting to see all territories and peoples within its political geography as essentially a part of the national organic being. Every part of India, therefore, must belong to the India story alone, or the Indian historical mainstream, and any other narrative that does not conform to this standard of national imagining thereby becomes deviant and alien, and must ultimately be brought into the mainstream. But the story of the Northeast cannot but be honestly told alongside those of the countries that straddle it on practically all sides. This is the problem of the Northeast story at its essence, defined by a core contradiction between what is projected as the Indian national mainstream and the different streams that the region expectedly has always also belonged to.

The nation, in this context, becomes akin to a cultural container.[1] Nothing spills outside it, and conversely, nothing from outside spills into it. Any historical stream that tends not to fit perfectly into this container becomes a problem area. Furthermore, it is another characteristic of the state to be suspicious of these 'deviant and non-mainstream' histories and peoples. The Indian state has been no exception. India's first home minister, Sardar Vallabhbhai Patel's letter of 7 November 1950 to the prime minister, Jawaharlal Nehru, is just one proof of this. In this letter, the leader reverentially referred to in India as the 'Iron Man', is unapologetic about an irredentist suspicion of the 'non-mainstream' Northeast.

Patel's political foresight is remarkable in almost predicting the 1962 war with China at a time when Nehru was befriending China and canvassing for bringing the country into the fold of the United Nations, making India the sole country outside of the Soviet bloc to do so. But in this 1950 letter, he also cautions Nehru to be wary of the population of the Northeast, whose loyalty to India, he says, has always been suspect: 'The people inhabiting these portions have no established loyalty or devotion to India. Even Darjeeling and Kalimpong areas are not free from pro-Mongoloid prejudices. During the last three years, we have not been able to make any appreciable approaches to the Nagas and other hill tribes in Assam. European missionaries and other visitors had been in touch with them, but their influence was in no way friendly to India or Indians'.[2] Elsewhere, the statesman does acknowledge the cross-border interrelatedness of histories, but this is seen as a matter to be wary of: 'All along the Himalayas in the north and north-east, we have on our side of the frontier a population ethnologically and culturally not different from Tibetans and Mongoloids. The undefined state of the frontier and the existence on our side of a population with its affinities to the Tibetans or Chinese have all the elements of potential trouble between China and ourselves'.[3]

Indeed, the conceptualisation of the nation as a cultural container becomes extremely problematic in the context of a multilingual, multiethnic, multireligious country such as India. Especially in dealing with peripheral provinces such as the Northeast, an approximate 98 per cent of whose physical boundary is international, there can be no other way of studying the place, its histories and peoples without doing so in consonance with those of territories beyond these international borders. In any case, most of these boundaries are mid-twentieth-century phenomena, and stories earlier than the period will not have them at all. In many ways, whatever their biases, colonial historians who worked on maps bigger than the confines of national boundaries provided a clearer picture of the pasts of these peripheral regions. Chroniclers of imperial history, such as Alexander Mackenzie, Edward Gait and Robert Reid, therefore, remain indispensable in any serious study of the Northeast region.

It is indeed fascinating to discover on this bigger map how Imperial Russia's interest in Mongolia had an impact on the evolution of the idea of the Northeast; how Britain's zealous and over-protective outlook towards its empire's frontiers in Afghanistan and Persia too had similar influences in the shaping of the Northeast; how the clash of interests between Russia and Britain and their decision to agree to a treaty-bound mutual exclusion of each other from Tibet ultimately left the field clear for China's entry into Tibet, and in turn, profoundly influenced the security environment of the Northeast as well as introduced an element of uncertainty to the northern boundary of the region.

Not many have tried to explore these connections. But, of the few, at least one has gone even beyond to suggest the Great Game has a sequel. In Bertil Lintner's 2012 book, *Great Game East*, the author argues that after the Great Game in Central Asia concluded in the early twentieth century with the changes in power alliances in Europe post–World War I, another one began unfolding in South and South-east Asia. This time, the rivalry is for the control of Asia's most volatile frontier – the Indo-Burma region.[4] This Great Game East is an extension of the Cold War between the Western and Eastern Blocs, and the Western Bloc's mission, at least in the beginning, was of combating the spread of communism in the world. One of the chief protagonists in this conflict theatre – as elsewhere – understandably was the United States, which through its undercover agency, the CIA, once ran operations supporting Tibetan resistance fighters even as the ultimate defeat of Chiang Kai-shek's Chinese nationalist party, the Kuomintang (KMT), at the hands of Mao Zedong's Chinese communists became imminent towards 1949.[5] Prior to the 1962 India–China war, when hostilities between India and China were still not open, this was done without the knowledge of India, and with the assistance of Sikkimese and Nepali sleuths. The operation headquarters then were in East Pakistan and Nepal. After the 1962 war, India too became party to this game.[6]

In reciprocation, China too, in the 1970s and 1980s, openly extended help to Northeast insurgents, beginning with the Nagas.[7] But here too, the power alignments would shift in the years after the 1962 war. China would fall out with the USSR even as India found itself drifting closer to the USSR. Consequently, the US would warm up to China. Before 1962, while the battle line of the Cold War was clearly marked between the Western democracies and the world communist movement, the equation was far more complex in South Asia. Immediately after World War II, the US, under President Harry Truman, and then, more urgently under President Dwight David Eisenhower, began identifying China as the major threat and challenge for the West in its fight against the spread of communism in Asia. The Americans first tried to fight the communists in China through Chiang Kai-shek's nationalist government. Chiang Kai-shek, a long-time ally of the West, a nationalist who abhorred the communists, and a devout Christian, fitted the bill well, especially during the Eisenhower-era propaganda war, when the conflict was projected consciously as a fight between the Godless communists and God-fearing 'free world'. The president, himself an orthodox Christian, even incorporated prominent evangelical leader of the time, Billy Graham, in his propaganda war against communism.[8] 'The Eisenhower administration also added the words "In God We

Trust" to all US currency, and the phrase "Under God" to the Pledge of Alliance, thus distinguishing Americans from the Little Moscovites who were solemnly pledging to their hammer and sickle flag'.[9] Truman, though also a devout Christian, unlike Eisenhower, declared the thrust of his campaign was to prevent a Third World War.[10] When Chiang Kai-shek's defeat at the hands of the communists became a foregone conclusion, America began looking to India for an ally. Both Truman and Eisenhower knew India's importance in this war, and thought that as a democratic and religious country, it was a natural ally. The prime minister of India during the period, Jawaharlal Nehru, however, remained unmoved, engrossed as he was in building up the Non-Aligned Movement (NAM), which he earnestly believed was the alternate world order.[11] Nehru was not a communist supporter, but he wanted to deal with communism on his own terms, not as a foot soldier of America's war. As an agnostic liberal, he was also uneasy with America's crusade with an overly religious hue. When America tried to enlist India as an ally in the wake of North Korea's invasion of South Korea, Nehru only offered to be the mediator to bring the West to the negotiating table with the communists, much to the annoyance of the Americans. Nehru's neutralism not only piqued the Americans, but it was also ultimately to drive them to lean towards Pakistan, when it became certain India would not be the anchor they needed so much in South Asia.[12] This, in turn, would spiral, and India would begin leaning closer to the USSR, and indeed, China.[13] The 1962 India–China border war would, therefore, not only break Nehru's heart, but also cause a radical shift in the power alignment in the region and the world. China would begin drifting from the USSR, and jumping at the opportunity, the US would begin covertly wooing China.

It is also said the controversial 1970 book by British Australian journalist reporting for a British newspaper from India during the 1960s Neville Maxwell's *India's China War*, which the then American secretary of state Henry Kissinger openly praised, has been one of the catalysts in this thaw in relation between the US and China.[14] It is significant that Kissinger in 1970 and the then US president, Richard Nixon in 1971 made their historic visits to China flagging off a new era of power alliance, paving the way for China opening up to the capitalist world. Maxwell's book, based almost solely on Indian sources, in particular, the still-classified 1963 General Henderson Brooks–Brigadier Prem Bhagat report on India's disastrous 1962 war with China, which apparently was leaked to him, is generally considered as a brilliantly written and researched book. Reviewers, however, have noted that he is too enthusiastic to agree with the Chinese views and equally enthusiastic to disagree with the Indian views. The book damns India as the aggressor and portrays China as the aggrieved in the 1962 war.

Empire and its colony

There were also other seemingly remote turns of events in the diplomacy of the British Imperial Government, sometimes a consequence of the Great Game and, at other times, related to internal political exigencies, which too had a telling effect on the evolution of the Northeast. The most important of these is what I call a clash of maps of concerns between the British Empire and its various colonies, which has already been cursorily touched upon in the previous chapter. This clash had to do with security perceptions as seen from London and Simla/Calcutta, in which the interest of the Empire almost always prevailed over that of its colony, quite tragically leaving the burdens of these decisions on the colony when the Empire ultimately dissolved. This conflict of the large and small maps of concerns in the case of India had very definite dramatis personae. The pitch of this conflict also changed with regime changes in London. As it has turned out, the Liberals generally were the most hurtful to British India's interest. There also emerged a broad pattern. Regardless of coming from a Liberal or Conservative background, executives who were posted in India turned to a stance closer to the vantage of the Conservatives on India's security while those who functioned from London tended to take a more detached and academic assessment of these same security scenarios, much to the frustration of those on the ground.

At one end of this spectrum of differing political outlooks was John Morley, Secretary of State for India between 1905 and 1910 and again in 1911 and Lord President of the Council between 1910 and 1914. His Liberal leanings were well known and 'he opposed imperialism and the Boer War, and his opposition to British entry into the First World War led him to leave the government in 1914'.[15] At the other end was George Nathaniel Curzon, 1st Marquess Curzon of Kedleston, known as Lord Curzon of Kedleston between 1898 and 1911 and as The Earl Curzon of Kedleston between 1911 and 1921. He was 'a British Conservative statesman who was Viceroy of India and Foreign Secretary'.[16] Morley remained in office long after Curzon retired and the tussle between these two vantages expectedly became unequal.

Relevant to this discussion are the circumstances that ultimately shaped British India's Tibet policy. As noted earlier, Curzon, who was deeply suspicious of Russian interest in Tibet, became certain Tibet either had to be under Indian control or, else, be made a protectorate state like Bhutan and Sikkim for India's future security. The British India administration from the time of Viceroy Lord Dufferin towards the closing decades of the nineteenth century had come to be of the opinion that the Chinese control of Tibet was just fiction. This opinion was catalysed further by the abject inability of the Chinese government to have the Tibetans honour two treaties the British signed in 1890 and 1893 with China, the first fixing the boundary of the British protectorate state of Sikkim and Tibet, and the second on regulating trade between Tibet and India. After Curzon took charge as viceroy, the need to deal with the Tibetans became even more urgent, as Curzon believed the 13th Dalai Lama incarnate, the spiritual and temporal leader of the Tibetans, was leaning towards Russia.

The Younghusband Mission of 1904, which forced the 1904 Lhasa Convention, by which Tibet became virtually a protectorate state of the British, is the first major outcome of this aggressive stance. If this invasion is landmark, the drama that followed revealed even more the innards of the British administration, and the various contrary pulls within it. In the years ahead, the India Office in London, with Morley at the helm as secretary of state, would undo all of what the Lhasa Convention 1904 was supposed to have achieved in securing India's northern boundary. All this on the plea that foreign policy interests of the Empire are not the same as those of the colonies and that the former was primary. The logic always was that the concession India seeks in Tibet would encourage other rival European powers to seek similar concessions in other areas of interest of the British Empire, such as in Persia, Afghanistan, Mongolia, China, Indo-China and so on. Continuing the duel after Curzon had departed, Morley wrote to Curzon's successor, Lord Minto, in October 1906 that these 'frontier men' forget 'the complex intrigues, rival interests and, if you like, diabolical machinations which make up international politics for a vast sprawling Empire like ours, exposing more vulnerable surface than any Empire the world ever saw'.[17] Ironically, Minto, once in India, would also begin to see India's security from similar lens as Curzon's.

It is not difficult to imagine this drama characterising policy friction between the big and small maps of concerns even today in the functioning of independent India's bureaucracy, which is, in very many ways, a replica of the British Empire's bureaucracy. Indeed, it is not uncommon to hear of policy proposals by the bureaucracy in Indian states, especially weak remote states such as those of the Northeast, being shot down unceremoniously by the secretaries and even joint secretaries in the union government's

Ministry of Home Affairs, often on the presumption of a better vantage to assess national interest from the centre. It is thus imaginable how, just as once upon a time, India's immediate interests were dismissed as myopic against the larger backdrop of the Empire's interest, what the states see as their immediate and urgent interests would have often ended up sidelined by the union government on the charge that they were parochial.

Great Game Northeast

There is plenty of scholarship available on the Great Game, but few that try to connect the Great Game with the shaping of the Northeast's physical and psychological geography. I will try to make this connection, and will primarily be depending on the works of some of these scholars to draw my conclusions. One is Alastair Lamb, whose two-volume monumental work *The McMahon Line: A Study in the Relations between India, China and Tibet* is rich in documentary details of politics that went into this complex relation between these countries. His only seeming weakness, as it were, is in his insistence that British India's boundary in Assam lay at the foot of the northern hills, thereby endorsing China's claim in the border dispute in this sector. I say this is a scholarship weakness not because he supports China's claim, but because there is not a single legislation or regulation on record which created this 'Outer Line', which he claims existed alongside the 'Inner Line'. The latter, unlike the former, definitely existed, having been created by the Bengal Eastern Frontier Regulation, 1873.

Another author who has left valuable information on the matter is Charles Bell, a Tibetologist and ICS officer who was once the British political officer in the British protectorate state of Sikkim. He was also the assistant of Henry McMahon in the Simla Conference of 1913–14, and is said to have been a friend of the 13th Dalai Lama and his representative to the Simla Conference, Lonchen Shatra. His book *Tibet Past and Present*, hence, gives an intimate and often personal account of the developments in Tibet during the crucial days of the Great Game, although there have been allegation that he was biased against the Chinese. There are Indian authors who have also looked into the matter in some depth. Of them, Parshotam Mehra stands out with his extensive work on Tibet affairs. Karunakar Gupta is another whose painstaking scholarship is far from being circumscribed by nationalistic interests. These authors were not writing about the Northeast specifically. Their accounts were of the Great Game as it played out on the vast canvas of Central and Inner Asia.

Westward roots

India, by and large, is a very Westward-looking country. This is not just in its march to modernity determined by an emphasis on science and technology, which is to be expected of any developing country, but also in its search for historical roots. Its dominant historical narrative, culture, and, indeed, people all trace their origin to the West. Therefore, while the Khyber Pass is imprinted prominently in the national archetypal memory as the route that gave India its soul, influences from the east in the making of India have never been given serious cognizance. This notwithstanding, culture being what it is, there have always been the osmotic ebbs and flows of mutual cultural influences in India's east too that no political boundaries could stop. This reluctance to look east inherent in the overall Indian character should explain to a good extent why the Northeast has remained India's area of darkness for so long. This outlook should again throw light on why before the British entered the region, India never had any serious Burma or Tibet policy. Whereas the outlook to Tibet changed drastically after 1962, India did not have a tangible Burma or South East Asia policy till the 1980s, when the idea of the much hyped 'Look East Policy' became current. Even this grand idea has not moved forward in any substantial way in the 30 years since, in the absence of any conscious drive from policymakers. Even if an increase in trade volume over the decades since 1980 does indicate a closer tie between the ASEAN and India, this connection has not been even remotely through the Northeast. In very many ways, the Northeast continues to remain an area of darkness, and this despite the fact that the dear price India paid for its blindness to the east is the disaster that befell it in 1962.

By contrast, British India had very definite, and often tough, policies for dealing with the east of its Indian Empire. As to how they dealt with Burma was touched upon in an earlier chapter. This one will look further into its relations with Tibet. For indeed, India's Tibet policies had, and still have, profound influences on the politics as well as psychological makeup of the Northeast. Until China declared its intent to send its People's Liberation Army into Tibet in the early 1950, and put this intent into practice in October 1950, India's attention on Tibet continued to lack any urgency. It does also seem that it presumed, until the entry of China into the scenario, that this boundary left behind by the British was a given and beyond controversy. India did express its disappointment when Peking announced its intent of a military takeover of Tibet in early 1950 and did try unsuccessfully to forestall the action. In a note, India tried to caution Peking that an incautious move, even in a matter which is within its own sphere, would be used by those unfriendly to China to prejudice her case in the UN and generally before neutral opinion.[18]

The Indian prime minister, Jawaharlal Nehru, was at the time canvassing for communist China's entry into the UN even at the cost of contender, nationalist China in Formosa. As Sardar Patel noted in his cautionary letter to Nehru quoted earlier, India was the only nation outside of the Soviet Bloc lending China its support for this cause.[19] India, in a memorandum of 21 October 1950, indicated it was consistent with the decision to forgo political interests in Tibet, but to consolidate the Indian position along its border. As a Belgian diplomat, W. F. Van Eekelen, writing of the development at the time noted, 'India had already conveyed to Peking, through diplomatic channels, that it would not insist on maintaining the rights Britain enjoyed in Tibet. But the sudden reduction of Tibetan autonomy must nevertheless have come as a most unpleasant surprise'.[20]

At the base of the controversy was the ambiguous nature of the boundary between India and Tibet left behind by the British at the time of transfer of power. In the western sector, the boundary between Tibet and India was a unilateral one, not demarcated on the ground, but presumed on paper by the British. For one, the Chinese refused to participate in any of the boundary commissions set up by the British to determine the boundary in this sector. The reasons for this lack of interest in the boundary demarcation included, as analysts have pointed out, a weak China's suspicion that it would end up forced into unequal treaties by the British as was happening in its far richer southern coastal provinces.

Another problem in the British dealing with Tibet has been one of not knowing how a state should conclude official agreements and treaties with an unrecognised state. This became evident even as late as 1959, after the Dalai Lama had established a government-in-exile in India, having fled from Tibet in the wake of a failed uprising against the Chinese, who were then in occupation of Tibet. On 9 September 1959, the Dalai Lama submitted his appeal to the UN against China's aggression and occupation of his country. The question then was, was Tibet an independent state? Pending a recognition of the Tibetan government in exile, this did not seem to be so, and on some excuse or the other, most of the Western nations, including the US, which was at the time covertly supporting the Tibetan resistance against the Chinese, refused to give this recognition in the sinister diplomacy of the Cold War era. The question was once again, how was a state to deal with a non-state on these matters? Was the Chinese occupation and atrocities on the Tibetans merely a question of Human

Rights violation, or else as aggression of one nation against another to be addressed and mediated by the UN?[21]

Lingtu blockade

Returning to the nineteenth century then, the British, to maintain a presence in Tibet, had sought to set up a trade mission to Lhasa in 1886 under the command of Colman Macaulay. This was in keeping with the agreement reached 10 years earlier in 1876 by the Chefoo Convention in Peking.[22] The Chinese, though not in a position to oppose the British then, had weakly conveyed their reluctance, saying the plan would be opposed by the Tibetans, indicating clearly they themselves were not sure Tibet was under their control. The British did not push the matter too hard and the mission was suspended. Some, however, say this was on a tacit understanding. The Chinese were spared the embarrassment for their inability to control the Tibetans and 'the British were compensated with Chinese recognition of the British annexation of Upper Burma, a region which the Manchus had long considered as falling within the sphere of their tributary states'.[23]

The Chinese apprehension of Tibetan opposition proved more than an excuse to discourage the British. Not knowing the Macaulay mission was abandoned, the Tibetans determined not to accept Chinese right to dictate foreign policy on them, took the matter in their own hands and 'sent a detachment into the British-protected State of Sikkim, a region to which they now reasserted ancient claims. In Sikkim, at the village of Lingtu, on the main road from Darjeeling to the Tibetan border at the Chumbi Valley, along which Colman Macaulay was expected to travel, the Tibetans set up a military post; and they refused to retreat even after there ceased to be any question of a British mission'.[24] The Tibetans, in their superstition, were reportedly instigated by 'the Ne-chung Oracle at Lhasa, which declared that its magic influence inside the fort would disarm any troops that the British sent against it, while the occupation would give them a commanding position in any negotiations that took place for the delimitation of the boundary between Tibet and Sikkim'.[25]

Pleas to the Chinese on the matter did not result in anything. To the British administration, it had become abundantly clear by 1888 that the Chinese 'had no longer the power to oblige the Tibetans to obey their wishes in matters of this kind. The British discovered that the only way to get the Tibetans out of Sikkim was by force'.[26] Lord Dufferin authorised the expulsion of the Tibetans in March 1888. The episode was the beginning of a change in British administration's attitude towards Tibet.[27]

Upon Chinese insistence, however, this new outlook did not immediately translate into a policy and the British continued to deal Tibetan affairs through the Chinese. Another influence on the British for this seeming lack of urgency is that the British considered trade potential with Tibet too small to risk antagonising China and jeopardise its commercial interests in the rest of the country, particularly its prosperous southern coastal regions. So, the two agreements mentioned earlier, the Anglo–Chinese Convention of 1890 and the Tibet Trade Regulations of 1893, were concluded not between the British and the Tibetans, but continued to be between the British and the Chinese. Moreover, a diplomacy that dealt with Tibetan issues directly with Tibetans would accord to Tibet a de jure sovereignty status in the eye of international law and this may encourage the Tibetans to enter into independent treaties with other European powers – a prospect which the British always have been keen to scuttle. The 1890 Convention confirmed the British position in Sikkim and defined the boundary between Sikkim and Tibet. The 1893 Trade Regulations provided for the opening of a trade mart at Yatung in the Chumbi valley just inside Tibet, where British and Indian merchants could come freely to trade with Tibetans. Both the Sikkim–Tibet boundary alignment and the Yatung trade mart were accepted by China on behalf of Tibet as a result of negotiations in which the Tibetans were not represented.[28] However, this complacent equation was destined to change drastically with the appearance of Russia in this political theatre.

Britain's Tibet anxiety

One of the determining factors behind Britain's Tibet policy towards the end of the nineteenth century and the early twentieth century is a fear Tibet would come under Russian influence. The British considered China the lesser and weaker danger, and preferred Tibet to continue to remain under loose Chinese control, or in the thinking of men such as Curzon, better still under British India's control as a protectorate state. The 1904 military invasion and conquest of Tibet by the Younghusband Mission at the behest of Lord Curzon was towards this end. Curzon, at the time, felt such a mission was urgent as he was certain Russian influence in Tibet had reached a flashpoint and that the loyalty of the 13th Dalai Lama, the spiritual and temporal ruler of Tibet, had swung conclusively towards Russia under the influence of a Siberian Buddhist monk, Dorjiyev (also spelled Dorjieff), of the Buddhist Buriat community. Dorjiyev had stationed himself in Lhasa as a close and trusted follower of the Dalai Lama and the British were certain he was a Russian spy.

The Buriat community has close ethnic ties with Buddhist Mongolian tribes and both come under the strong influence of what Alastair Lamb calls the Tibetan Buddhist Church,[29] at the apex of which is the Dalai Lama incarnate. The British suspected that this connection was being exploited by Russia to gain influence in Tibet. These worries were not so much about losing business as Tibet did not command much British commercial interest. What was of more concern for the British was that Tibet had considerable cultural and religious sway in the Himalayan states of Nepal, Bhutan and Sikkim and the entry of Russia into Tibet may amount to loss of prestige for the British in these small mountain states as well. Nepal's loyalty was especially important for the British, for it was a rich base for recruitment for its prized Gurkha Regiment. 'An increase of Russian influence in Lhasa might well suggest to the Durbar at Kathmandu the advantages of a policy of playing off Russia against Britain to the Nepalese benefit'.[30]

Curzon became convinced by the turn of the twentieth century that Tibet had to be taken by force and kept under the British control as a protectorate. This was despite clear assurances from Russia that they had no interest in Tibet.[31] Francis Younghusband, an old hand at the Great Game, who, a decade earlier, as a captain had conducted an extensive survey of the Karakoram sector of the British India frontier as part of the British effort to establish a linear boundary there, enjoyed Curzon's full confidence and was the officer chosen for the Tibet mission. He entered Tibet from Sikkim in early December 1903 with 3,000 troops. The outcome was predictable as the Tibetans were ill-equipped and ill-trained. They ended up brutally massacred. The 13th Dalai Lama fled to Mongolia before Younghusband entered Lhasa, but the latter forced the Tibetans to sign a convention, the terms of which virtually made Tibet a British protectorate. The convention, signed on 7 September 1904, and ratified in Simla on 11 November the same year, has in all 10 articles of agreements.

The most important articles say: One, the British would be allowed to trade in Yadong, Gyantse, and Gartok. It is however common knowledge these trade centres would couple up as the observatory posts for the British. Two, Tibet was to pay an indemnity of Rs. 7,500,000. Chumbi valley was to remain under British control until this indemnity was paid in full. The amount was to be paid at an annual instalment of Rs. 1,00,000, effectively ensuring Chumbi valley would remain in British hands for 75 years at least or longer if the indemnity was not paid up. Three, the boundary between Sikkim and Tibet, which resulted from the Anglo–Chinese Convention of 1890, was to be recognised. Four, and most importantly, Tibet was to have no relations with any other foreign powers without the consent of the British government.[32]

The terms of the convention would no sooner come to be drastically diluted by those in the British administration who did not see British foreign policy as Curzon and other Conservatives did. The indemnity, for instance, would be voluntarily reduced to Rs. 2,500,000 by Lord Ampthill, the officiating viceroy in the absence of Lord Curzon, who was on leave then, with the nod of the British home government, not long after Younghusband forced the Lhasa Convention in 1904. The provision for the British trade agent at Gyantse to make visits to Lhasa, which was meant to be a symbolic show of the extent of British hold over Tibet, would also come to be withdrawn soon enough. One of the reasons for British hesitation to keep the Lhasa Convention unaltered was again for the fear that it would have given Tibet the status close to a sovereign country with independent powers to conclude international treaties. 'Lansdowne at the Foreign Office felt that the precedent of Tibet having a right to conduct its own foreign relations without reference to its suzerain might be undesirable; the Afghans, for example, might quote it as an argument for their claim to the right to enter into direct relations with the Russians'.[33]

The Great Game, indeed, was beginning to get more complicated. The Lhasa Convention of 1904 quite clearly revealed in its making, as well as its immediate aftermath, a clash of interests and visions between British India and the British home government with profound consequences for the future of India.

Lhasa 1904 undone by Peking 1906

China, meanwhile, played a masterly stroke of diplomacy in the wake of the 1904 Lhasa Convention. First, its representative, T'ang Shao-yi, parleyed hard to pave the way for the Anglo–Chinese Convention in 1906, in which it sought to make the Lhasa Convention legal only after ratification and recognition by China.[34] Proposal for a settlement to this effect came from the Chinese and talks began in Calcutta in February 1905, but under Curzon, it did not bear the fruit the Chinese were after. Curzon wanted the Chinese to unconditionally ratify the Lhasa Convention. He was determined that the Lhasa Convention should not amount to 'British endorsement of Chinese control (of Tibet) which the Chinese were themselves unable to make effective'.[35] The negotiations had to be abandoned without any result in November 1905.

Fortune, however, was on the Chinese side. By late 1905, Curzon's term as viceroy came to an end, and in England, there was a change of regime, ushering in a Liberal cabinet, which 'decided upon a policy of settling the major problems of British policy towards Central Asia through negotiations with the Russians'.[36] If not for these changes in the British government outlook, and 'in the English political climate which had obtained in 1903 or early 1904 the Lhasa Convention might perhaps have been allowed to stand unsupported by Chinese adhesion. Had Curzon continued as Viceroy, the Indian Government would certainly have fought hard against the reopening of negotiations in Peking or London'.[37]

The Calcutta talks resumed in Peking, and on 27 April 1906, the British renegotiated the Lhasa Convention, and the Chinese accepted it after modification. Interestingly and significantly, the 1906 agreement on the Lhasa Convention was a bilateral affair between China and Britain, and Tibet was not included either in the discussions or in the signing of the renegotiated agreement. China, thus, managed to turn adversity into advantage and, before international law, managed to impress that Tibet was under China.[38] China also bargained and persuaded the British administration to allow China to pay up the reduced indemnity of Rs. 2,500,000 owed by Tibet as per the term of the Lhasa Convention of 1904. Not only this, it also persuaded the British to allow the amount to be paid in just three instalments, therefore ensuring the return of Chumbi valley to Tibet in three years.

This turn of events is to have a profound implication on the political future far beyond the boundaries of Tibet. Had the British been unambiguous about its stand on the status of Tibet at this time, and had there been no conflict of visions between British home government and British India, there probably would not have been any need for the Simla Conference of 1913–14, which resulted in the controversial McMahon Line, and the tragic consequences of a border dispute. Liberal Britain, in this sense, was not abandoning just Tibet, but also the interest of its prized colony – India. Sizing up the 'Tibet Anxiety' of the British and apprehension of a Russian takeover of Tibet, even Neville Maxwell, a man generally considered an India baiter, dismissively observes that the concern had been only that of 'strategists and statesmen seeing the interest of the sub-continent in terms of Britain's stake there, concerned with the repercussions of the threat from Russia or China on British investments, or on Parliament in London. The national interests of Indians were not a factor in British calculations, except in so far as it occurred to Englishmen that it would not do for the people they ruled to come into unsettling contacts with either Russians or Chinese across the border'.[39] The strategy was to ensure 'the prestige indispensable to the rule of the British over India demanded that their subjects should not be allowed to see on any horizon the rise of a power even remotely comparable to that of the British empire'.[40]

Another interesting insight from the episode was that even after Curzon's departure from India and the change of regime in London, the dichotomy of vision between London and Shimla/Calcutta continued. Curzon's successor, Minto, was as reluctant to reopen negotiations with China on the Lhasa Convention as Curzon had been. But London prevailed and the negotiations were indeed reopened and culminated in the 1906 Peking Convention. The gulf between how Calcutta and London saw Indian affairs was clear and the Tibet development 'must have seemed to many of Minto's advisers that the British Foreign Office in London posed at least as great a threat to the security of the Indian borders as ever did Russia'.[41]

But the 1906 Peking Convention was not all. The British bound themselves up further with a 1907 treaty with Russia, ensuring they remove themselves out of Tibet still further, prompted again by their 'Tibet Anxiety', to have Russia to agree they too would never enter Tibet. This was so in spite of signs that the Great Game was tapering off towards a conclusion. Russia had already suffered a humiliating naval defeat, followed by a routing on land at the hands of the Japanese in 1904–05 and was retreating from its earlier aggressive postures in Central Asia. The treaty of 1907, by ensuring both Russia and Britain would lay their hands off Tibet, left the field wide open for Chinese entry into Tibet, unhindered by any foreign powers. On the chessboard of the Great Game in far off places as Mongolia, Afghanistan and Persia was thus determined the fate of British Tibet policy, and therefore, the shadow of the Great Game too came to fall on the future of India's Northeast.

In summary then, Britain's object for a long time had been to keep the Russians out of Tibet at any cost, even if it meant giving China more leverage in the region. By the end of the Curzon's term and the ushering in of a Liberal government in London, this outlook softened considerably, and the emphasis soon came to be on a settlement of the Russian problem through negotiations in Europe. 'Where Minto and the Indian Government, perhaps inevitably, were still inclined towards a basically Curzonian solution of meeting the Russian threat by means of counter-measures on the Indian frontier, Morley advocated negotiation in London and St. Petersburg while the frontier was left strictly alone. The only permanent answer to the Tibetan problem, he felt, was a mutual Anglo-Russian agreement to keep Tibet neutral, an agreement efficacy of which depended upon the good faith of the two sides'.[42]

For the next few years after the 1907 Anglo–Russian Convention, things remained quiet on the Tibetan front and Morley's policy of non-interference did seem like it had paid off. The receding of the undeclared rivalry between the two powers was undoubtedly complemented by developments in Europe where new military alliances were taking shape ahead of World War I. Significantly, Russia fell out of the Triple Alliance alongside Germany and Austria-Hungary, and joined Britain and France to form the Triple Entente.

Chinese forward policy

British complacency in Tibet, however, would soon be broken again, this time by a forward policy of the Chinese, which began taking shape in 1906 after the Peking Convention, and peaked in 1910, when Tibet was overrun under the military leadership of Chao Erh Feng.[43] Not only did China take over Tibet again, but it also began probing into neighbouring Himalayan kingdoms of Bhutan, Sikkim and Nepal, as well as into the 'un-administered areas' of the northern Assam hills, now the Indian state of Arunachal Pradesh. The British would then realise how much their decade of non-interference policy in Tibet had cost them, and begin the effort to undo some of its consequences.

At one point, it had even seemed it was only a matter of time before the British would have to abandon the Anglo–Russian Convention 1907 so as to give itself a freer hand in evolving a more engaging Tibet policy. But another turn of fortune saved the British of further alarm, for just when a complete takeover of Tibet by China seemed a foregone conclusion, the Republican Revolution in China broke out, leading ultimately to the fall of the Manchu dynasty in 1912. The Tibetans seized the opportunity and banished all official presence of China in Tibet. China at the time was plunged into an existential crisis, and there were speculations that the country may disintegrate. It was at this juncture, when China was at one of its weakest, that the tripartite Simla Conference, represented by the plenipotentiaries of Tibet, British India and China, was proposed and held – a fact that China was never to forgive. China was clearly the underdog in this conference, therefore another reason for the sympathy for the country among a good section of independent scholars.

In retrospect, many observers now feel Britain's suspicion of Russia's territorial interest in Tibet was overreaction. They are of the opinion that Russia had only an indirect interest in Tibet. The Buriat tribe of Russia's Siberian region were Buddhist, and like the Mongolian Buddhists, their ethnic cousins, come under the 'Tibetan Buddhist Church', of which the Dalai Lama is the leader. Russia had deep interest in Mongolia and needed the goodwill of the Dalai Lama to extend and preserve its interest there. Still, as noted earlier, Tibet remained a backwater region and commanded no great commercial interest of either the British or the Russians. However, towards the end of the nineteenth century, it suddenly became a grave cause for worry for the British when, as noted earlier, Agvan Dorjieff, the Russian Buddhist monk from the Buriat community, arrived in Lhasa and based himself there. This monk 'was a native of the Buriat tribe, which, though of Mongolian origin, is included in the Siberian territory of Russia. To the Tibetan he is known as Tse-nyi Kem-po, which indicates that he is a professor of metaphysics. He had been one of the tutors of the young Dalai Lama, and had always been recognized as a man of ability'.[44]

Dorjieff became a trusted aide of the Dalai Lama, and the Dalai Lama being the supreme spiritual and temporal leader of Tibet, the British had reasons to be concerned. In time, the British became certain this monk was a Russian agent. This suspicion, as we have seen, was ultimately to lead to the drastic British action of sending the Younghusband military mission to Tibet and the Dalai Lama fleeing Lhasa and seeking refuge in Urga, Mongolia.

The 13th Dalai Lama did give the British reasons to be suspicious of his Russian loyalty. Under Dorjieff's influence, the Dalai Lama did come to distrust the British and incline towards the Russians. He refused to communicate with the British authorities when the Curzon administration tried to contact him to discuss the Tibetan refusal to recognise or adhere to the terms of the 1890 and 1893 treaties British India signed with the Chinese. He even returned unopened a letter from Lord Curzon himself in 1899, who, by the time, had come to believe Chinese had no control of Tibet and obtained permission from London to communicate directly with the Tibetans.[45]

Charles Bell explains this conduct, saying the Tibetans were, by nature, distrustful of foreigners and wanted to be left alone. They, thus, distrusted both British India as well as China, but their extra suspicion of the British may have been catalysed by Dorjieff, who spread the story that Russia was a Buddhist country, was much more powerful than the British and that it would most readily aid Tibet in its troubled times.[46]

In 1901, Dorjieff was entrusted a mission from the Dalai Lama to the Tsar of Russia.[47] The leader, who had earlier refused to even open a letter from Curzon, was sending an envoy to the Russian monarch, and this would have annoyed the British still further. When Dorjieff returned, he brought back gifts from the Tsar. 'Among the goods brought by the Mission to Lhasa on their return from Russia was a consignment of Russian arms and ammunition'.[48] The Russians assured the British that the mission was of a purely religious character, but this would have sounded hardly convincing to the British. The Curzon administration then resolved to deal with the Dalai Lama, and the Younghusband mission to Lhasa was precisely with this intent.

But if the India Office and the Foreign Office in London did not foresee these consequences of its policy of non-interference in Tibet, or did not see them as worth losing sleep over, the British India Government in Simla did. Minto was distressed by the terms set for the British negotiators to achieve at the Anglo–Russian Convention. 'The Indian Government did not believe that the problems of the security of the Indian borders could be solved by talks in St. Petersburg'.[49] The Indian government was of the opinion that the set objectives of the talks would amount to surrendering British position of strength, in Afghanistan as much as in Tibet.

Morley, the chief architect and advocate of the liberal policy, had to administer a rebuke to India. He said to Minto in July 1906, 'Britain cannot have two foreign policies. The decision to discuss Central Asia questions with Russia had been made, and the Indian Government would have to abide by that decision. Be we right or wrong, that is our policy'.[50] But this claimed diplomatic victory of the Liberal Henry Campbell-Bannerman government would soon turn sour, and in 1914, Lord Charles Hardinge, who as permanent under-secretary in the foreign office and despite his conservatism had worked closely with Edward Grey,[51] after becoming viceroy, would seek a renegotiation of the 1907 Convention with Russia. But before the 1907 Convention, much harm to Indian interest had been done by the 1906 Peking Convention, which set off the bold and aggressive stance of China on Tibet. The 1906 Convention was pushed through despite strong protests by the Tibetans for they were excluded from the negotiations, and also because it 'provided that the preservation of Tibet's integrity should rest with China, and that China, but no other Power, should have the right to concessions in Tibet. The old mistake of concluding a treaty with China about Tibet without consulting the Tibetan Government was repeated'.[52]

As we have seen, the Chinese lost no time thereafter to launch its forward policy. It appointed an able administrator and nationalist, Chang Yin Tang, as the new High Commissioner, or Amban, for Tibet, and Tang arrived in Lhasa in the autumn of 1906. Here, he worked to gain control over the Tibetan administration, enfeebled as it was by the 1904 Expedition and the absence of the Dalai Lama, who fled Lhasa for Tibet when Younghusband attacked Lhasa. He lost no time to begin working 'to lessen British influence in Tibet, a policy in which he was aided by the Peking Convention and the unwillingness of the British Government of the day to take any part in Tibetan affairs'.[53] The first step Chang took after arriving in Lhasa was to introduce trade regulations in the existing British trade centres in Tibet. He made sure that there would be no more direct dealings between the British and the Tibetans, and all commerce were from then conducted through Chinese intermediaries and at prices fixed by the Chinese authorities.

So harassed were British subjects trading in Tibet that a need to renegotiate the Tibet trade agreement of 1893, signed between China and the British, soon arose. When the renegotiation of the new trade agreements did happen in 1908, the British again found themselves straitjacketed by the both the Peking Convention of 1906 and the Anglo–Russian Convention of 1907. The home government in London too continued to hector the Indian administration, distressing Lord Minto.[54]

The general effect of these regulations introduced by Tang 'was still further to push British and Indians out of Tibet'.[55] One of the clauses of the new agreement even agreed that British officers and subjects (including Indians) should be barred from travelling in Tibet beyond Gyantse. Such restrictions were unprecedented. Till that time, 'Indian pilgrims were accustomed to visit the sites sacred to Hindus at Manasarowar and elsewhere. Such pilgrimages now became illegal'.[56] The Tibetans were obviously disappointed. 'For matters which they regarded as within their own control were placed under the control of Chinese officers. In one way and another they were placed under Chinese domination, and the British were primarily responsible for putting them there, first by the Lhasa Expedition and next by the treaties which followed it up'.[57]

Tang's campaign to return lost Chinese prestige in Tibet while obliterating whatever remained of the prestige the British acquired after the Younghusband Mission was very well coordinated and timed. It may be recalled, in the 1906 Peking Convention, China had, in a masterly stroke of diplomacy, agreed to pay up the reduced indemnity sum of Rs. 2,500,000 the Tibetans were to pay the British as part of the Lhasa Convention of 1904. Until this indemnity was cleared, the British were to, as security, occupy the Chumbi valley in Tibet, a narrow valley wedged between Sikkim and Bhutan, forming a vital lifeline of the trade between Tibet and India. The generous Chinese overture, apart from the political and juridical credits China won for itself, also obviously impressed the Tibetans favourably. The Chinese also had negotiated successfully, especially with Morley as moderator, to pay up the entire amount in just three instalments. In February 1908, even as the Amban was pushing his campaign hard, the last instalment was paid up and the British evacuated the valley, increasing further the Chinese prestige in Tibet and reciprocally depleting those of the British.

As Charles Bell notes, 'The absence of the Dalai Lama from Lhasa and the payment by China of the Younghusband indemnity strengthened the Chinese position. All Chinamen who entered Tibet preached to the Tibetans that China was now run on modern lines, that it had modern guns and up-to-date troops which could hold their own against any country, statements which Tibetans, living like hermits in their own country, had no adequate means of testing. . . . Many Tibetans who had lost faith in the power of China, now began to look to that country to protect them'.[58] The British officer is, however, quick to note in all fairness that 'it may be freely conceded that China's work in Tibet had its own good points. The Chinese officials of the modern school, who came in now, lessened the bribes taken by the Tibetans officials from the poorer classes, and in ordinary non-political cases gave straighter justice than that dealt out by the Tibetan magistracy. There was no doubt some foundation for the Amban's claim that the poorer classes in Tibet were in favour of China'.[59]

In this changed atmosphere in 1909, the Dalai Lama was on his way back to Lhasa only to find to his utter dismay as he entered Tibetan territory that in the name of administrative modernisation and social reformation, the Amban was also on an agenda of Sinification of the Tibetan population. Chinese schools, Chinese language, Chinese customs as well as costumes were forced on the Tibetans. He immediately started contacting foreign emissaries in Peking, British, French, Russians and Japanese, requesting that 'the invading Chinese troops may be compelled to withdraw from Tibet'.[60] The most serious charges of all he made against the Chinese was that they wished to abolish the religion of the Tibetans.[61]

At about the time Tang began pushing reform agendas in the Lhasa region, Chinese troops under Chao Erh Feng were pushing their way towards Lhasa. When the Dalai Lama reached Lhasa at the end of December 1909, Feng's army had already taken Eastern Tibet and were making their way towards Lhasa. When the army reached the periphery of Lhasa on 12 February 1910, fearing arrest and imprisonment, the Dalai Lama and his ministers, taking with them their official seals, fled the Tibetan capital along with 200 soldiers towards India, where they were given refuge in the British hill station of Darjeeling.

Bhutan Treaty 1910

Morley in the India Office in London would have remained unperturbed by these developments if the Chinese did not begin probing the neighbouring principalities of Sikkim, Bhutan, Nepal and the Assam hills. The Chinese, it soon became apparent, considered these principalities and even Upper Burma as their tributaries. China, 'appears to regard the Mongolian peoples that border on her own and the Tibetan frontiers, Nepal, Sikkim, Bhutan, and even Burma, as within her natural sphere. And with Bhutan, inhabited by people of Tibetan stock and revering the Dalai Lama as their spiritual head, past centuries had given her a connexion which might well have been magnified into a suzerainty of the shadowy Chinese type'.[62] Bell writes of the development at the time, reasoning further why this would be a cause for alarm for British India: 'Bhutan, garrisoned by Chinese troops, peopled more and more by Chinese colonists, and overhanging the tea gardens of Assam and Jalpaiguri, would have been a new and very disturbing factor on the Indian frontier'.[63] Bell further notes: 'These were no imaginary perils. Two months earlier the Chinese Amban at Lhasa had addressed the Chiefs in Bhutan in somewhat the following words: The Bhutanese are the subjects of the Emperor of China, who is the Lord of Heaven. You, Deb Raja and two Penlops, think you are great, but you cannot continue without paying attention to the orders of your Ruler. Bhutan is the gate on the south which prevents entry (by the British)'.[64]

British relations with Bhutan at the time were marked by one treaty alone, signed after a British military expedition into the kingdom in 1865 to punish and forbid it from harassing British subjects in adjoining Cooch Behar and Sikkim, often looting and taking slaves. However, the 1865 treaty would not have been enough to keep China from extending its influence in Bhutan. It merely made Bhutan agree to refer disputes with all neighbouring states to the British for arbitration, and for this, the British would increase subsidies to the kingdom, something akin to how the traditional Posa arrangement of the Ahoms with neighbouring hill tribes were transformed and monetised by the British. Bhutan had remained a quiet ally since then, cooperating with the British in every possible way, including the use of its territory to launch the Younghusband Expedition in 1904.[65]

Bell's administrative report on the development, and his proposal for negotiating a new treaty with Bhutan to take care of the new concerns, was accepted by the Foreign Office, then under a new secretary, Harcourt Butler, and subsequently, by the Indian government, but Morley delayed a decision for 10 months. However, he too finally relented.[66] A very brief treaty was signed on 8 January 1910, at Punaka, Bhutan and ratified at Calcutta on 24 March 1910, which merely revised Article VIII of the 1865 British treaty with the kingdom. Bhutan was to remain independent, but it was to conduct its foreign affairs only on the advice of the British. In the revised paragraph, the British pledged 'to exercise no interference in the internal administration of Bhutan. On its part, the Bhutanese Government agrees to be guided by the advice of the British Government in regards to its external relations. In the event of disputes with or causes of complaints against the Maharaja of Sikkim and Cooch Behar, such matters will be referred for arbitration to the British Government, which will settle them in such manner as justice may require, and insist upon the observance of its decision by the Maharaja named'.[67]

Unlike the case of Bhutan, the British were not so much afraid for Nepal, for the country had a robust military, therefore would not be easily subdued. It was, on the contrary, afraid that Nepal may go ahead and attack Lhasa, leaving the British at a quandary whether to honour its alliance with Nepal and take its side, thus abrogating its commitment to the 1907 Anglo–Russian Convention, or else remain neutral, and thus, lose a good ally and rich recruiting ground for its prized Gurkha Regiments. If it was the latter course of action, there was the likelihood of China and Nepal forming an alliance, with grave implications on the strategic and security positions of India.[68] Sikkim was already a protectorate state, so it too was not much a cause for worry. The British, however, as noted earlier, were to be saved the prospect of having to deal with the Chinese immediately, for just as China assumed a menacing presence in its northern frontier, the Republican Revolution broke out in China, ultimately toppling the Manchu dynasty, forcing Chinese power to recede from Tibet and other outlying provinces.

However, if the British were spared an immediate confrontation, the experience was a vital lesson. They had themselves laid the ground for this uncertainty with the ambiguous Tibet policy pushed disinterestedly by the India Office in London under a Liberal government. The Simla Conference of 1913–14 was a result of this new-felt urgency to make the effort to give a semblance of permanence to this unsettled and incomplete agenda along India's Northeast frontier. It, however, proved too late. The damage was already beyond full recovery and the border issue in this sector lingers on even to this day.

Notes

1 See Peter J. Taylor, *The State as Container: Territoriality in the Modern World-System* (University of Newcastle, 1994), online version published by Sage Journals, http://www.sagepub.com/dicken6/Sage%20articles/Chap%206/CH%206%20-%20Taylor.pdf (accessed 30 December 2014).
2 The text of Sardar Vallabhbhai Patel's letter available at http://www.friendsoftibet.org/main/sardar.html (accessed 30 December 2014).
3 Ibid.

4 See Bertil Lintner, *Great Game East: India, China and the Struggle for Asia's Most Volatile Frontier* (HarperCollins, 2012).
5 See Lezlee Brown Halper and Stephan Halper, *Tibet: An Unfinished Story*, for a detailed account of the US decisions taken on the matter to support Tibetan insurrection against China.
6 Bertil Lintner, *Great Game East*, pp.1–37.
7 Ibid.
8 Lezlee Halper, *Tibet: An Unfinished Story*, p. 174.
9 Ibid.
10 Ibid.
11 Ibid.
12 Ibid., p. 143.
13 Ibid.
14 Claude Arpi, http://www.claudearpi.net/maintenance/uploaded_pics/Henderson_Brooks_Bhagat.pdf (accessed 30 December 2014).
15 http://en.wikipedia.org/wiki/John_Morley (accessed 5 June 2012).
16 http://en.wikipedia.org/wiki/George_Curzon,_1st_Marquess_Curzon_of_Kedleston (accessed 3 April 2012).
17 Morley Papers (as quoted in Alastair Lamb, *The McMahon Line*, Vol-1, p. 59).
18 W. F. Van Eekelen, *Indian Foreign Policy and the Border Dispute with China*, p. 30.
19 http://www.friendsoftibet.org/main/sardar.html (accessed 30 May 2013).
20 Van Eekelen, *Indian Foreign Policy*, p. 30.
21 See, Lezlee Brown Halper and Stephan Halper, *Tibet: An Unfinished Story*, pp. 217–23.
22 Alastair Lamb, *The McMahon Line*, Vol. 1, p. 6.
23 Ibid.
24 Ibid., p. 7.
25 Charles Bell, *Tibet Past and Present*, p. 60.
26 Alastair Lamb, *The McMahon Line*, p. 7.
27 Ibid.
28 Ibid.
29 See Alastair Lamb, *The McMahon Line*, Vol. 1.
30 Ibid., p. 9.
31 Charles Bell, *Tibet Past and Present*, p. 65.
32 Ibid., full text of the 1904 convention attached as Appendix-VII, pp. 284–7.
33 Alastair Lamb, *The McMahon Line*, p. 34.
34 Charles Bell, *Tibet Past and Present*, pp. 287–9, full text of 1906 convention attached as Appendix VIII.
35 Alastair Lamb, *The McMahon Line*, p. 45.
36 Ibid., p. 48.
37 Ibid.
38 See ibid., pp. 36–42 for an account of the diplomacy and negotiating skills of Chinese negotiator T'ang Shao-yi.
39 Neville Maxwell, *India's China War*, p. 67.
40 Owen Lattimore, *Inner Asian Frontiers of China*, p. 236 (as quoted in Neville Maxwell, *India's China War*, p. 67).

41 Ibid., p. 55.
42 Ibid., p. 66.
43 See http://en.wikipedia.org/wiki/Zhao_Erfeng and http://www.friend softibet.org/main/tibet.html (accessed23 July 2013).
44 Sir Charles Bell, *Tibet Past and Present*, pp. 62, 63.
45 Ibid., p. 62.
46 Ibid., p. 70.
47 Ibid., p. 63.
48 Ibid., p. 64.
49 Alastair Lamb, *The McMahon Line*, p. 110.
50 Ibid.
51 http://en.wikipedia.org/wiki/Charles_Hardinge,_1st_Baron_Hardinge_of_Penshurst (accessed 7 July 2013).
52 Charles Bell, *Tibet Past and Present*, p. 88.
53 Ibid.
54 Alastair Lamb, *The McMahon Line*, p. 147.
55 Charles Bell, *Tibet Past and Present*, p. 91.
56 Ibid.
57 Ibid.
58 Ibid., p. 93.
59 Ibid.
60 Íbid., p. 96.
61 Ibid.
62 Ibid., p. 100.
63 Ibid.
64 Ibid., p. 101.
65 Ibid.
66 Ibid., p. 102.
67 Text of treaty between Great Britain and Bhutan, reproduced as appendix XI in Ibid., p. 297.
68 See Alastair Lamb, *The McMahon Line*.

6

LINGUISTIC NATIONALISM VERSUS RELIGIOUS NATIONALISM

Partition trauma and the Northeast

Like its northern boundary, the evolution of the southern boundary of the Northeast too has its own history of intrigues and trauma. The northern boundary, as we have seen, resulted from the controversial Simla Conference of 1913–14 and is generally referred to as the McMahon Line. The southern boundary is known as the Radcliffe Line, drawn by the boundary commission headed by Cyril Radcliffe in 1947, when India was partitioned into two nations along religious lines. A convenient landmark from which to begin this study is, yet again, the arrival of the British in the political arena of the region and the signing of the Treaty of Yandabo in 1826, by which, among others, the Ahom kingdom came to be part of British India.

The Ahom kingdom was, however, not coterminous with the spread of the British province of Assam. British Assam included territories beyond what was the traditional domain of the Ahoms. Under the British province were included the present states of Meghalaya, Arunachal Pradesh, Mizoram and Nagaland, and for a time, Sylhet in Bangladesh. The two other Northeast states of Tripura and Manipur were independent kingdoms then, though under loose British monitoring from its Assam province, and came to be part of the Indian union only in 1949, a little over two years after Indian independence. Sikkim, which is also now administratively considered a part of the Northeast, having been admitted into the North East Council, was also an independent proto-Tibetan Himalayan monastery state, though a British protectorate. Till 1874, when it was made a chief commissioner's province, Assam was clubbed with the British province of Bengal and administered from Calcutta. These distinctions, though not profoundly important, still do make a difference, for in the evolution of the Northeast's southern boundary, the rise of modern Assamese linguistic nationalism and political consciousness, as Amalendu Guha and other writers call it, had a very big role.[1]

There are generally two largely divergent strands within which analysts of the history of modern Assamese nationalism fall into. One disagrees that the birth of modern Assamese political consciousness is a recent phenomenon and traces its roots in the antiquity of the great Aryan culture – therefore, even earlier than the Ahoms, who arrived in Assam through the Patkai Ranges under the leadership of Sukapha (AD 1228–68), in the mid-thirteenth century, to establish a kingdom for the next 600 years until the advent of British rule. This school sees Assamese cultural evolution as closely aligned with the great Indic culture of Aryan India, and consequently, the birth of modern Assamese nationalism as very much a part and parcel of Indian nationalism, therefore little to distinguish it from the forces that propelled and remodelled modern Indian nationalism, which culminated in the epochal Indian freedom struggle against British colonialism. Udayon Mishra, a scholar of this school, for instance, in his *The Periphery Strikes Back* even goes to the extent of arguing that Assam should not be clubbed in the same regional category as the rest of the Northeast states on the plea of its much more pronounced cultural and political proximity to mainstream India from historical and proto-historical times.[2] The merits of this argument are, however, outweighed by the dangers it overlooks, and this will become more evident in the course of this chapter. For, from this same vantage, even the present state of Assam cannot be, with any justification, called a single cultural or political entity. The stark demographic and cultural differences between the Brahmaputra valley and the Barak/Surma valley and even within the Brahmaputra valley itself, which have thrown up violent assertions of independent identities by the Bodos, Tiwas, Karbis, Rabas and many more, tell of this shortcoming.

The second school sees the genesis of modern Assamese nationalism quite differently. Scholars of this school generally conclude that Assamese nationalism is a function of Bengali nationalism or a reaction to Bengali cultural hegemony. Amalendu Guha and Sajal Nag would rank among the foremost who hold this view.

Neither of the two can, however, be dismissed totally, but the latter does seem to provide more satisfactory explanations to many seismic historical events Assam has witnessed in modern times, such as the politics that went behind the award of the populous Sylhet district to Pakistan at the time of the 1947 Partition and the six-year-long anti-foreigners agitation led by the All Assam Students Union (AASU) in the early 1980s, which literally paralysed the state administration for as many years. Unlike the former, the narrative in the case of the latter can be, and has been, charted out more precisely in chronological historical time. However, this is not to say all viewpoints on Assam's modern nationalism have to fall within these two frames only. There are others who also have identified independent factors contributing to its making. Sanjib Baruah, for instance, argues how the germ of political turmoil in the state, to a great extent, is also a function and reaction to land tenure policies introduced by the British, which left the Assamese peasantry in the plains as well as tribal communities in the hills under severe land alienation pressures, and they either had to adapt to the new system under circumstantial duress or, else, resort to violence to preserve their domains.[3]

To recall Curzon's Romanes lecture again and draw an inference, Western states and empires are, by nature, uneasy about un-demarcated and undefined boundaries of the extent of their rules. By this same attribute, they were also uneasy about undocumented spaces within the territorial bounds over which they exercised sovereignty. Every bit of land had to be accounted for by deeds of landownership, which also are pledges for tax obligations to the state by individual landowners, and whatever space remained without private ownership was treated as state-owned by default, or khaslands. We have seen in the introductory chapter on how this approach to land played out in India's western sector in Kashmir. It may be recalled when the British inherited Kashmir from the Sikhs after defeating them in 1846, and found no demarcated boundary to mark the kingdom's extent, they immediately began a fruitless exercise of setting up boundary commissions and expeditions to delimit and demarcate a boundary to establish the extent of the empire's new acquisition. Of the latter imperial unease of undocumented land within their sovereign territories, what unfolded in Assam after the British annexed it in 1826 is an illustrative demonstration and, in many ways, led to tragic consequences.

The pre-colonial world had little knowledge or use of precisely demarcated and documented land revenue mechanism. They were, by and large, and in varying degrees, non-monetised, pre-modern economies, and they had hardly any need, intention, compulsion or the technology for creating excessive surpluses. The notion of wasteland and khasland, therefore, did not exist. In more primitive societies, mostly in the hills, the economy was one of hunter-gatherer, augmented by subsistent slash-and-burn shifting agriculture. In the fertile alluvial plains, agriculture was far more developed and productive, leading to the emergence of feudal states with a fair, but varying degrees of centralised bureaucracies. Still, the land tenure mechanisms that evolved in these principalities were far from the intensive tax- and revenue-driven economies that the colonial economy was characterised by. This was very much the state of the economy the British found Assam in when they took over its administration. One of the first initiatives of the colonial administration was, hence, about reforming their newly acquired territory's land tenure mechanisms. They saw little potential for raising revenue from the hills, so tended to leave them, as well as the communities living there, in their isolation, designating these lands as un-administered areas, or the 'Backward Tracts' by the Government of India Act 1919.

The colonial administration would soon evolve a method for governing the lawless lands in a way that needed as little administrative energy as possible, and the Bengal Eastern Frontier Regulation, 1873, is one of these. In 1936, the 'Backward Tracts' were graded as 'Excluded Area' and 'Partially Excluded Area', when the Government of India Act 1935 came into force. The 'Excluded Areas', which included the present-day Arunachal Pradesh, Nagaland, Mizoram and the North Cachar Hills, were to be governed directly by the imperial authority through the provincial governor and would have no representatives in the Assam Legislative Assembly to be set up under a new provision introduced in the Government of India Act 1935, and conversely, the Assembly would have no legislative jurisdiction in matters concerning the 'Excluded Areas'. Garo Hills, Mikir Hills and part of Khasi and Jantia Hills came under the 'Partially Excluded Area', and these districts were allowed to send a few representations to the Assam Legislative Assembly, and these representatives were to be placed under ministers, subject, however, to the governor's discretionary control.[4]

Land reforms and khaslands

In the fertile flatlands of the valleys, the colonial administration was quick to seize the opportunity to augment and tap the till-then underutilised, revenue potential. It therefore introduced modern land revenue laws, marked by long-term land deeds, and therefore, tax liabilities on the title holders. These laws were premised on the presumption of settled agriculturist communities familiar with intensive multi-crop cultivation, and this came into conflict with the traditional non-sedentary or partly sedentary agricultural practices among the Assamese peasantry, not just in the hills but also among plains communities.[5]

In the plains, while the new British system demanded intensive multi-crop cultivation, the traditional practice was for single crop cultivation, and this too, far between long rotation cycles of fallow intervals, sometimes extending several years. Initial resistance to conform to the newly introduced British norms of long-term land title system in the Assam plains led first to the dispossession of Assamese peasantry, who refused to register their land and acquire these land titles, for without these titles, their traditional underused agricultural lands, by default, became government khasland.[6] Then, to their further dismay, the British administration began encouraging Bengali peasants from East Bengal, who were much better acquainted and skilled with modern and more productive agricultural methods as well as the British land tenure system, to fill in the vacuum the Assamese peasants thus left.[7] These immigrants not only engaged in intensive multi-crop agriculture still quite alien among the Assamese peasantry, but also introduced cash crops, especially jute, and this suited the colonial administration's revenue drive.

Not only did the Assamese peasants discover they were losing out land to these immigrants, Baruah writes, but these years were also marked by large-scale reclamation and transfer of forest as well as arable land to tea gardens. Here too, the Assamese peasants, as well as tribal communities, found themselves on the receiving end. 'As one mode of resource use comes into contact with another mode organized on very different social and ecological principles, we expect the occurrence of substantial social strife. In fact the clash of two modes has invariably resulted in massive bursts of violence and sometimes genocidal conflicts',[8] Baruah quotes from Madhav Gadgil and Ramachandra Guha, and further notes, 'The violent encounter between the Nagas and the British – a process that colonial rulers described as the "pacification" of the Naga "savages" – can be best understood in these terms. There were ten "punitive expeditions" between 1835 and 1851. After a period of relative quiet, there was an uprising by Angami Nagas in 1879, when they seized the British military base in Kohima, leading to the last major military encounter'.[9]

Besides tea, British entrepreneurs at the time were also prospecting rubber in the hills, and together, the two enterprises led to serious encroachment of land in the foothills, causing disruptions in the hunting-gathering lifestyles of the tribal communities in these hills, therefore evoking hostility towards British subjects. This was one of the reasons for the introduction of the Inner Line system under the Bengal Eastern Frontier Regulation of 1873. The legacy of this friction of land alienation, resulting out of the 'new property regime imposed by the colonial land settlement project', was to remain long after British colonialism ended, Baruah continues:

> the fallout of this shift continued to be a sub-text in the political instability in the area till this day; notably the insurgencies that blame the Indian government for its economic underdevelopment and indeed sometimes of treating the area as a colony,

the perennial tension between immigrants and the indigenous peoples and the unrest among 'tribal' people such as Bodos and Karbis whose reliance on shifting cultivation had historically been more pronounced than that of the rest of the population. Indeed one reason why the economic grievances of the Bodo people did not come to a head till the 1980s was that for nearly a century many of them were able to move around cultivating land formally designated as protected forests. Only in the 1980s, following Assam's long campaign against 'foreigners', these most indigenous of Assam's inhabitants came to be treated as encroachers by the Assam government – provoking the anger of many Bodo activists.[10]

The Treaty of Yandabo, 1826, however, remains an important pivot for any study of modern Assamese nationalism, regardless of whichever of these vantages Assam's history is seen from. The British entered Assam not out of economic interest, but by the compulsions of military considerations. To protect its own interest in Bengal, it had to intervene in Assam to halt the advance of an invading Burmese Army, which had already overrun Manipur, Assam and other small principalities in the region, and was already threatening the eastern frontiers of Bengal. Once the threat perception of external aggression was eliminated after the comprehensive defeat of Burma, the British wished to maintain some armed presence, as we have seen in the chapter on militarisation of the Northeast, even though maintaining the military it brought into Assam during the war was becoming redundant and cost-ineffective. This was when a plan to raise a civil militia came to be considered seriously. The Cachar Levy was thus raised in 1835. The discovery of tea and other forest wealth soon elicited a permanent administrative interest of the British in Assam, and in direct reciprocity, the Cachar Levy grew in size and sophistication until at the end of World War I, it was renamed the Assam Rifles, a paramilitary unit officered by officers of the Indian Army on deputation, and closely linked to the Gurkha Regiments of the Indian Army, with combined responsibilities of military as well as police duties.[11]

With a growing British commercial interest in Assam, especially after the discovery of tea, the expansion of the British administration there too became essential. Assam was already devastated economically and spiritually by a reign of terror under Burmese occupation before the British rescued it. The entry of the British, therefore, though a relief for Assam in the initial stages, also had a huge toll with far-reaching ramifications. The interest that drives any colonial government is primarily revenue extraction, and in Assam too, the British immediately set about looking for means to do just this. As already briefly discussed, the first move of the administration was to effect land reforms to raise a tax base and also to make the land productive and revenue-generating. 'The peasants were taxed for their landed property, products, transport system, etc.'[12] Agrarian tensions and revolts were the natural consequences.

There were to be more woes for the Assamese. The British administration soon enough discovered an acute shortfall of local recruits with Western education and familiar with the working of the British bureaucracy. By the 1830s, the British administration began looking to adjoining Sylhet, Dhaka and Mymensing districts of Bengal for recruits. 'Soon all the principal offices of the Government were manned by Bengalees as they were found to be efficient and competent colonial functionaries'.[13] By 1834, when Francis Jenkins was appointed the new commissioner of Assam, 'almost all departments of the government were manned by the Bengalees'.[14] The scene was thus set for an eventual clash of interest on ethnic lines. A situation in which local communities were literally pushed aside and a new imported influx of another community foisted as the intermediary of the colonial power structure can only be predicted to cause dangerous discontent among the original population.

Grow more food

This ethnic equation was to become far more complex. In the British effort to extract more revenue from the land by making it more productive, and since the local Assamese populations were still not ready for more modern techniques of farming or land tenure mechanisms, the British stepped up their initiative of encouraging East Bengali peasants to immigrate to Assam to bring more land under modern intensive farming. In the build-up to World War II years, under a 'Grow More Food' programme as part of the British war effort, this immigration policy was to reach a zenith, so much so that it met with strong objection from Congress leaders complaining that the programme was actually amounting to 'Grow More Muslims' – a sentiment which was to echo in the observation of the then viceroy, Lord Wavell, after a visit to Assam at the time. The Muslim League government in Assam then was, however, encouraging this immigration policy, bringing in another dimension to the accumulating dark clouds of conflict in the region. 'The Muslim cultivators from East Bengal were encouraged by the Muslim League government of Mohammad Sadullah in Assam ostensibly for the Grow More Food Campaign. However, Viceroy Lord Wavell said in his Memoirs that Sadullah was much more interested in growing more Muslims'.[15]

Most of the earlier immigrants were middle-class Bengali Hindus from the East Bengal district of Sylhet, whose immigration was encouraged by the British administration in Assam. Not long after the British takeover of Assam, 'Sylheti middle-class economic migrants to the Brahmaputra valley and Cachar areas were a population in motion in colonial Assam, moving back and forth, many with simultaneous homes in both Sylhet and the Brahmaputra valley districts and Cachar since the late nineteenth century. As early as 1901, the Census of India recorded that Sylhetis who are good clerks and enterprising traders are found, in small numbers, in most of the districts of the province'.[16]

Anindita Dasgupta, who has done extensive research and interviews of surviving Sylhetis of the Indian Partition era in both Bangladesh and India, points out that the Sylheti Hindu migrants to Assam did not treat themselves in the least as refugees, and instead, assumed an air of superiority over the local Assamese. One 78-year-old (in 2001) gentleman Sylheti migrant in Guwahati, Bijoy Kumar Das, whom she interviewed, for instance, said they 'came like tourists, camera in hand, clicking random pictures of the city. They thought Assam was a jungle and were so excited'.[17] In another interview by her in Silchar about the same time, a 75-year-old gentleman, Paritosh Ral Choudhury, confirmed this peculiar distance between the middle-class Western-educated Sylheti migrants and the local Assamese. 'The Assamese did not know how to eat *Chal-kumra*. So, they would give it away to us . . . At the time when we migrated to Cachar, the Assamese would eat curds that were so rotten that insects would be swimming in it'.[18] Another 65-year-old woman in Shillong, Shorbani Das, remembers whenever any Assamese person came to her house to meet her father for some work, 'her father would shout loudly to the servants to give the man a *moorha* (cane stool) on the verandah to sit on and the Assamese man would sit outside and wait for her father patiently'.[19]

When the then fledgling Assamese middle class came to be their own, having acquainted themselves with the colonial ways, they quite predictably came to consider the Hindu Bengali migrants from Sylhet, who had, by then, come to have a stranglehold on the colonial bureaucracy's ranks and files, thereby its local-level power structure, as their usurpers and bitter rivals. This divide would prove pivotal in many crucial turns of history of the region in the years that followed. The shifting complexions of this rivalry would even, at points, appear to be counter-intuitive when considered against the political trends in the rest of the Indian subcontinent, especially as the freedom struggle against British colonialism approached its zenith. Some of the consequences, such as the fate of Sylhet, which was ultimately awarded to (East) Pakistan, in which this rivalry came to be a major determinant, borders on the tragic. Not only Sylhet, at one juncture, the turn of history showed the potential of much more drama, with the possibility of the whole of Assam being awarded to Pakistan coming under active administrative consideration and public discussions.

Two parallel developments, one at the local regional level, and the other on the larger canvas of the Indian national freedom struggle, unfolding simultaneously became pronounced. The rivalry between the Bengalis and Assamese in Assam, which began as a middle-class contest for jobs and the levers of power of the colonial state, soon transformed into a linguistic nationalistic rivalry in which the Assamese began to feel threatened of being colonised and marginalised into insignificance by the numerically expanding and increasingly hegemonic presence of the Bengali immigrants.

This rivalry would become further complicated because of another latent division within the Bengali immigrants along religious lines coming to the fore. The English-educated Sylheti Bengalis, largely Hindus, who filled the administrative jobs and the land-hungry Bengali Muslim peasant settlers would soon begin to see differently on issues of their nationality. But before this division came about, the two categories of immigrants, though professing different religions and belonging to different economic classes, spoke the same language, and as a linguistic community, they began seriously upsetting the demographic balance of the province, and at one point, threatened to reduce the local Assamese to a minority. However, it was the earlier immigrants of middle-class Bengali origin who became the targets of initial resentment of the new Assamese middle class, who were finding themselves losing out practically on all fronts. Amalendu Guha sums up the scenario in the following words:

> The period from 1826 to 1873 was a period of transition for the Assam's pre-capitalist economy into its colonial phase. British capital penetrated the economy and started building an infrastructure to sustain the exotic capitalistic set-up. Collaborating traders, bankers, lawyers and clerks from other Indian provinces came as camp-followers. Bullock carts, a novelty for the region, were introduced. The economy was monetised. The closed society was exposed to immigration of labour, new skills, new vices and new ideas. Marwari trader-cum-moneylenders monopolised

the internal trade as agents of the British trading houses in Calcutta, who in turn worked for their metropolitan counterparts in London. Bengali clerks, doctors and lawyers, with the advantage of their early initiation to English education and British-Indian administrative system, monopolised Government jobs and professions. In this context, the new-born, rickety Assamese intelligentsia of the period found itself to be an insignificant minority in the 'urban' sector.[20]

Language agitation

Before going into the nature of Assamese reaction, a little foregrounding on certain structural developments on the political front would be helpful in understanding the situation. When the British incorporated Assam into its Indian Empire, it was not made into a separate province. Instead, it was absorbed into its Bengal province. From the British point of view, moving populations from East Bengal to Assam would have been just a matter of inter-district skill relocation for optimum performance of its provincial administration. They were probably not too concerned about the social consequences this may bring about, but the reality was Bengali middle-class immigrants came to dominate Assam almost completely. At their behest, Bengali was made the official language as well as the medium of school education in Assam from 1837, and this was done on the plea that Assamese was only a dialect of Bengali, a presumption of the Bengali middle class, who made sure this was soon the opinion of the British administration in the province as well. This was a major stab to the Assamese sense of self-esteem, already wounded by the manner they had been usurped from state power by Sylheti Bengali immigrants.

Understandably, the Assamese middle class began rallying against this language policy. In this campaign, Christian missionaries were to take a lead role in the Assamese fight-back, urging the British administration to rescind the decision of making Bengali the official language of the province. Other than the probable reason of their coming to identify with the cause of the people among whom they worked, the missionaries who, at the time, had begun spreading their wings in both the hills and plains of Assam, would have found it difficult to preach other than in Assamese, which had come to be the lingua franca of the local communities. 'Therefore, the missionaries took up the task of establishing a separate identity for the Assamese language'.[21] This resonated well with the nascent Assamese middle class. A series of articles started appearing at the time on the need to resurrect the Assamese language from oblivion under Bengali hegemony:

On 1 August 1853, 'An Assamese Gentleman' from Calcutta wrote about the necessity of the Assamese learning their own language. In December 1855, Gunabhiram Borua published an article comparing Assamese and Bengali languages. The Article of Puranananda Sharma, 'Asomiya Bhashar Kotha' in March 1856 and Gunabhiram's 'Matri Bhashar Shkti' in March 1857 reflected the sentiments of the local people. On 25 May 1855, Miles Bronson of the American Baptist Mission in Assam published a letter in favour of the Assamese language. Earlier, on 10 May, the same paper published an article 'Progress of the Education Scheme in this Presidency' on the situation in Assam. Ananda Ram Dhekial Phukan, educated in Hindu College, Calcutta and a government servant since 1847, in his memorandum to A.J.M. Mills regretted that education in Assam under English Rule was in a 'retrograde state'.[22]

The language agitation only became stronger in the years ahead. But most British officials remained adamant that Bengali should be the preferred official language, insisting there was virtually no difference between Assamese and Bengali. The argument was that 'Assamese was not the language that the Ahom rulers brought with them. It was the local language of Assam which the Assamese had developed through intercourse with Bengal'.[23] The campaign for return to Assamese language, however, only spread and grew stronger.

Assamese peasantry joins stir

Towards the later part of the nineteenth century, the tide began to turn in favour of Assamese. This was on account of several factors, not just as an acknowledgement of the merit of the campaign that Assamese was an independent language. Among these was a shift in the British outlook to its Bengal Presidency, where a radical anti-colonial movement was already building up, much to the alarm of the colonial government. Yet again, the Assamese middle class was also able to win over and bring in the Assamese peasantry into the campaign. With the unabated immigration of land-hungry Muslim peasants from East Bengal, mainly from Sylhet and Mymensingh, aided by new land laws introduced by the British, the Assamese peasantry were finding themselves increasingly dispossessed. Their

LINGUISTIC NATIONALISM VS RELIGIOUS NATIONALISM

insecurity and anxiety soon found a common cause with the middle-class campaign for the restoration of Assamese language, sowing the seed for a larger Assamese linguistic nationalism.

In the face of these developments, in July 1873, Assamese was restored as the official language of five valley districts of Assam, namely, Kamrup, Darrang, Nowgong, Sibsagar and Lakhimpore.

The next year, on 6 February 1874, Assam was separated from Bengal. The reason cited for this by the colonial government was administrative convenience. Assam was 'remote and difficult to access, and few Lieutenant-Governors ever visited it. The local conditions were altogether different from those which prevailed in Bengal, and were quite unknown to the officers responsible for the government of that province, who had not the time, even if they had the inclination, to make themselves acquainted with them'.[24] At the time two options were considered as to the administrative future of Assam. One was 'to raise the position of Bengal Government by amalgamating the Board of Revenue with it, and the other was to lower it by lopping off some of its more remote territories. The Government of India preferred the latter alternative'.[25] Quite obviously, the growing tea industry in Assam, and therefore, the need for a more efficient revenue management, was also a consideration. But later in the same year, the colonial administration took another decision, which would have a long-standing impact on the history of modern Assam, and indeed, the entire Northeast region. 'On 12 September of the same year Sylhet was incorporated in the new province'.[26]

The amalgamation of Sylhet with Assam, however, was bitterly resented both by the Sylhetis – especially the educated, Hindu middle class – and the Assamese, but for radically different reasons. The Sylhetis, on their part, thought it was a degradation for them to be attached to a backward state such as Assam, and that they would be much better off as part of Bengal, then at the peak of what is generally referred to as the Bengali Renaissance. The Assamese, on the contrary, were worried Assam would become a Bengali province, leaving them marginalised demographically, linguistically, politically and culturally.

A bitter struggle was triggered off by this decision. Making it even more intriguing was also the fact that this struggle was unfolding against the canvas of the Indian freedom struggle, and its changing internal dynamics. When the Indian freedom struggle progressively became polarised on religious lines, and a partition of India on religious lines became inevitable, with the Hindus remaining in India and Pakistan created for the Muslims, Assam failed to respond to this new and radically repolarised alignment. Linguistic Assamese nationalism, defined by its memories of antagonistic opposition to the hegemony of Bengali immigrants from Sylhet and other East Bengal provinces, continued to hold sway in Assam. When, at the appointed hour of the partition of India, the only hope of the Hindu population of Sylhet to remain with India was to be treated as a part of Assam, the latter would disown the idea. Sylhet, ultimately, was destined to become part of East Pakistan. 'Under the constant shadow of the Bengali-Assamese conflict, the growth of nationalism in 19th-century Assam was a two-track process. People were increasingly turning as much to the great nationalism at the all-India level as to the little nationalism at the linguistic regional level'.[27]

Bengali elite and peasantry

While the growing rivalry between the Assamese middle class and the educated Bengali Hindu immigrants was taking the centre stage of politics in Assam, curiously, another fissure became visible in this ethnic equation. The difference in class interests between the middle-class Bengalis from Sylhet and the Bengali peasants from Sylhet and adjoining district of Mymensingh soon became apparent. While the former tended to lord over the Assamese politically and culturally, the land-hungry Muslim peasants were happy with the promise of land in Assam, and even began identifying themselves as Assamese. So, while the Sylheti Hindus nostalgically longed to return to Bengal and continued to condescendingly look down upon the Assamese, the Bengali Muslim peasants began seeing things differently.

When the merger of Sylhet to Assam was announced, Sylhet was the first to protest the 'amalgamation with Assam and its people with whom they had no similarities – social or linguistic'.[28] They were candid in their objection to the transfer that it would be to their disadvantage to be part of a backward province and people, thereby losing the benefits of the much more established and advanced laws and institutions of Bengal. While this was the attitude of the upper crust of the Bengali community in Sylhet, the peasantry, which had little share in the power structure of Bengal, found their predicament more promising in Assam, with its abundance of land for them to cultivate.

The Assamese too resented the amalgamation of Sylhet to Assam, but as noted earlier, for an entirely different reason. They were apprehensive of being demographically marginalised. A demographic profile of Assam at the time will make the picture clear:

> Thus the province that emerged was an amalgam of four disparate elements: (i) the preliterate hill districts, speaking diverse tongues,

(ii) the five Assamese-speaking districts of the Brahmaputra Valley together known as Assam proper, (iii) Goalpara of the same Valley where the Bengali and the Assamese cultures overlapped, and (iv) the two Bengali-speaking districts of the Surma Vallley – Sylhet and Cachar.

The Hill districts, inhabited by various tribes together, had an insignificant population. There, a middle class competing for jobs and higher education was yet unborn. The rest of the provincial population was, more or less, evenly balanced between the two Valleys. However, the Surma Valley, in this respect, had an edge over the others until 1911.[29]

But the 'Bengali linguistic group rapidly increased in number from Census to Census through immigration. It continued to outnumber the Assamese even in the new province well until the partition in 1947'.[30]

The revenue potential of Assam in the meantime also made quantum increases. Not only was there tea to trade but coal, oil and timber. It was also a time the partition of Bengal had become imminent. The creation of a Muslim-majority province by breaking up Bengal had become a necessary strategy for the British colonial rulers to deal a blow to the rising Indian nationalism, heavily tinted as it was with Hindu spiritual content. 'In 1892, some officials in the foreign department suggested that the Chittagong Division of Bengal be transferred to Assam. When the idea was discussed in details at the official level during 1896–97, the then Chief Commissioner of Assam further suggested that the districts of Dacca and Myamensingh be also transferred along with Chittagong Division'.[31]

After some initial opposition from certain quarters within the government, by 1903, this proposal began gaining legitimacy. Such a merger, it was thought, would facilitate the completion of the Assam–Bengal Railway, which was under construction then. It would also give Assam 'a maritime outlet in order to develop its industries in tea, oil and coal'.[32] The planters were also keen to have this merger happen. When Lord Curzon, the then viceroy 'visited Assam in 1903, they put into his head the idea that if Chittagong was tagged to Assam and developed as an outlet to the sea, the prohibitive transport cost of tea could be substantially reduced'.[33]

Bengal was partitioned on 16 October 1905, and with it, Assam's status as a separate province came to an end, as it was as per the Curzon Plan, which in a nutshell was 'to split up and thereby weaken a solid body of opponents to our rule',[34] and Assam was merged with Eastern Bengal. The partition of Bengal was met with unprecedented opposition from Hindu

Bengalis, and by contrast, as expected, a muted response from the Muslims. The explanation for this is that all positions of power in the colonial establishment had come to be monopolised by the caste Hindus in Bengal, sowing the seeds of communal distrust. Under the circumstance, 'the prospect of Muslims outnumbering the Bengali Hindus in the new province had its appeal to the former'.[35]

In Assam too, the Bengalis reacted vehemently to the partition of Bengal, but the Assamese initially stayed aloof. Some Assamese leaders such as Manik Chandra Borua and Jagganath Borua even went ahead and supported the Curzon Plan,[36] much to the annoyance of the Bengalis. The protest, hence, remained confined to Bengali pockets in urban areas of the province, but soon, the Assamese middle class began taking a stand against the reorganisation of Assam, although, again, for a totally different reason than that which led the Bengalis to protest. The Assamese saw this would further marginalise them demographically. The apprehension was also of a threat to Assamese identity and language. The feeling was that the inclusion of Sylhet in Assam was a bad enough threat but the amalgamation of Assam with East Bengal sounded the death knell of Assamese identity.

The British finally relented against the incessant agitation in Bengal against the Curzon Plan, and on 12 December 1911, the partition of Bengal was annulled by a royal declaration. 'Assam, inclusive of Sylhet, was also formally reverted to its old status as a Chief Commissioner's province with effect from 1 April 1912'.[37] Bengal received a respite, but not Assam, where the seed of Bengali–Assamese antagonism – the Sylhet question – still remained unresolved.

The Sylheti Bengalis remained firmly united on the question of re-drawing the provincial boundaries on a linguistic basis. One of its members in the Assam Legislative Council, 'B.N. Chaudhury moved therefore a resolution in July 1924 for the transfer of Sylhet to Bengal ... Difficulty arose, however, from the side of Bengali-speaking Cachar which was not keen on the vivisection of the province'.[38] If Sylhet were to be transferred, the Bengalis of Cachar did not see any point in remaining in Assam, therefore the original resolution had to be modified to include Cachar. Of the three Cachar members in the Council, two decided to support the modified resolution, but the third still opposed it. 'The Council voted 22 to 28 to pass the amended resolution'.[39]

Curiously, the Assamese did not oppose the motion, as long as Assam's status as a separate province remained unchanged, despite the loss of territory. In fact, one Assamese member, Nilmoni Phukan, voted for the resolution.[40]

The issue, however, remained complex and unresolved. There was no clear-cut consensus on the question of the territory of Cachar. There was no certainty on the future official status of Assam in the event of the campaign to severe the Bengali provinces becoming a reality:

> A special session of the Council in January 1926 voted, 26 to 12, to recommend only Sylhet's transfer to Bengal. A second resolution recommended that in no case should Assam lose its major province status . . . All Sylhet members, except two Muslims, and all Indian members from the Brahmaputra Valley, except Saadulla and two other Muslim members, voted for the motion. All the three Cachar members – two Hindus and one Muslim – voted against. They were opposed to Sylhet's transfer to Bengal, unless Cachar also was transferred. Another motion recommending also the transfer of Cachar was, however, defeated.[41]

Likewise, 'In the Surma Valley Political Conference held on 1 July 1928, a resolution recommending the inclusion of both Sylhet and Cachar into Bengal was defeated by an overwhelming majority. The Conference voted for the transfer of Sylhet alone'.[42]

It is clear then, on the question of the transfer of Sylhet back to Bengal in the early twentieth century, there emerged a consensus among both the Bengali and Assamese communities in Assam in the Surma as well as the Brahmaputra valleys. Both communities were for the proposal, but for entirely different reasons. However, with the increasing polarisation of politics on communal lines in the rest of India at the time, and the widening visions of the future of India held by the Hindus and Muslims, it was only a matter of time before the situation in Assam changed. But the polarisation was not so straightforward as on the larger Indian canvas.

Muslim leaders in Assam, such as Syed Muhammad Saadulla, the first chief minister (then called prime minister) of Assam, began opposing the transfer of Sylhet to Bengal on the plea that the continued presence of the Muslim majority district in Assam would put the political future of the Muslims of the province in better stead. With the ascendency of this outlook, Assam's already dangerous ethnic and communal friction was set to see yet another chapter. The shape of politics that spun off from this development would ultimately lead to a campaign at the time of Partition, by Saadulla, who had joined the Muslim League by then, and his supporters, for Assam to be awarded to Pakistan. This was opposed tooth and nail by the Assamese, rallying under the leadership of Gopinath Bardoloi of the Congress, who was Saadulla's able match in the high drama of this political theatre during Partition, and ultimately, Assam stayed with India.

'Bardoloi's conflict with Saadulla did not stem from a personal rift. It reflected a broader division: the ideological battleground between Congress and the Muslim League and the politics of the times. The British saw Saadulla as the ideal foil for Bardoloi and Congress'.[43] After Indian independence, Saadulla, though he lost in his campaign, and thereafter, retired from active politics, stayed on in India and did not migrate to East Pakistan.

Political developments in Assam in the years leading to Indian independence and Partition were intense as much as they were peculiar. They cannot certainly be depicted with justice using the same brush strokes Indian history of the time is portrayed, as has often been the tendency. At the time the boundary commission under Cyril Radcliffe was set up to determine the dividing line between the soon-to-be-independent India and Pakistan, Sylhet district was marginally Muslim majority, and therefore, under the terms of Radcliffe's commission, it would have had to go to Pakistan. But if Sylhet were to be treated as part of Assam, then, in the combined province of Assam, Hindus would be majority; therefore in awarding Assam to India by the same principle followed by the boundary commission, Sylhet would have remained with India. But memories of a century of bitter rivalry, and the Assamese apprehension of losing Assam and their Assamese identity to a hegemonic Bengali population remained unchanged, and they continued to vehemently oppose the idea of Sylhet as part of Assam, at the civil as well as at the political levels.

The cynicism of the time is reflected in interviews of refugees from the Partition period in Assam and Bangladesh by Anindita Dasgupta. She notes: 'Another significant insight thrown up by my fieldwork was the implicit recognition that the separation of Sylhet from Assam in 1947 was caused not so much by a rivalry between Hindus and Muslims, but between the speakers of two major languages in colonial Assam, the Bengalis and the Assamese'.[44] Curiously, the Sylheti Bengali's disdain for the Assamese and Assam remained even after the Partition, and Sylhet was awarded to Pakistan. The Sylheti 'bhodrolok'[45] who opted to migrate to Assam refused to see themselves as refugees.

The circumstance was tragic, but not unforeseen. For 'while the Bengalees grew from an insecure immigrant group into a formidable political force, the Assamese grew from a disintegrated and frightened indigenous population into an incipient nationality with economic and political ambitions. The Assamese had to fight for their recognition as a full-fledged nationality',[46] writes Amalendu Guha. The writer quotes the Delimitation Committee of 1936, 'the line of division in Assam politics is primarily not between Hindu and Muhammedan or on caste lines, but between the inhabitants of Assam Valley and those of the Surma Valley'.[47] The Brahmaputra valley is the traditional home ground of the Assamese while the Surma valley (Barak valley) is predominantly Bengali.

Census figures reveal quite clearly this embedded linguistic tension in Assam of the time. By 1901, 48 per cent of the population of Assam spoke Bengali and only 22 per cent spoke Assamese.[48] 'Under the circumstances, the "Valley jealousy" which was formerly limited to job-seeking middle classes alone, was slowly being percolated and transformed into a cult of aggressive and defensive linguistic nationalism'.[49] Quite expectedly, in the 1930s, 'the demand for containment of further influx of East Bengal Muslim immigrants into Goalpara, and the rest of the Brahmaputra Valley, was increasingly raised as a political issue. If the immigration continued unrestrained, would not the Assamese be turned into a linguistic minority in their own homeland – the Brahmaputra Valley? This was the question which plagued the minds of not only its urban middle classes, but also the peasant masses'.[50]

Against the rising tides and changing colours on the larger canvas of the Indian freedom struggle, these rivalries in Assam too were destined to acquire new hues. The Muslim question soon came to complicate the equation between the Assamese and the Bengali. The Sylheti bhodroloks were a different class altogether, but an estimated 85 per cent of the later economic immigrants, mostly of land-hungry peasants from over-populated East Bengal to land-abundant plains of Assam, were Muslims. 'All that they wanted was land. From their riverine base, they further pressed themselves forward in all directions in search of more of living space in the areas held by the autochthones. It was then that an open clash of interests began to take place'.[51]

The line system

The need to introduce an administrative device to control this continued influx began to be felt soon enough. This administrative initiative came in the shape of the Line System, the idea of which 'was first mooted in 1916 and adopted in 1920'. Under this system, 'a line was drawn in the districts under pressure in order to settle immigrants in segregated areas, specified for their exclusive settlement'.[52] Despite these restrictions, in the next 10 years, 'the number of settlers, including children born after their arrival, increased from an estimated three lacs in 1921 to over a half a million in 1931'.[53] The influx of the Bengali population during this period was phenomenal and the Assamese were justified in being alarmed that demographically they would be left in minority if the trend was not halted. In some of the target areas of the immigrants, such as Barepta subdivision, 'the percentage of Bengalee Muslims increased from 0.1 percent in 1911 to 49 percent in 1941'; likewise, 'about 87 percent of the population in the Surma Valley were Bengalees'.[54]

Many commentators feel the illegal immigration problem Assam and the rest of the Northeast face even today could have ended in 1947, or at least, have been substantially different, if not for the politics that ended up with Sylhet awarded to Pakistan. India lost the territory of Sylhet, but much of the Sylheti Hindu Bengali population the Assamese did not want for fear of being outnumbered, in any case, migrated to India after Partition, not wanting to remain in a theocratic Islamic country. Most of them landed in Assam. From economic migrants, they overnight transformed into refugees. The thinness of the line dividing the two also became more than apparent. The territory was, in this sense, lost, but not the problem.

This thin line that divides the notion of legality, or the lack of it, with regard to moving populations came to the fore in exchanges of notes between the Assam chief minister, Gopinath Bardoloi, and the first prime minister of India, Jawaharlal Nehru, and then between the deputy prime mnister, Sardar Vallabbhai Patel, and Bardoloi's successor, Bisnuram Medhi, on the question of settling Partition refuges in Assam. Jawaharlal Nehru, is said to have remarked, 'I suppose one of these days we might be asked for the independence for Assam'.[55] In a similar vein, Deputy Prime Minister Sardar Vallabbhai Patel called Bordoloi's successor, Bisnuram Medhi, a narrow-minded parochial person,[56] author Sanjib Baruah notes.

Baruah's own trite commentary on these remarks, alluding to the rise of secessionist movement in the state in contemporary times, sums up the lack of understanding of these towering Indian leaders of the Assamese insecurity, and indeed, the insecurity of the entire region, on a matter that goes far beyond legality or even concerns of the popular understanding of Indian nationalism: 'The idea of Assam's independence, of course, did not remain a joke for long, and nor could the label of "parochialism" smother the desire for independence among a younger generation of Assamese'.[57]

But before I move on, a still closer look at the nature of the struggle for Assam's future on the eve of Partition may be rewarding as these events are very much a prelude to the shape of politics in the state long after Partition. As we have seen, by the turn of the twentieth century, the influx had become so alarming that fearing backlashes from the Assamese, a Line System was introduced in 1920, by which the immigrants were restricted from settling beyond certain demarcated lines, preventing them from encroaching into traditional grazing grounds, reserved forests and long fallow fields of traditional Assamese communities. The line system, however, was to soon become a bone of contention. Muslim leaders demanded its abolition while the Assamese, now leaning towards the Congress, under the leadership of Gopinath Bardoloi, wanted the system maintained more rigidly, warning that 'short of a rigid Line system, the linguistic problem would become in the coming years a source of constant friction resulting in violence, incendiarism and crimes of all kind'.[58]

As the political polarisation between Hindus and Muslims grew in the rest of the Indian subcontinent, in Assam too, an Assamese civil society organisation, the Asamiya Samrakshini Sabha, complained that the Muslim League was giving communal colour to local issues and 'the Bengali Muslims immigrants who were all along willing to identify themselves with the Assamese people in matters of language and culture, were now being persuaded and forced to read Bengali'.[59] Other Assamese civil society organisations also made representations to Nehru that if the Congress were to agree to separate Sylhet and Cachar plains from Assam and to stop the mass immigration into the Brahmaputra valley, the Assamese people would pledge to be the staunchest supporters of the Congress.[60]

Congress leaders were aware of the desperate immigration situation in Assam and were clearly worried:

> The proportion of Muslims in the population of the Brahmaputra Valley had increased from 9 percent in 1881 to 19 percent in 1931. It increased to 23 percent by 1941 and remained the same in 1951. In 1911, Muslims constituted 0.1 percent of the population of Barpeta subdivision; but by 1941, they constituted nearly 49 percent. The area of land settled with immigrants from other provinces was about 1.1 million acres in 1940–41m i.e., one-fifth of the total temporarily-settled area, inclusive of wasteland grants, in the Brahmaputra Valley. East Bengal immigrants alone accounted for nearly half a million acres.[61]

The overtones of political concerns were definitely taking a communal turn, including in the Congress camp. There, however, remained a major complication. As noted earlier, Bengali immigrants were not just Muslims. There was also a sizeable section of influential largely urban Bengali middle-class Hindus who continued to demand equal status of the Bengali and Assamese language even in the Brahmaputra valley. They continued to vow to resist any attempt to make Assamese the language of Assam. 'By and large, the Muslim immigrants were more concerned with acquiring land rights than preserving their language. It was particularly so in Assam proper. The attitude of a major section of the Bengali Hindu settlers, particularly its influential urban section, was quite different. Their leaders viewed the Brahmaputra Valley as a bilingual area'.[62]

As the Partition of India became inevitable, this three-way political equation in Assam was threatening to prove explosive, and tragic in equal measures. Summing up the situation, Amalendu Guha writes: 'Never was the communal situation in Assam so tense as in the last year of the British rule. In the 1940s the demand for the abolition of the Line system had converged on the demand for a six-province Pakistan that would include Assam. In January 1946, the province's Muslim electorate stood, in a massive way, behind these demands and their champion – the Muslim League. If Assam could be yoked with Bengal in one and the same Section that had a 51 percent Muslim majority under the Cabinet Mission Plan, these demands would be substantially achieved'.[63]

On 23 March 1940, the All India Muslim League passed the Lahore Resolution, also known as the Pakistan Resolution, demanding that a geographically contiguous region with Muslim majority both in the north-western as well as eastern sectors of India be demarcated as to constitute a separate sovereign Muslim state, during the League's 22–24 March general session in the city of Lahore.[64] Saadulla, who was leading his third ministry in Assam at the time, supported the resolution and worked to have Assam included in Pakistan, by showing the province as Muslim-majority. He therefore continued to encourage Muslim immigrants from East Bengal to occupy uncultivated government khasland.

Not only this, he was also accused of scheming to have the 1941 Census falsely show a higher Muslim population figure, leading to an uproar and wide protest, led by the Congress, headed by Gopinath Bardoloi, as well as various Hindu organisations. Saadulla had 'instructed that population be classified on the basis of community rather than religion. This was done to hide the actual growth of Muslim population from the Assamese protectionists. As a result, a large number of tribal people who earlier entered as Hindus, Christians or Buddhists in the earlier census, were now merely shown as "Tribals". This means that Hindu-tribals were shown as non-Hindus in the 1941 Census. The total number of Hindus thus went down in comparison with the Muslims'.[65]

The 1946 election in Assam was crucial. The Congress, which campaigned on the plank of opposing the threat of Assam's inclusion in Pakistan, emerged victorious convincingly and Gopinath Bardoloi formed a coalition government. This victory somewhat assured Assam's place in India as and when the country is partitioned, but not so that of Sylhet. Once in power, Bardoloi set about on a campaign to evict illegal Muslim settlers from grazing grounds and reserved forests, as well as to have Sylhet separated from Assam on the slogan of 'Assam for Assamese', heightening social tensions further. It was in this atmosphere that the Sylhet referendum was held on 6 and 7 July 1947 to decide the district's fate.

'It was virtually a vote on the twin issue of the reorganisation of India on a communal, and of the province of Assam on a linguistic basis. Sylhet Hindus who had for decades agitated for a re-union with Bengal now clung to Assam. On the other hand, Sylhet Muslims who were, on political considerations consistently opposed to the move since 1928, now reversed their position'.[66] Assamese public opinion too remained unchanged in desiring Sylhet separated from Assam, and this opinion was represented by the ruling Congress.

The result of the referendum was on expected lines. Muslims voted for Pakistan and Hindus for India, and the Muslims won by a margin of 55,578 votes, almost perfectly reflecting the communal composition of the district population. 'Only the three thanas of Patharkandi, Ratabari and Badarpur and about one half of the thana of Karimganj were to remain in Assam, as per terms of the award, and the rest of the district went to Pakistan'.[67]

The residue of bitterness that remained from the referendum among Sylheti Hindus is also on expected lines. They remained convinced that 'Muslim communalism was thought to be incited by the Assamese political leaders who had wanted to get rid of Sylhet for many years now. Even where there is recognition of the partisan role played by the Muslims, it is never the Sylheti Muslims but more distant players like the Bihari Muslims, Muslim League leaders . . . ',[68] summarises researcher Anandita Dasgupta. She further notes: 'The clearest example of the perfidy of the Assam government towards Sylhetis was the disenfranchisement of some 1.5 lakh of non-Muslim tea-garden labourers who could have been crucial in nullifying the eventual verdict of the Sylhet Referendum'.[69]

Assam agitation

The perception of a grave threat to the Assamese linguistic identity and their bitter rivalry with the Bengali speakers in Assam, however, was not destined to end even after the severing of Sylhet. A good percentage of Hindu Bengalis, trapped in theocratic Muslim Pakistan, would move across the border to India into Assam. Other than the Partition refugees, the old stream of economic migrants of Muslim peasants continued, because of the political and economic uncertainty East Pakistan continued to be in.

Writing in the 1990s, and reflecting on the sensitive issue of Bangladeshi immigration, Sanjoy Hazarika notes from an interview he did of an academic in Dhaka: 'The economic viability of Bangladesh has long been in question because of its over-population, poor natural resource base, vulnerability to natural disasters and undiversified economy dependent on the production of two crops, rice and jute'.[70] Such a state of uncertainty is predicted to result in a tendency for outward migration and into neighbouring countries. Assam, with its vast, under-populated, fertile flatlands would naturally come to be looked by the besieged population of Bangladesh as their *Lebensraum*.[71]

Assamese insecurity therefore continued, and the community's response to this would begin to have immediate as well as deeper, longer-term ramifications. The Congress Party, which ascended to power on the plank of addressing this Assamese state of mind, continued to return to power in Assam till late into the 1970s, probably also because the party held sway in the entire country in the early decades of its independence. In 1960, the third Congress chief minister of the state, Bimala Prasad Chaliha, introduced the Assam Official Language Bill, which sought to have Assamese as the sole official language of the state, much to the dismay of the state's Bengali population. Nonetheless, the bill was pushed through the Assam Assembly to become the Assam Official Language Act in 1961.[72] The Bengali population of Cachar (Barak valley) rose in revolt, and on 19 May 1961, 11 language protestors were killed at the Silchar railway station. In the aftermath of this tragedy, the Assam Official Language Act was partially withdrawn in October of the same year. In the Barak valley, a dual language policy was adopted and Bengali was made the 'other official language'.[73] Resentment continued and language frictions and riots plagued Assam well into the 1970s and 1980s.

The language friction between the Assamese and Bengalis, however, also had other grave consequences for Assam. It laid the seeds for tribal majority hill districts of the state to break away to become separate states in 1972. In the colonial era, if these non-Assamese ethnic communities of Assam, including the Nagas, Lushais, Khasis, Jantias and Bodos, had no particular love for the Bengali language, they were not happy with the prospect of Assamese being imposed on them either. A prominent politician of Meghalaya state,

P.A. Sangma, summed up the mood thus: 'We all spoke Assamese, we still can. But we are not Assamese, so we could not accept the imposition of Assamese. That's why Assam broke up'.[74] In the continued language agitation after the Silchar incident, 'the tribal groups joined the Bengalis'.[75] Sections of the Bodos even began demanding Hindi as the official language.[76]

Meanwhile, the acute instability of East Pakistan, among other reasons, was to ultimately lead to the 1971 war of liberation, which culminated in the birth of Bangladesh. This war, and the carnage that preceded it, which many describe as genocide, drove yet another wave of refugees, making Assam's already full cup of woe overflow. Predictably, Assam would begin to churn again. Beginning in the late 1970s, spearheaded by the All Assam Students Union (AASU) and another civil body, the All Asom Gana Sangram Parishad (AAGSP), launched a six-year-long agitation for the detection and deportation of illegal immigrants from East Bengal, then termed 'foreigners', literally paralysing the state administration for as many years. The agitation concluded with the signing of the Assam Accord in 1986.

Recalling the heady days in Guwahati, the capital of Assam, in the 1970s, Yasmin Saikia writes how, in her childhood, she remembers not too infrequent outbreaks of street violence, and frightened Bengali students often desperately seeking shelter in their house in fear of their Assamese friends, who wanted to kill them: 'Assamese violence against Bengali speakers was part of the political landscape of Assam until the late 1970s. In the 1980s, the rhetoric changed to "anti-Bangladeshi" and a religious flavour was introduced in the Assamese agitation led by the All Assam Students Union (ASSU). The demand of expulsion of the so-called illegal Bangladeshi immigrants became the motivating slogan of the Assamese public'.[77]

Other than the continued influx of migrants, the insecurity and frustration of the Assamese was compounded by many other dysfunctions of the society and that of the Indian state in the wake of independence. Assam found itself marooned and having to deal with a radically new political geography. Its rail line to the rest of India was snapped and could only be restored in 1950 through the Siliguri corridor. Its access to the sea and the port of Chittagong, once part of a natural economic region, and a convenient export route for Assam's produces, mainly tea, too was shut abruptly. So too, its elaborate river transport system developed by the British. Instead of trying to understand and 'help the Assam government to face these problems, the Central leadership seemed hell-bent on browbeating the state on the refugee issue'.[78]

Still accentuating this insecurity and frustration further, and paving the way for these to turn into anger was a spiralling unemployment figure.

There was soon born a growing sense of not only negligence by the union government, but also of Assam's rich resources being exploited, with the state benefitting little from it. 'As a result, popular anger at what had now come to be termed the stepmotherly treatment of Assam, mounted and found its first expression in the movement for the first oil refinery in Assam which occurred in 1957'.[79]

This was when, as noted earlier, a movement to make Assamese the official language of the state, gathered momentum. This met with expected resistance from the Bengalis and the hill tribes of undivided Assam. The directionless fury building up in the society was also again demonstrated in attacks on the trading community in the state, the Marwaris. In Udayon Misra's words, 'The feeling of being let down endured nevertheless and would soon find violent expression in yet another upsurge of nationalistic feeling – this time in the form of attacks on Marwari business houses in Guwahati and other towns of Assam in January 1968'.[80]

When little or nothing changed to improve the situation on the ground, by the 1970s, calls for Assam to secede from the Indian union began to be heard. It was in this political milieu that the six-year-long Assam Agitation was born, and the AASU came into prominence like never before. It was also the time when the militant incarnate of this discontent, the United Liberation Front of Asom (ULFA), came into existence – to be precise, on 17 April 1979.

At the end of the Assam Agitation in 1986 with the signing of the Assam Accord, leaders of the AASU stepped forward to form the political party Asom Gana Parishad (AGP) almost as the new vehicle to carry forward the fruits of the AASU's struggle to the next battlefield. The AASU, AGP and ULFA, indeed, were siblings and belonged to the same constituency, sharing the state of mind of a society under siege. 'There is always the danger of simplifying in arriving at such conclusions without trying to understand the inner workings of organisations such as ULFA. The fact, however, is often overlooked that right from its inception, the ULFA maintained close links with the AASU and the AGP, occasional differences notwithstanding, and during the first few years most of the ULFA recruits were drawn from the ranks of the AASU'.[81]

Nellie massacre

The cataclysmic moment of the Assam Agitation came in February 1983, a dark page in Assam's beleaguered history, often referred to as the Nellie Massacre. Tragic though the event may be, it provides a gruesome summary of the modern history of Assam. It tells in a nutshell a tale of tearing anxieties and identity insecurity the land has been struggling to come to terms with ever since. Researcher Makiko Kimura, in her 2013 book, *The Nellie Massacre of 1983, Agency of Rioters*,[82] analyses the politics that went into the massacre, which left an estimated 2,000 Bengali Muslim immigrants in a cluster of villages in the Nowgong district, about 70 km from the capital city of Assam, Guwahati, killed in a single day's organised attack by neighbouring villagers, most belonging to the Tiwa (or Lalung) tribals, but including some other local communities as well. She also comes up with a fascinating flashback of this history of turmoil.

Kimura does not solely give a documentary account of what happened, but also attempts to understand the psychology of what went into the carnage. This approach is expected and understandable, for in the 30 years since the incident, much has already been written on the factual status of the subject, including reports by two commissions of inquiries, an official one, headed by an IAS officer, T. P. Tewary, whose report was rejected by the then 'anti foreigners' agitators, who too instituted their own enquiry through an organisation called the Asom Rajyik Freedom Fighters Association, headed by a retired chief justice of the High Court of Himachal Pradesh, T. U. Mehta. In terms of documentary details then, there would have been little left to be said.

The year 1983 was the height of the anti-foreigners movement in Assam. In January of the year, the Congress-led government in New Delhi announced election to the 126-member Assam Legislative Assembly and the 12 Lok Sabha constituencies in the state. The leader of the agitation, AASU, and AAGSP decided to boycott the election, unless the electoral roll was first revised and launched a widely supported agitation to press for their demand.

A few days later, on 6 January, the Assam government arrested the movement leaders, including Prafulla Kumar Mahanta and Bhrigu Phukan, president and general secretary, respectively, of the AASU, and went ahead with the election with polling in three phases on 14, 17 and 20 February. The Nellie massacre happened immediately in its wake, on February 18, with just one phase of the polling left to be concluded.

The days preceding the massacre were marked by extreme tensions, with the agitators not just organising street agitations, but also trying to coerce candidates either not to file nominations or, if they have already done so, to withdraw them. According to the Tewari Commission, during the disturbances, there were 545 attacks on roads and bridges; 140 kidnappings; 193 attacks on election staff and candidates, their relatives, or political workers; 274 bomb explosions or recoveries or explosives; and so on.[83]

The movement leaders also managed to have the two Lok Dal factions, namely, the Bharatiya Janata Party and the Janata Party, boycott the election, leaving only the Congress, the six-party Left Democratic Alliance and a local party among indigenous tribal groups, the Plains Tribal Council of Assam (PTCA), to contest the election. Under the circumstance, there were only 630 candidates who filed nomination compared to 1,049 in the 1978 Assembly election.[84]

When the anti-foreigner movement broke out towards the end of the 1970s, the linguistic nationalism friction in Assam remained very much as a strong undercurrent, but because the Partition had happened, there was a shift in the legal facade of this resentment against outsiders, and it came to be sublimated as a fight against the presence of illegal foreigners in the state. The focus of the movement, therefore, came to slowly, but surely fall on Muslim Bengali immigrants, at least on the surface.

Are the dynamics of this clash of linguistic nationalism between the Assamese and Bengalis shared by the tribal communities of Assam? Can the Nellie Massacre incident be treated as purely an extension of this friction or did the Tiwa and other perpetrators of the massacre have other reasons for their act? The broad picture that emerges is that there were some shared concerns between the anti-foreigners movement, spearheaded by AASU and AAGSP, and the tribal attackers, but the latter had independent reasons too. For the latter, it was not so much a linguistic nationality tussle, and more to do with land alienation. They saw the immigrant settlers as aggressive land encroachers, kidnappers of girls, petty thieves and so on. These attackers also believed that the settlers were merely waiting for their time to attack and usurp them altogether, and therefore, believed what they did was a pre-emptive strike. They also saw the immigrants as 'Miyas', almost an independent ethnic category signifying land-hungry Muslim peasants from Mymensingh, and not to be absolutely equated with what the mainstream Assamese understood a Bengali or foreigner to be.[85]

This dichotomy of interests between mainstream Assamese and various other communities of the state is still not resolved. It is indeed curious that the rise of aggressive Assamese linguistic nationalism largely in reaction to Bengali linguistic chauvinism caused a reciprocal spiral of insecurity among non-Assamese-speaking indigenous communities in the state. It led, as noted earlier, to the breaking away of the state's hill districts and the creation of new hill states. It must also be noted that the insecurity spiral is far from contained and there are still centrifugal tendencies at work, and tribal groups such as the Bodos, Tiwas and Karbis now are fighting for further bifurcation of Assam to create new states for themselves, resulting periodically in murderous ethnic clashes, exposing, in the process, the anachronism and dangers of a proliferation of ethnic homelands demands. Many of the intractable ethnic feuds the Northeast has seen, and still is seemingly destined to see, are driven by this passion.

Demands for homeland states are indeed a tragic predicament, which the Northeast is beset with today. 'In Assam two narratives run parallel; one is the inclusive philosophy of *manabata* or humanity/humanism and the other is an exclusionary rhetoric of *bidexhi* or outsiders/strangers',[86] writes Yasmin Saikia. She continues: 'Assam's history is a story of migrants communities who travelled from far and near and settled along the alluvial plains of the rich Brahmaputra valley to eke out a living . . . Migration to the Assam valley is within this story of the human search for a future. Multiple communities of settlers – Ahoms, Brahmins, Muslims, Rajasthanis, Punjabis, Bengalis, Manipuris, Nepalis . . . and many more groups of documented and undocumented people have made their home in Assam. The diverse people have made Assam what it is today, a blended and rich world of settled and settling communities'.[87] This innocence and harmony is what stands lost, and what the state is struggling to recover desperately today.

Chittagong and Chakmas

Other than the Sylhet trauma in the creation of the southern boundary of the Northeast by the boundary commission headed by Cyril Radcliffe in 1947, there is another controversial transfer of territory, even lesser known to the world outside of the Northeast. This has to do with the award of the Chittagong Hill Tracts (CHT) to Pakistan by the commission, though these sparsely populated hill ranges are inhabited by Buddhist-aligned tribes, mainly the Chakmas, not remotely Bengali or Muslim. In the entire hill tract, the 'Muslim population was only 3 per cent of the whole'[88] as the chairman of the Boundary Commission, Cyril Radcliffe, wrote to the viceroy, Lord Mountbatten on 12 August 1947. But the report notes, this territory 'was difficult to assign to a State different from that which controlled the district of Chittagong itself'.[89]

Earlier in the same report, Radcliffe prefaced his intention of awarding the CHT to Pakistan with the following qualification: 'The question of drawing a satisfactory boundary line under our terms of reference between East and West Bengal was one to which the parties concerned propounded the most diverse solutions. The province offers few, if any, satisfactory natural boundaries, and its development has been on lines that do not well accord with a division by contiguous majority areas of Muslim and non-Muslim majorities'.[90]

Radcliffe also noted that, often, discussions on the award of territories that did not clearly fall within the terms of reference of the commission he headed, such as the majority status of Hindu or Muslim community inhabiting a territory, contiguity of the territory with other Hindu or Muslim population concentration territory, and so on, were fruitless, and he was asked by the other members to exercise his own best judgement in these cases: 'in the absence of any reconciliation on all main questions affecting the drawing of the boundary itself, my colleagues assented to the view at the close of our discussions that I had no alternative but to proceed to give my own decision'.[91]

In these cases, he also wrote, he took care that while 'drawing the line to eliminate any avoidable cutting of railway communications and of river systems, which are of importance to the life of the province but is quite impossible to draw a boundary under our terms of reference without causing some interruption of this sort, and I can only express the hope arrangements can be made and maintained between the two States that will minimize the consequences of this interruption as far as possible'.[92]

That the Chakmas and other CHT tribes themselves were keen to be left with India was not given priority. They had unambiguously expressed this opinion in representations they made to the Indian leaders in the tense pre-Partition days, and both Nehru and Patel assured them they would be with India. On 15 August 1947, the day India attained its independence, Chakma leader, 'Sneha Kumar Chakma hoisted the Indian flag at Rangamati. . . . The Indian flag was lowered by the Pakistani Army on August 21 at gun point against violent protest'.[93]

On the evening of 12 August, the day he received the report from Radcliffe, Lord Mountbatten held a meeting of his staff, and informed them CHT had been awarded to Pakistan. He wrote in his personal report No.17 August 16, 1947, that his Reforms Commissioner, V. P. Menon, who was present at the meeting, warned him that this was unlikely to be taken lightly by the Congress leaders, and that 'Nehru and Patel were certain to blow up, since they had only recently assured a delegation from Chittagong Hill Tracts that there was no question of their being allotted to Pakistan'.[94] Menon also warned Mountbatten that if the award of CHT to Pakistan came to be known, Nehru might even refuse to attend the meeting of the Constituent Assembly, which the Viceroy was to attend. The Congress leaders may even boycott the state banquet and the evening party, Menon further cautioned the viceroy.[95] Upon Menon's advice,

Mountbatten decided to hold on to the news of the award till the final day, 15 August. 'On August 13, I therefore wrote to Jinnah and Nehru telling them that I had not received all the awards by the time I left for Karachi, though I expected them that afternoon'.[96]

But the news of the award of CHT to Pakistan apparently leaked out, and true to the warning of Menon, Mountbatten wrote that he received an angry and 'incredible' letter from Patel, threatening that if the people of CHT were to resist being 'put into East Bengal the people would be justified in resisting this award by force and that the Central Government would be bound to support them'.[97]

Years later, the Indian foreign policy with regard to the CHT came very close to this eventuality, as Subir Bhaumik writes in *Troubled Periphery, Crisis of India's North East*. 'Within four years of the liberation of Bangladesh, India unleashed another guerrilla campaign in that country. The immediate provocation for the Indian sponsorship of the Shanti Bahini guerrillas, made up of Chakma, Marma and Tripuri tribesmen, was the military coup that killed Sheikh Mujib-ur-Rehman and many members of his family'.[98] The tribes of CHT, who were still longing to be united with India, and having been rudely and definitively denied autonomy by the Awami League government after the liberation of Bangladesh in 1971, were willing partners in India's plan. A representation lead by the Chakma leader, Manabendra Narayan Larma, in 1972, was flatly told by the new president of independent Bangladesh, Sheikh Mujib-ur-Rehman, 'go home and become Bengalis'.[99]

After the coup in Bangladesh and the installation of a military dictatorship unfriendly to India, the then prime minister, Indira Gandhi, was even prepared to liberate the CHT as she did Bangladesh in 1971. 'There is no denying that the strategic location of the CHT was an obvious temptation for any government in Delhi. Almost the entire tribal population of the CHT wanted to be part of India rather than an Islamic country whose military rulers were beginning to change the demography of the area by systematic re-settlement of Bengali Muslim plainsmen'.[100] If not for the defeat Mrs. Gandhi suffered in 1977, and the takeover of the Indian premiership by Morarji Desai, the history of these hill tracts may have been very different, Bhaumik further speculates.[101]

The stated reasons for which Radcliffe awarded the CHT to Pakistan were 'that the whole economic life of the people of the Hill Tracts depended upon East Bengal, that there are only one or two indifferent tracts through the jungles into Assam, and that it would be disastrous for the people themselves to be cut off from East Bengal . . . In a sense Chittagong, the only port of East Bengal, also depended upon the Hill Tracts; for if the jungles of the latter were subjected to unrestricted felling, I am told the Chittagong port would silt up'.[102] In retrospect, it is, however, obvious the decision is behind much of the Chakma refugee problem in Northeast India today. Facing systematic erosion of their base in the CHT, Chakmas have fled to neighbouring regions across the border in India as refugees. They are today scattered all over the Northeast, particularly in Tripura, Mizoram and Arunachal Pradesh, more often than not as unwelcomed guests, constantly threatened by vigilante groups, to be evicted and driven back to their original homes.

It is interesting how another study, the Report of the Excluded and Partially-Excluded Areas Sub-Committee (A.V. Thakkar Committee), which submitted its report on 18 August 1947, differed on its perception of the CHT from the Radcliffe report. The CHT were among the very few pockets of land inhabited by very backward aboriginal populations, which were demarcated as 'Excluded Areas' in pre-Partition India. The committee concluded quite differently from Radcliffe on which state the CHT should preferably go:

> Now Bengal is to be partitioned, the future administration of the Hill Tracts appears to lie with Assam. The Lushai Hills form in part the hinterland of this district and though communications to the east are not easy, they are not more difficult than with Chittagong. Karnafuli provides a waterway to Demaguri which is connected with Lungleh in the Lushai Hills. The Chakma, Magh and Mro of these Hills have probably their tribal origin in common with the Lushais and in any case the province of Assam is the home to many different tribes. It is obvious the Hill Tracts should not go to East Bengal in view of its predominantly non-Muslim population. The people themselves are strongly averse to inclusion in Bengal.'[103]

There were also other stretches of territory where the terms of reference of the Radcliffe boundary commissions were rendered ambiguous. One of the most important terms was to award to either Pakistan or India territories as per the wishes and religious affiliations of the majority inhabitants of the place. The problem faced in applying the term in CHT was also very much the case in Darjeeling and Jalpaiguri regions. Darjeeling and certain police stations areas in the Mymensingh district, which border the Garo Hills of Assam, were then classified as 'Partially Excluded Areas of Bengal' and 'the tribal population of the district seems to consist largely of labour employed in the tea gardens and some Lepcha and Bhotia'.[104] Like in the CHT, here too, 'the Muslim population amounted to 2.32 per cent of the whole in the case of Darjeeling, and to 23.08 per cent of the whole in the case of Jalpaiguri, but which constituted an area not in any natural sense contiguous to another non-Muslim area of Bengal'.[105] Here however, unlike in the case of CHT, Radcliffe used his discretion as chairman of the Bengal Boundary Commission to award them to India.

Another place put on the edge at the time of Partition was the Khasi Hills, as noted civil servant, Nari Rushtomji, wrote. He observed that the most important cash crops of the Khasi Hills were oranges and betel-nuts, and their main market before Partition was the district of Sylhet skirting their southern border. Pakistan campaigners imposed a virtual blockade on the Khasi Hills with the object of putting 'pressure on the Khasis and create among them a feeling that they would be better off in Pakistan'.[106]

Rushtomji recounts how he travelled to these hills to assure the Khasis, who too were not Muslims, that they would get an airstrip to facilitate transport of their produces and assuage their apprehension of their future welfare. These hills, as we know, have remained with India.

Like its northern boundary, the southern boundary of the Northeast is a legacy of the colonial government and was forged on an anvil of extremely layered Partition politics. The violence that accompanied the process was not as overt as in the West Bengal or the Punjab sectors, but it was not devoid of its own share of trauma. Its history is indeed replete with human miseries, much of which – though not evident immediately or explosively – are still unfolding and continually growing in their complexities, often threatening to throw the entire region into a spiral of chaos and mayhem. The unregulated immigration problems leading to myriad consequences, often deadly in nature, such as the periodic murderous riots in the Bodo areas, the unresolved Chakma refugee problem, the unending cycles of ethnic clashes in Assam and Manipur, the violent assertions of exclusive ethnic identities with potentials for ethnic cleansing feuds, are just some of the residual consequences of this dismal chapter in the history of the making of the Northeast.

Notes

1 Amalendu Guha, *Planter-Raj to Swaraj: Freedom Struggle and Electoral Politics in Assam 1826–1947* (People's Publishing House, 1977).
2 See Udayon Mishra, *Periphery Strikes Back: Challenges of the Nation State in Assam and Nagaland* (Indian Institute of Advanced Study, 2000).

3 Sanjib Baruah, *Durable Disorder: Understanding the Politics of Northeast India* (Oxford University Press, 2005), pp.83–97.
4 Robert Reid, *History of the Frontier Area Bordering on Assam*, p. 18; see also The Government of India Act, 1935 (26 Geo V&Edw. VII, Ch. 2) and http://en.wikipedia.org/wiki/Government_of_India_Act_1935.
5 Sanjib Baruah, *Durable Disorder*, pp. 83–97.
6 Ibid.
7 Ibid., pp. 90–91.
8 Madhav Gadgil and Ramachandra Guha, *This Fissured Land: An Ecological History of India* (as quoted in Ibid., p. 93).
9 Ibid., pp. 93–4.
10 Ibid., p. 95.
11 See chapter, *History of Militarisation of the Northeast* for a detailed discussion on Assam Rifles.
12 Sajal Nag, *Roots of Ethnic Conflict: Nationality Question in North-East India* (Manohar 1990), p. 35.
13 Letter issued to the Government of India, Vol. 7, No. 236. Jenkins to William Grey, 7 December 1854, ASR (as quoted ibid., p. 37.)
14 Ibid.
15 D. N. Bezbaruah, 'Demographic Threats in Assam', *Dialogue*, January–March 2005, Volume 6 No. 3, http://www.asthabharati.org/Dia_Jan%2005/d.n.htm (accessed on 29 November 2013).
16 Anindita Dasgupta, 'Denial and Resistance: Sylheti Partition "Refugees" in Assam' (*Contemporary South Asia*, 2001) p. 343, Taylor and Francis Ltd.
17 Ibid., p. 345.
18 Ibid., p. 349.
19 Ibid., p. 350.
20 Amalendu Guha, *Planter-Raj to Swaraj*, p. 25.
21 Sajal Nag, *Roots of Ethnic Conflict*, p. 52.
22 Ibid., p. 53.
23 Ibid., p. 55.
24 Edward Gait, *A History of Assam*, p. 387.
25 Ibid., pp. 387,388.
26 Ibid.
27 Amalendu Guha, *Planter-Raj to Swaraj*, p. 69.
28 Sajal Nag, *Roots of Ethnic Conflict*, p. 59.
29 Amalendu Guha, *Planter-Raj to Swaraj*, p. 28.
30 Ibid.
31 Ibid., p. 70.
32 Note of Home Secretary to the Government of India on March 28, 1903 (as quoted in Sajal Nag, *Roots of Ethnic Conflict*, p. 60).
33 Amalendu Guha, *Planter Raj to Swaraj*, p. 70.
34 Sir A. Frazer's note of 6 Dec. 1904 (as quoted in Amalendu Guha, *Planter Raj to Swaraj*, p. 71).
35 Ibid. Amalendu Guha, *Planter Raj to Swaraj*, p. 71.
36 Ibid. Nag, p. 60.
37 Ibid., Amalendu Guha, *Planter Raj to Swaraj*, p. 81.
38 Ibid., p. 166.

39 Ibid.
40 Ibid.
41 Ibid.
42 Ibid., p. 167.
43 Sanjoy Hazarika, *Strangers of the Mist: Tales of War & Peace from India's Northeast* (Penguin, 2003), p. 49.
44 Anindita Dasgupta, *Denial and Resistance*, p. 344, http://dx.doi.org/10.10 80/09584930120109559 (accessed on 19 November 2012).
45 Bhodrolok, or bhadralok, is the word for the educated, affluent Bengali middle class.
46 Sajal Nag, *Roots of Ethnic Conflict*, p. 79.
47 Amalendu Guha, *Planter Raj to Swaraj*, p. 204.
48 A Gazetteer of Bengal and North East India (as quoted in Anindita Dasgupta, *Denial and Resistance*, p. 350.
49 Ibid., p. 205.
50 Ibid.
51 Ibid., p. 206.
52 Ibid.
53 Census of India, 1951 report (as quoted in Amalendu Guha, *Planter Raj to Swaraj*, p. 206).
54 Imperial Gazetteer of India, 1908 reprint (as quoted in Sajal Nag, *Roots of Ethnic Conflict*, p. 99).
55 Nirode Barooah's *Gopinath Bardoloi, Indian Constitution and the Centre-State Relations, 1990* (as quoted in Sanjib Baruah, *Durable Disorder*, p. 167).
56 Sanjib Baruah, *Durable Disorder*, p. 167.
57 Ibid.
58 Gopinath Bardoloi's 13 November 1937 letter to Rajendra Prasad (as quoted in Amalendu Guha, *Planter Raj to Swaraj*, pp. 256–7).
59 Excerpts from a memorandum presented to Nehru on 28 November 1937 (as quoted in Ibid., p. 257).
60 Ibid.
61 Ibid., p. 258.
62 Ibid. Guha, *Planter-Raj to Swaraj*, p. 259.
63 Ibid., p. 315.
64 Wikipedia, http://en.wikipedia.org/wiki/Lahore_Resolution (accessed 27 August 2013).
65 *Assam Tribune*, article of 10 October 1941 (as quoted in Sajal Nag, *Roots of Ethnic Conflict*).
66 Amalendu Guha, *Planter-Raj to Swaraj*, p. 319.
67 Ibid., p. 320.
68 Anindita Dasgupta, *Denial and Resistance*, p. 351.
69 Ibid.
70 Sanjoy Hazarika, *Strangers of the Mist*, p. 13.
71 Ibid.
72 Nabanipa Bhattarcharjee, *Assam's Language Warriors*, http://www.indiaseminar.com/2012/640/640_nabinipa_bhattacharjee.htm (accessed on 15 November 2013).

73 Ibid.
74 Purno Agitok Sangma, press conference 1996 (as quoted in Subir Bhaumik, *Troubled Periphery: Crisis of India's North East* (Sage, 2009), p. 75.
75 Subir Bhaumik, *Troubled Periphery, Crisis of India's North East* (Sage, 2009), p. 75.
76 Ibid., p. 76.
77 Yasmin Saikia, Outlook India, *Blame 'Em, Bludgeon 'Em*, August 13, 2012 issue, http://www.outlookindia.com/printarticle.aspx?281846 (accessed 3 February 2014).
78 Udayon Misra, *The Periphery Strikes Back*, p. 116.
79 Ibid., p. 117.
80 Ibid., p. 119.
81 Ibid., p. 134.
82 See Makiko Kimura, *The Nellie Massacre of 1983: Agency of Rioters* (Sage, 2013).
83 Ibid., p. 74.
84 Idid.
85 Ibid., pp. 80,81.
86 Yasmin Saikia, *Blame 'Em, Bludgeon 'Em, Outlook India*.
87 Ibid.
88 Report by Cyril Radcliffe, Chairman of the Bengal Boundary Commission, on 12 August 1947, to the viceroy, Lord Mountbatten (as reproduced in Larry Collins & Dominique Lapierre, *Mountbatten and the Partition of India, March 22–August 15, 1947*, Tarang Paperbacks, 1983, p. 274).
89 Ibid.
90 Ibid., p. 273.
91 Ibid., p. 274.
92 Ibid., p. 275.
93 Mohsin, Amena, *Politics of Nationalism: The case of Chittagong Hill Tracts. Bangladesh* (as quoted by Md. Nazmul Hasan Chowdhury in 'The Resistance Movement in the Chittagong Hill Tracts: Global and Regional Connections' (*Asian Affairs*, Vol. 28, No. 4, 36–51, October–December 2006).
94 Viceroy's personal reports, Report No. 17, 16 August 1947 (as reproduced in Larry Collins & Dominique Lapierre, *Mountbatten and the Partition of India*, p. 278).
95 Ibid.
96 Ibid.
97 Ibid., p. 279.
98 Subir Bhaumik, *Troubled Periphery* (Sage, 2009), p. 165.
99 Ibid., p. 28.
100 Ibid., p. 167.
101 Ibid.
102 Viceroy's personal reports, Report No. 17, 16 August 1947 (as reproduced in Larry Collins & Dominique Lapierre, *Mountbatten and the Partition of India*, p. 279).
103 Report of the Excluded and Partially-Excluded Areas Sub-Committee (A.V. Thakkar Committee) (18 August 1947, as reproduced in, N.P. Bhange, *Tribal Commissions and Committees in India* (Himalaya Publishing House, 1993), pp. 3–4.

104 Ibid., p. 5.
105 Report by Cyril Radcliffe, Chairman of the Bengal Boundary Commission, on 12 August 1947, to the viceroy, Lord Mountbatten, (as reproduced in Larry Collins & Dominique Lapierre, *Mountbatten and the Partition of India*, p. 274).
106 Nari Rushtomji, *Enchanted Frontiers*, p. 110.

7

CONCLUSION

In the end is the beginning

This end note is not only a summary of what has been said in this book, but also an explanation of what has not been said and why. As many would have taken note, I have, in the preceding chapters, only on very few occasions, touched on the complex contemporary conflict situations prevalent in the Northeast. My attempt has been to sketch a picture of the larger geopolitics that have determined the political destiny and general psychological makeup of the region, which, in many ways, predicated these later day postcolonial conflict scenarios. I will, however, very briefly profile this culture of protest endemic in the entire Northeast region in modern times. Since I will not have the space to attempt profiling all the myriad conflict theatres in the region, I will pick as examples the three states of Nagaland, Mizoram and Manipur, which form the eastern frontier of the Northeast. They have been, in colonial history as well as now, generally treated as a sub-region of the Northeast. Nagaland is where the resistance to absorption to India was spontaneous and the most fundamental. Currently, this conflict is in a state of animated suspension following a peace talk between the government and the rebels initiated in 1997. In Mizoram, a similar conflict raged for 20 years before it was put to a conclusive end in 1986 with the signing of the Mizo Accord. In Manipur, straddled by these two states, insurrection not only continues to fester, but has become more complex.

Telling of the distant past, however tumultuous, and telling of burning contemporary issues, for many obvious reasons, require very different approaches and resources for they present radically different challenges. While the tumults of the past come invariably sublimated and mellowed by time, without the advantage of hindsight and the detachment only time can bring, current conflicts, by their very urgency, can be blinding as much as they are prone to be coloured by emotions, especially for subject analysts or writers who are part of the conflict environment they write about. As it is, trauma history writing is not easy, and is today evolving as an autonomous and specialised subject, leaning heavily towards the academic subject of psychology. As trauma scholars now inform us, the witnesses and other subject informants suffer from many forms of psychological inhibitions, more often than not, making them incapable of articulating their experiences completely.

The challenge, then, to recall Maurice Blanchot's words, is 'to keep watch over absent meanings',[1] for sometimes, these inhibitions and resultant silences are themselves eloquent testimonies of the scale and pitch of the trauma behind their stories. Objective and prosaic accounts, though necessary and important, have been less than adequate in representing these experiences, and often, it is literature and the arts that have increasingly proven to be the more versatile medium for the expression of these experiences. For all these reasons and more, writing of the endemic conflict issues of the Northeast has never been easy. But it is not the nature of the challenge which made me not to take up the issue in this volume. The project I set out to explore initially at the IIAS, Shimla, was more inclined to this idea of trauma representation, quite different, though related, from what I ended up accomplishing. I started exploring the intangibles that go into the making and shaping of traumatic experiences in the making of history of the Northeast, and how these experiences are not always possible to be calibrated faithfully through objective tools of standard history writing, and therefore, tended to remain as 'unclaimed experiences'.[2] Months into my fellowship, I was left at a difficult crossroads with the choice of deciding whether to take my inquiry towards the initial goal of discovering 'unclaimed experiences' or, else, to steer it towards discovering the influences geopolitics and geography had in the evolution of the idea of the Northeast, which I increasingly became fascinated by as my reading list grew. I chose the latter finally, but without giving up the desire or intent to return to explore the former in another project in the near future.

Naga imbroglio

The Nagas were the first to raise the banner of revolt against the idea of becoming part of India. The Naga insurrection also undoubtedly has been the most fundamental and, therefore, has been able to sustain its energy through six decades. The Naga rebellion, unlike the other similar insurrections spawned in the region in the decades after Indian independence, cannot be, for this reason, just a question of the 'periphery striking back',[3] and instead, is more like the periphery seeing itself as fundamentally different.

IN THE END IS THE BEGINNING

The former picture is probably a lot closer to the rebellions in Manipur and Mizoram, as also Assam and the rest of the Northeast. Currently, most factions of the Naga underground organisations are on ceasefire with the government, and the most powerful among them, the National Socialist Council of Nagalim, led by Isak Swu and Thuingaleng Muivah, has been holding peace negotiations with the Government of India since 1997. There is, therefore, relative peace in Nagaland at the moment, but the undercurrents of hostilities are far from resolved. I will not speculate on what the outcomes of the Naga peace talks would be, though the hurdles before it and the compromises to be made before any success can be hoped for are extremely challenging. The problem is further compounded by the fact that during more than a decade and a half of maintaining a ceasefire, the Naga underground movement has been splintering at an alarming rate. I do not intend to do a progress report of the Naga movement, or for that matter, the other insurgencies, but instead, restrict myself to sketching very brief psychological profiles of them and the factors that led to their emergence.

In the nineteenth century, when British administrators came in contact with the group of tribes in the hills of Assam they would come to refer to generally as Nagas, these tribes did not know they were being referred to as Nagas even though before the British, the name was apparently already in use by people in the plains to refer to them. Except among the powerful Angami villages where, the British noticed, a loose confederation had evolved, Naga villages elsewhere were still self-contained and had little contact or interaction with each other except in hostility, making violent murderous raids on each other. British sub-assistant commissioner at Nowgong, who was given the responsibility of leading the first expedition into the Angami Hills in 1839 to take stock of these violent raids, E. R. Grange, officially noted of these raids by the Angamis that 'the villages most frequently attacked were small settlements of Naga stock occupying clearings in the south of Tularam's Hills'.[4] He also noted that these raids were related to a slave-taking tradition among the tribes.[5]

As a policy, as noted in an earlier chapter, the British continued to leave these hill tribes alone to the greatest extent possible. This policy, however, changed after the spread of tea gardens and British interest reached the foothills. The raids, then with increasing frequency, began to be on the tea gardens, prompting the British to change their policy and begin a campaign of subjugating and keeping these hill tribes in check.

Till the turn of the twentieth century, unless they encroached into British interests in the plains and invited punitive expeditions, these tribes

IN THE END IS THE BEGINNING

remained as they were in their splendid isolation in the mutually hostile environment in the hills. There was, therefore, no cause for a unified identity to evolve among them and the Naga nomenclature remained largely an identity marker outsiders reserved for them and not one internalised among them.

Analysts generally agree World War I was the first occasion for these tribes to realise their common predicament and develop a fraternal bondage. The British had enlisted Naga villagers in their Labour Corps and took them for porter service in Europe. There, in Europe, treated as a group and given the same responsibilities, exposed to the same dangers, these disparate tribes, speaking mutually unintelligible languages though from a common hill home, discovered the commonness in their identity and the nomenclature that signified that commonness. 'It was during the First World War, that Nagas, some say 5000, had their first Western exposure, in France, serving in the Allied Labour Corps. Along with the sexually transmitted diseases, which, for the first time, some Nagas contracted during their time in Europe, there was also, obviously, a lot of mind-stretching done by these "Coolies"'.[6] Other sources give a lower figure of Nagas in the Labour Corps. 'The British Government recruited a number of labourers and porters from the Naga tribes. As part of the labour corps, around 2000 Nagas were sent to France, where, alienated from the other British Indian troops, they developed a sense of unity. They agreed that after returning to their homeland, they will work towards unity and friendship among the various Naga tribes. These Nagas, together with the British officials, formed the Naga Club in 1918'.[7]

The Naga Club was the first institution among the Nagas to symbolise this baptism into modern nationhood. But even after this, the Naga identity still remained fluid and far from possessing any definite boundary. In 1929, when the Simon Commission visited the region, in its first official demonstration of nationalistic aspiration, the Naga Club submitted a memorandum, essentially asking the commission to not include them in the purview of the commission's recommendation for administrative reforms for India, as they did not identify with India. Among the 20 signatories of various tribes then considered as Nagas was a Kuki.[8] The Kukis are no longer treated as Nagas today, though many other tribes in south Manipur, who the Kukis consider as their kin, linguistically and culturally, have been incorporated as Nagas.

The memorandum, besides pleading for the Naga Hills not to be treated as part of the Indian administration, also talked of eight known Naga tribes in the administered areas and more unknown tribes in the un-administered areas. They underscored their identity as distinct from the plainsmen among whom their staple diets of beef and pork are taboo, and their apprehension that they would lose their land if placed under Indian administration.[9] These shifts and realignments of identity in what is an essentially new identity should come as nothing strange. Otherwise, the Naga identity formation in which a set of linguistically disparate hill tribes, once mutually hostile, come together around a name given to them by outsiders to call themselves an ethnic family is, at once, unique and heroic. Such an identity does have dangerous foreboding ahead, not the least in its expanding nature, incorporating more and more groups within its umbrage, but in the process diluting the hold its core has on its peripheries, threatening the appearance of fault lines between its different constituents. The other problem has been that this identity, though at one level, has been expanding; at another, it has also become very exclusionary, therefore placing it in antagonistic positions with many neighbouring communities. The bloody clashes in the 1990s between Naga and Kuki tribes whose traditional homelands overlap spatially, especially in Manipur, were an indicator of the violence exclusionary ethnic identity politics can lead to, but this is another story.

By the mid-twentieth century, the Naga identity solidified further and there was little ambiguity left as to what this identity is among the tribes who call themselves Nagas. In 1946, the Naga Club became the Naga National Council (NNC), a social and political organisation 'to put forward the demand for a special status for the Naga Hills district'.[10] Till this time, there were no hints of separatist tendencies in the organisation as evident from a four-point memorandum submitted to the Cabinet Mission on 19 June 1946.[11] But in the next one year, the entire complexion of the Naga aspiration would radically change. The NNC would then begin to insist on self-determination. A letter to the Assam government on 21 May 1947, for instance, said, 'the Nagas who were determined not to allow themselves to be involved in a divided and chaotic India, are prepared to declare their own Independence and can only think of entering into a ten-year Treaty with an Independent Assam'.[12]

The entry of A. Z. Phizo, the charismatic Naga nationalist into the Naga political firmament at the time, may have catalysed this change. Phizo was educated in Shillong, but went to Burma in search of a profession before returning to the Naga Hills with the Japanese and Indian National Army during World War II. When the Japanese and the INA lost the war on this front, Phizo was captured by the British forces, but released in 1946.[13] In 1950, Phizo became the president of the NNC, but even before that, the influence of his extremist thoughts in the NNC became discernible.

Phizo campaigned as a leader to convince his people that 'the Naga people belong to the Mongolian stock, and for the 52 generations of their remembered history they have lived according to their own proud, simple and utterly independent way of life' and that 'historically, Nagaland has no connection with India, and even the part of Nagaland which for a time came under British administration was kept separate from British India'.[14] In the years that followed, Phizo would sweep aside all his opposition, with violence, when necessary. He then campaigned and conducted a plebiscite in 1951 in which the Nagas voted 99 per cent to be independent of India, called a successful boycott of the Indian election in 1952 and finally, when all these did not give him his goal of Naga sovereignty, declared the Federal Government of Nagaland in 1956, parallel to the Government of India. Open hostility then broke out between Phizo's followers and the Government of India, who had, by then, brought in the army into the Naga Hills.

Under intense military pressure, Phizo would escape to England on 10 June 1960, but the Naga struggle would continue.[15] In the next decade, the Naga Hills would see some of the most tumultuous time until in 1975, when the NNC and the Government of India decided to end the conflict with the signing of the Shillong Accord. This peace bought at such a high price would, however, not hold, for the radical among the Naga fighters would break away to continue the struggle under the banner of the National Socialist Council of Nagaland (NSCN) in 1980. The NSCN itself would split eight years later in 1988 into two factions. Naga independence remains elusive, but in the bargain, the biggest tangible reward the Nagas got from this struggle so far is the constitution of a Nagaland state in 1963 by merging the Naga Hills district of Assam and the Mon & Tuensang district of the then North Eastern Frontier Agency (NEFA). It is yet too early to say if there will be more rewards and what shape these would be, if at all.

Mizo struggle

The Mizo identity project parallels the Naga story quite closely. But unlike the Naga tribes, who were, for a long time, referred to as Nagas by outsiders, the Mizos were not referred to as Mizos. The dominant tribe among them were the powerful Lushais. Besides the Lushais, among whom the Sailos had emerged as the dominant clan, there were also the Hmars, and further north, the Baites, Sukte and many more tribes and clans. The nomenclature Mizo was indeed a product of conscious political mobilisation by tribal elites in the Lushai Hills to evolve an inclusive identity for the different kindred tribes living in these hills in the mid-twentieth century.

This identity was, in many ways, a response to the despotic hold over these hills by the Lushai chieftains and was, thus, a movement initially spawned among the non-Lushai tribes. This movement would soon come to be under the banner of a newly formed organisation, the Mizo Union (MU). The word Mizo is derived from two monosyllabic terms – 'Mi' meaning man in many of the Tibeto-Burman languages spoken in the Northeast, including the tribes of the Lushai Hills, and 'Zo', which signifies mountains. Mizo, hence, means 'man of the hills, and had little ethnic value'.[16]

Among the significant markers in the Mizo identity building project by the MU were having chieftainship abolished from the Lushai Hills district, and with it, ushering in land reforms biased towards the commoners and away from the chiefs. The MU also had the name of their district changed from Lushai Hills to Mizo Hills, besides persuading the centrally appointed Census Commission to recognise Mizo as a tribal category in the Schedule Tribes list of Assam in 1951. The success of these campaigns can be gauged from the 1961 Census survey outcome. Unlike in early censuses, which recorded large number of ethnic categories, 'by 1961 most people had begun to call themselves Mizos, so much so that the Lushai, Ralte, and Paite categories were recording nil figures'.[17] All these developments understandably were opposed by the lobbies of chiefs who were increasingly being sidelined by the brand of politics brought in by the MU that transferred power to the commoners who now began to form the new elite.

This polarity brought about by the ascendency of the 'commoners' would continue to inform politics in these hills, but it tells of the resilience of the society that the two ultimately reconciled without detriment to the larger Mizo society. History has been witness everywhere that often it is certain cataclysmic events that help flatten out such differences, and in the modern history of these hills, the devastating famine of 1959 and the apathy with which the Assam government responded to the situation, eventually leading to the outbreak of violent Mizo nationalistic uprising led by the Mizo National Front in 1966, in many ways, served this part, convincing these tribes that when it came to the crux, they were in the same existential boat.

Like in Nagaland, the Mizo rebellion too would invite brutal intervention of the Indian Army. The experiment that began in the Naga Hills to counter the NNC guerrillas, that of regrouping villages, would become a sustained strategy to contain the Mizo insurgents. This involves destroying small and widely dispersed villages and regrouping the villagers in a few central and concentrated villages with the intent of keeping vigil of these villages easier and, more importantly, to deprive the insurgents their natural sanctuaries.

While the pressure this would have put on the insurgent fighters in their hideouts in the jungles is expected, the psychological and social consequences of this atrocious strategy on the entire civil population can only be imagined. Tribal villagers removed and dislocated from their traditional grounds, which provided them their livelihood either in the form of arable lands or else hunting grounds, would find themselves helplessly living off rations from the government. It is not difficult to believe, as many have argued, that this would have been a factor in the introduction of a parasitic culture among the tribes. In the Mizo Hills, to overcome the terrain disadvantage, the government even deployed its airpower to strike remote bases of the MNF fighters. There is little to doubt the nature of the extreme crisis these counterinsurgency measures would have brought to the Mizos, as also in the case of the Nagas, but it arguably also would have further cemented the sense of being one people, consolidating the Mizo identity further.

Two other important factors that catalysed this identity formation, common to both the Naga Hills and the Lushai Hills must be mentioned here. One is the arrival of Christian missionaries in these hills in the late nineteenth century. Not only is it a question of introducing a common cosmological and theological belief system among the tribes, thus further ensuring a commonness, but for their own convenience, the missionaries' foremost efforts have also always been, at the very start of their missions, towards developing a lingua franca for these disparate tribes. This was absolutely necessary for it would have been technically impossible for them to spread the words of the Gospels in several dozen dialects.

In Assam, for instance, the Christian missionaries stood solidly behind the Assamese resistance against the replacement of their language by Bengali as the state's official language and as a medium for teaching in schools. One of the reasons was that Assamese was known across many tribes of Assam whereas Bengali was not. Under the circumstance, the missionaries' contribution to the emergence and ascendency of Nagamese, a pidgin Assamese dialect that in time became the lingua franca in the Naga Hills, is not a surprise at all. The Naga Hills, after all, were part of the Assam province at the time.

In the Lushai Hills, though also part of Assam at the time, the missionaries discovered soon enough that the different tribes and clans, though they had their own and different dialects, knew the Lushai Duhlian, the language of the dominant Lushai tribe. 'Early mission work was, therefore, concentrated on developing a viable medium for education and for spreading Christianity. The pre-eminent position of Duhlian made it the natural choice for missionaries. They set about standardizing the language by devising a primer and developing its dictionary. Bible and hymn books were translated into Duhlian and soon were to find their way into the far corners of the district, further popularizing the language. Today Duhlian is the official language of the state'.[18]

The Naga Hills and the Lushai Hills were similar in other ways, not just for being a part of the Assam province. They were both territories lying outside the Inner Line, and were classified as 'Backward Tract' by the Government of India Act, 1919, and then 'Excluded Area' by the Government of India Act 1935, excluding them from the legislative process of the Assam government, and therefore, any sense of self-governance, and were ruled directly by the governor of the province. Many of the discontents in these hills, therefore, were a direct response to the administration dictated from the plains of Assam. This would include the Mizo's sense of outrage at government apathy at the time of famine in their hills in 1959 – a fury which ultimately led to the 20-year Mizo secessionist movement in 1966. Again, the rise of aggressive Assamese linguistic nationalism, and the introduction of Assamese as the official language in 1961 as a response to what the Assamese felt was a threat to the Assamese identity from Bengali dominance, resulted in leaving non-Assamese hill tribes in Assam alienated, paving the way for the creation of separate tribal hill states out of Assam, and among these was Mizoram as a Union Territory in 1972 and full-fledged state in 1987, after the MNF signed a truce with the Government of India in 1986.

This, then, is a brief sketch of the Mizo story of how a number of disparate, mutually hostile tribes decided to forge a unity under a single ethnic identity. Like the Naga story, it has been heroic so far. This does not, however, mean there are no longer any daunting challenges ahead. So long as an identity is new and in the formative stages, it is malleable and ductile, therefore ready to adjust and accommodate. But as the identity matures and solidifies, its boundaries tend to become rigid and exclusionary. The alienation of the Brus, Chakmas, Chins and even the Hmars in contemporary times in Mizoram is the alarm bell for this identity project. It is too early to say anything for certain yet, but the resilience of the Mizo identity is set to be determined by how it accommodates or rejects these new challenges.

Manipur enigma

Neighbouring Manipur is a study in contrast. Its identity is not recent, which is a blessing as well as a curse in nation-building. A crystallised identity with a long history as a state does give it stability as long as epochs remain unchanged and paradigms of statehood and peoplehood are not challenged. In imagining pre-colonial Manipur, the picture evoked is of James C. Scott's 'Zomia' with a central paddy state surrounded by non-state ungoverned tribes in the hills, evading as Scott suggests, the reach of the state and its influence to the extent possible.

Manipur's identity problem in modern times has been its abject inability to re-imagine and reinvent itself outside of Scott paradigm of hill–valley relationship, long after this epoch has concluded, and a new one of democracy has dawned. History teaches us epochal changes do invariably cause trepidations and have been known to take several generations before a new equilibrium is found. It remains to be seen if the state and its people are resilient enough to last out the turmoil of this epochal transition and settle to a new creative calm, or disintegrate as so many doomsday pundits so enthusiastically predict of the state with barely disguised glee.

I will not go into describing the ethnic relations in the state again. Much has already been said of Manipur's hills in the descriptions of the Naga Hills and Lushai Hills. For indeed, there are considerable overlaps of concerns, topography and demography between Manipur and its two neighbours. It cannot be merely a coincidence that British colonial administrators and writers have always tended to treat the three as a composite region, with Manipur as the controlling hub. I will instead take a tour of how the native state of Manipur responded to the prospect of becoming part of the newly independent Republic of India.

At the time of Indian independence, there were only three principalities in the Northeast – united Assam, Tripura and Manipur. Even as late as 1949, the latter two princely states were still to join the Indian Union. But although the two at the time were yet to sign a Merger Agreement with India, their kings had earlier signed the Standstill Agreement and the Instrument of Accession, agreeing in principle they would join the Indian Union, indicating spiritually they were already very close to the idea of India.

It was a time the then home minister of India, Sardar Vallabhbhai Patel, was on a frantic campaign to have the process of getting all princely states to merge with the Indian Union and the campaign reached the Northeast too. Tripura's merger was uneventful. It was the Manipur case that became distasteful, as Lt. Col. Haobam Bhuban puts it in his book *The Merger of Manipur*.[19]

The king of Manipur at the time, Maharaja Bodhachandra Singh, during one of his visits to Shillong, the then capital of Assam province, in

IN THE END IS THE BEGINNING

September 1949, was kept under house arrest, and after six days of 'persuasion', made to sign the Merger Agreement, thereby formally merging Manipur with the Union of India. Repeated pleas by the king that it was his desire to ultimately sign the agreement, but he be first allowed to go home and consult his assembly was turned down as the job had to be done under all circumstances immediately. Sardar Patel had already readied an Indian Army brigade to take over charge in case the king created problems.[20]

Manipur at the time was already a constitutional monarchy, having hastily given itself a democratic constitution and an elected assembly in keeping with the demands of the time. The king, as it happened in Bhutan in 2007, had voluntarily agreed to limit his role in the administration as only a constitutional head. The real power was to vest with the assembly.

Indeed, many of the rebel groups among the Meiteis, the dominant community of Manipur, today argue that the Merger Agreement is legally invalid as the king had no authority then to sign any treaty independent of the elected Manipur Assembly (parliament). Lt. Col. Haobam Bhuban and many others argue that had India been a little more tactful, much of the insurrections witnessed in Manipur today would have had a different hue and moral legitimacy.[21] Manipur, hence, began its postcolonial history as a wounded society.

What then is Manipur exactly unhappy about today? The question needs a much deeper probe than the usual and familiar escape into the overstated loss of sovereignty story. Would, for instance, things be for the better had history taken a different turn in 1949? Would the multi-fractured ethnic strife and mutual suspicions among communities be any different? Would many of the chronic problems, including that of the perennial fund crunch, be any better? No honest effort has been forthcoming to try and answer these painful questions, hence the resonating lament continues to be of lost glory of the past. Few seem willing to admit that the imagined old glory, the claims of aeons-old amity between ethnic communities, old values, are all things of the past and that the new mission must be to try and locate the new paradigms on which Manipur must base its new relations and politics.

On 21 September 1949, the then king of Manipur, Maharaja Bodhchandra signed the Manipur Merger Agreement under controversial circumstances in Shillong and without the knowledge of his people back in Manipur. The development was not revealed till 15 October 1949, the day the agreement was to come into force; some believe this was because the king was afraid. On 15 October, however, Manipur woke up to a new reality. Their recently constituted assembly was unceremoniously done away with, and a Union of India representative became their administrative head.

Protests were not immediate; in fact, contrary to expectations, the transition passed off rather uneventfully. One reason could have been that the institution of monarchy was already suffering from an unprecedented unpopularity, so a regime change came as a welcome development. There were also pro-merger political parties, such as the Manipur State Congress Party, campaigning for such an outcome. Except for some mild statements of resentment by a communist movement taking shape at the time under the charismatic leadership of Hijam Irabot, which too ultimately faded out after his death in exile in Burma, there were hardly any protests against the merger worth mentioning.

But the calm was not to be for long, although it was initially not remotely to do with any secessionist sentiment.

After the Manipur Legislative Assembly, consisting of members elected under the Manipur Constitution, was dissolved, all its powers lapsed into the hands of Major General Rawal Amar Singh, who was foisted on the state as its chief commissioner. When the Constitution of India finally came into force on 26 January 1950, Manipur was declared as a Part-C state under the provision of Article 240 and the First Schedule to the Constitution. Consequently, from a responsible and representative government, Manipur's history relapsed to a minor province with a mere bureaucrat as head of its administration.[22]

Expression of resentment, though not immediate, all the same came in the form of a mass movement in 1954. In response, the centre had to concede to cancelling the Part-C status of Manipur and upgraded it to a Union Territory in 1957 under the State Re-organisation Act of 1956. The former princely state was henceforth administered by a chief commissioner and a territorial council. The centre's concession was, however, not seen as adequate and the agitation continued into the 1960s under the leadership of the Socialist Party and the Assembly Demand Co-ordination Committee, demanding a full-fledged assembly.

In spelling out the alienation of Manipur resulting out of the insensitivity of central policies, the committee even warned in its various representations and memorandum to the central government of the possibility of secessionist sentiments surfacing. A 1962 memorandum of the agitation leaders to the governor at the time said, 'Manipur is situated in the international border. Any step-motherly treatment to the people will produce harmful consequences to the integrity and solidarity of India. Manipuris are also within free India and they are entitled to the civic and political rights enjoyed by all the people in the rest of India. But why do you impose such autocratic diarchal rule on the Manipuris read one of them'.[23]

The agitation gained momentum, and the Government of India became alarmed, considering it was also the time the Naga movement in the neighbouring Naga Hills district of Assam was at its heights.

In 1962, the Government of India made the 4th Amendment to the Constitution, by which Article 239-A was inserted to create a Legislature and a Council of Ministers in the Union Territories; hence, Manipur came to have a 30-seat Union Territorial Legislature in 1963.

However, the resentments were not put to rest. By then, another demand for full-fledged statehood was building up under the leadership of an organisation called the All Manipur Peoples' Convention, which felt that to be subjects of a union territory meant second-class citizenship in the country. The increasingly popular demand was picked up by the Manipur Territorial Assembly, which took a resolution to demand for statehood on 2 September 1966.

By the following year, almost all the political parties in the state joined hands and made common cause of the issue. Then, on 29 February 1968, four opposition parties together formed the All Manipur Statehood Demand Committee to spearhead the agitation. In 1969, another body called the United Action Committee was formed by the opposition parties to press for the same demand.

The agitation intensified by the turn of the decade, and in March 1970, the ruling Congress and the United Action Committee combined forces to form the All Parties' Statehood Demand Co-ordinating Body. Henceforth, the agitation turned a new leaf. This body organised a massive rally on 18 May 1970. Here, the protestors decided all employees of the Imphal Municipality as well as all other memberships to the advisory town committees and notified town committees should tender their resignations. It also called upon members of parliament from the state to relinquish their seats. Further, it called for the boycott of all national festivals, the elections to the Imphal Municipality and the Legislative Assembly. It also resolved to launch a non-cooperation movement from 26 August 1970.[24]

In accordance with its resolves, on 1 August 1970, the commissioners of Imphal Municipality, members of the town committees of Moirang, Bishenpur, Nambol, Kakching, Lamlai and members of advisory councils to the Government of Manipur resigned from their respective posts to press the Government of India to grant statehood to Manipur. The committee then called a Manipur bandh on 3 August, and again, on 3 September. Only when the issue got too hot to handle did the Government of India give in to the demands of the people of the state, and full-fledged statehood was granted to Manipur on 21 January 1972, making it the 20th state of India.

By then, an unhealthy conditioning had set in – the belief henceforth was nothing would make the union take notice of its peripheral provinces if a demand is not predicated by violent protests. This became stark especially in Manipur, when the Naga Hills became the 16th full-fledged state of India in 1963, although historically, politically or economically, the Nagas were much less a cohesive entity. 'The Nagas had one advantage. They took to arms earlier. At least this is what had seemed in Manipur'.[25]

A culture of protest was thus introduced. Though the first resistance group among the Meiteis emerged in 1964 with the formation of the United National Liberation Front (UNLF), armed campaigns broke out only two decades later in the late 1970s, by which time several other revolutionary groups had formed.

Footnote

These are three conflict scenarios from the Northeast that I have very briefly sketched – traumas that are part and parcel of any epochal change, but in these cases, made acute by the abruptness and unfeeling manner these changes were introduced and handled. The question is, which way from here? Of the three states, Mizoram, free of historical burdens so far, seems to be the one most successful in 'working through' and coming to terms with its present. Manipur and Nagaland, it does seem, in their own ways, are stymied by the psychological condition, which Dominick LaCapra calls 'fidelity to trauma',[26] a condition in which the victim develops a self-defeating sense of betrayal at the thought of leaving memories of a traumatic past behind and moving on. An unconscious desire to remain tied down by the memories of sacrifices and traumas of a past generation, the grandeurs of their resistance, lost glories of the past and so on thereby resulting in shrinking scopes for present and future reconciliations. There must come a time when everybody, without disowning their past, is able to leave it behind, to get up and move on to meet the challenges of the present and the future. This is the challenge before the present generation of these two states, and indeed, the entire beleaguered region.

Notes

1 As quoted by James E. Young, in *Between History and Memory: The Uncanny Voices of Historian and Survivor, History and Memory*. Vol. 9. No. 1/2, Passing into History: Nazism and the Holocaust beyond Memory – In Honor of Saul Friedlander on His Sixty-Fifth Birthday (Fall 1997), pp. 47–58, Indiana University Press, http://www.jstor.org/stable/25680999 (accessed on 21 Mar 2012).

IN THE END IS THE BEGINNING

2 See Cathy Caruth, *Unclaimed Experience; Trauma, Narrative, and History* (Johns Hopkins University Press, 1996).
3 See Udayon Mishra, *The Periphery Strikes Back*.
4 Alexander Mackenzie, *History of the Relations of the Government...*, p. 104.
5 Ibid.
6 Charles Chasie, *The Naga Imbroglio: A Personal Perspective* (Standard Printers & Publishers, 1999), p. 26.
7 Neivetso Venuh; Bonita Aleaz, *British Colonization and Restructuring of Naga Polity*. Mittal Publications. pp.55–65 (as quoted in http://en.wikipedia.org/wiki/Naga_nationalism).
8 Charles Chasie, *Naga Imbroglio*, full text of memorandum reproduced as Appendix Group A 1, pp.165–7.
9 Ibid.
10 Ashikho Daili Mao, *Nagas: Problems and Politics* (Ashish Publishing House, 1992), p. 34.
11 Ibid.
12 Ibid., p. 35.
13 Ibid., p. 49.
14 Nirmal Nibedon, Nagaland: The Night of the Guerillas, p. 29.
15 Ashikho Daili Mao, *Nagas: Problems and Politics*, p. 55.
16 Sajjad Hassan, *Building Legitimacy: Exploring State-Society Relations in Northeast India* (Oxford University Press, 2008), p. 145.
17 Ibid., p. 149.
18 Ibid., p. 148.
19 See Lt. Col. Haobam Bhuban, *The Merger of Manipur (Pritam Haobam, 1988)*.
20 Sanjib Baruah, *Durable Disorder: Understanding the Politics of Northeast India* (Oxford University Press, 2005), p. 59.
21 See Lt. Col. Haobam Bhuban, *The Merger of Manipur*.
22 Ibid.
23 The information in this and following paragraphs were gleaned from an interview by the author with a former president of the Manipur People's Party, MPP, L. Chandramani Singh, who was also part of these agitations.
24 Ibid.
25 See R. Constantine, *Manipur: Maid of the Mountains* (Lancer 1981).
26 LaCapra, *Writing History, Writing Trauma* (The Johns Hopkins University Press, 2001), p. 22.

BIBLIOGRAPHY

Books

Agamben, Georgio. (2005) *State of Exception*, Chicago: University of Chicago Press.
Anderson, Benedict. (1983) *Imagined Communities: Reflections on the Origin and Spread of Nationalism*, Verso.
Assam Rifles DG. (2003) *Guardians of the North East, The Assam Rifles 1835–2002*, Directorate General Assam Rifles, Laitumkhrah Shillong-11, in association with Lancer Publishers & Distributors.
Barpujari, H. K. (1981) *Problem of the Hill Tribes: North-East Frontier, 1873–1962, Vol. III: Inner Line to McMahon Line*.
Baruah, Sanjib. (2001) *India against Itself: Assam and the Politics of Nationality*, Oxford University Press.
Baruah, Sanjib. (2005) *Durable Disorder: Understanding the Politics of Northeast India*, Oxford University Press.
Baruah, Sanjib (ed.). (2009) *Beyond Counter-insurgency: Breaking the Impasse in Northeast India*, Oxford University Press.
Bell, Charles. (1924) *Tibet Past and Present*, Oxford University Press.
Bhaumik, Subir. (2009) *Troubled Periphery, Crisis of India's North East*, Sage.
Bhuban, Lt. Col. Haobam. (1988) *The Merger of Manipur*, Pritam Haobam.
Carr, E. H. (1961) *What Is History, The George Macaulay Trevelyan Lectures Delivered in the University of Cambridge January – March 1961*, Penguin Books.
Caruth, Cathy. (1996) *Unclaimed Experience; Trauma, Narrative, and History*, Johns Hopkins University Press.
Chakravarti, P. C. (1971) *The Evolution of India's Northern Borders*, London: Asia Publishing House.
Chasie, Charles. (1999) *The Naga Imbroglio: A Personal Perspective*, Standard Printers & Publishers.
Chellany, Brahma. (2011) *Water: Asia's New Battleground*, HarperCollins.
Constantine, R. (1981) *Manipur: Maid of the Mountains*, Lancer.
Eekelen W. F. Van. (1964) *Indian Foreign Policy and the Border Dispute with China*, Martinus Nijhoff.

Engels, Friedrich. (1948) *The Origin of the Family, Private Property and the State*, Moscow: Progress Publishers. First published 1948 (reprinted 1950, 1952, 1954, 1959, 1962, 1968, 1972, 1977).

Fanon, Frantz. (1990) *The Wretched of the Earth*, Penguin Books.

Fukuyama, Francis. (1992) *The End of History and the Last Man*, Penguin Books.

Gait, Edward A. (1933) *A History of Assam*, Calcutta: Thacker Spink & Co. P. Ltd.

Geertz, Glifford. (1980) *Negara, The Theatre State in Nineteenth-Century Bali*, Princeton University Press.

Guha, Amalendu. (1977) *Planter-Raj to Swaraj: Freedom Struggle and Electoral Politics in Assam 1826–1947*, People's Publishing House.

Guha, Ramachandra. (2008) *India After Gandhi: History of the World's Largest Democracy*, Picador.

Haksar, Nandita.(2011) *The Judgment That Never Came: Army Rule in North East India*, New Delhi: Chicken Neck, imprint of bibliophile South Asia.

Hall, D. G. E. (1964) *A History of South-East Asia*, London: Macmillan & Co. Ltd.

Harvey, G. E. (1967) *History of Burma*, Frank Cass & Co. Ltd.

Hassan, Sajjad. (2008) *Building Legitimacy: Exploring State-Society Relations in Northeast India*, Oxford University Press.

Hazarika, Sanjoy. (2003) *Strangers of the Mist: Tales of War & Peace from India's Northeast*, Penguin.

Johnstone, James. (1983) *Manipur and the Naga Hills*, Cultural Publishing House.

Kamei, Gangmumei. (2002) *Jadonang a Mystic Naga Rebel*, Gangmumei Kamei.

Kaplan, Robert D. (2012) *Revenge of Geography: What the Map Tells Us about Coming Conflicts and the Battle against Fate*, New York: Random House.

Kimura, Makiko. (2013) *The Nellie Massacre of 1983: Agency of Rioters*, Sage.

LaCapra, Dominique. (2001) *Writing History, Writing Trauma*, The Johns Hopkins University Press.

Lamb, Alastair. (1968) *Asian Frontiers: Studies in a Continuing Problem*, London: Pall Mall Press.

Lamb, Alastair. (1966) *The McMahon Line, A Study in the Relations Between India, China and Tibet 1904 to 1914*, Routledge & Kegan Paul.

Larry, Collins and Dominique Lapierre. (1983) *Mountbatten and the Partition of India, March 22-August 15, 1947*, Tarang Paperbacks.

Lezlee Brown, Halper and Setphan Halper. (2014) *Tibet: An Unfinished Story*, Hachette India.

Lintner, Bertil. (2012) *Great Game East: India, China and the Struggle for Asia's Most Volatile Frontier*, HarperCollins.

Lisam, Komdam Singh. (2011) *Encyclopedia of Manipur.*, New Delhi: Kalpaz Publication.

Mackenzie, Alexander. (1999) *History of the Relations of the Government with the Hill Tribes of the North-East Frontier of Bengal*, Mittal Publications.

BIBLIOGRAPHY

Mao, Ashikho Daili. (1992) *Nagas: Problems and Politics*, Ashish Publishing House.

Maxwell, Neville. (1970) *India's China War*, Jaico Publishing House.

Mehra, Parshotam. (2007) *Essays in Frontier History – India, China and the Disputed Border, India's Imperial Legacy and China's Frontier Gains*, Oxford University Press.

Mishra, Udayon. (2000) *Periphery Strikes Back: Challenges of the Nation State in Assam and Nagaland*, Indian Institute of Advanced Study.

Myint-U, Thant. (2011) *Where China Meets India, Burma and the New Crossroads of Asia*, Faber and Faber.

Myint-U, Thant. (2001) *Making of Modern Burma*, Cambridge University Press.

Nag, Sajal. (1990) *Roots of Ethnic Conflict: Nationality Question in North-East India*, Manohar.

Nariman, Fali S. (1913) *The State of the Nation*, Hay House India.

Nibedon, Nirmal. (1978) *Nagaland: The Night of the Guerillas*, Lancer.

Noorani, A.G. (2011) *India-China Boundary Problem, 1846–1947*, Oxford University Press.

Prabhakara, M.S. (2011) *Looking Back into the Future*, Routledge.

Reid, Robert. (2013) *History of the Frontier Areas Bordering on Assam from 1883–1941*, Bhabani Books.

Rushtomji, Nari. (1971) *Enchanted Frontiers, Sikkim, Bhutan and India's North-Eastern Borderlands*, Oxford University Press.

Rushtomji, Nari. (1983) *Imperiled Frontiers, India's North-Eastern Borderlands*, Oxford University Press.

Scott, James C. (2009) *The Art of Not Being Governed: An Anarchist History of Upland Southeast Asia*, Orient Blackswan.

Sen, Amartya. (2005) *The Argumentative Indian*, Penguin Books.

Shakespear, Col. L.W. (1929, 1977) *History of Assam Rifles*, Firma KLM Private Ltd, on behalf of Tribal Research Institute, Government of Mizoram.

Taylor, Peter J. (1994) 'The State as Container: Territoriality in the Modern World-System', *Progress in Human Geography* 18(2): 151–62.

Thakkar, A.V. (1993) *Report of the Excluded and Partially-Excluded Areas Sub-Committee* (A.V. Thakkar Committee) (18 August 1947), in N.P. Bhange, *Tribal Commissions and Committees in India*, Himalaya Publishing House.

Articles

Bezbaruah, D.N. (2005) 'Demographic Threats in Assam', *Dialogue*, January–March, 6(3).

Bhattarcharjee, Nabanipa. (2012) 'Assam's Language Warriors'. http://www.india-seminar.com/2012/640/640_nabinipa_bhattacharjee.htm (accessed on 3 September 2015).

Brownlie, Ian.(1988) 'The Rights of Peoples in Modern International Law', in James Crawford (ed.), *The Rights of Peoples*, Oxford University Press.

Chowdhury, Md. Nazmul Hasan. (2006) 'The Resistance Movement in the Chittagong Hill Tracts: Global and Regional Connections', *Asian Affairs*, 28(4), 36–51, October–December.

Dasgupta, Anindita. (2001) 'Denial and Resistance: Sylheti Partition "refugees" in Assam', *Contemporary South Asia*, 10(3): 343–60.

Falk, Richard. (1988) 'The Rights of Peoples (In Particular Indigenous Peoples', in James Crawford (ed.), *The Rights of Peoples*, Oxford University Press.

Goswami, Namrata. (2012) 'China's Territorial Claim on Arunachal Pradesh: Alternative Scenario 2032', IDSA Occasional Paper No. 29, November.

Gupta, Karunakar. (1980) 'Distortions in the History of Sino-Indian Frontiers', *Economic and Political Weekly*, 15(30) 26 July.

Gupta, Karunakar. (1974) 'Hidden History of the Sino-Indian Frontier I-1947–1954', *Economic and Political Weekly*, 9(18), 4 May.

Gupta, Karunakar. (1974) 'Hidden History of the Sino-Indian Frontier II-1947–1954', *Economic and Political Weekly*, 9(19), 11 May.

Gupta, Karunakar. (1982) 'India-China Border', *Economic and Political Weekly*, 17(32), 7 Aug.

Gupta, Karunakar.(1971) 'The McMahon Line 1911–45: The British Legacy', *The China Quarterly No. 47*.

Kar, Bodhisattva. (2011) 'When Was the Postcolonial? A History of Policing Impossible Lines', in Sanjib Baruah (ed.), *Beyond Counter-insurgency: Breaking the Impasse in Northeast India*, Oxford University Press.

Karlsson, Bengt G. (2013) 'Ethnicity in Northeast India through the Lens of James Scott', *Asian Ethnology*, 72(2).

Lokendra, N. (1993) 'Manipur During World War II (1942–45): Socio-Economic Changes and Local Responses', Manipur State Archives.

Lord Curzon. (1907) 'Frontiers', Romanes Lecture. https://www.dur.ac.uk/resources/ibru/resources/links/curzon.pdf (accessed on 3 September 2015)

Nora, Pierre. (1989) 'Between Memory and History: Les Lieux de Memoire', Special Issue: *Memory and Counter-Memory*, no. 26, Spring.

Wouters, Jelle J.P. (2012) 'Keeping the Hill Tribes at Bay: A Critique from India's Northeast of James C. Scott's Paradigm of State Evasion', *European Bulletin of Himalayan Research*, 39: 41–65.

Young, James E. (1997) 'Between History and Memory: The Uncanny Voices of Historian and Survivor', *History and Memory*, 9(1/2), Passing into History: Nazism and the Holocaust beyond Memory – In Honor of Saul Friedlander on His Sixty-Fifth Birthday, Fall.

INDEX

AFSPA 4, 10, 33, 49, 53, 55–62; see also Armed Forces Special Powers Act 1958
Ahom kingdom 5, 63, 74, 75, 79, 80, 81, 82, 83, 84, 85, 86, 87, 102, 105, 116, 155, 159, 160, 169, 186
Aksai Chin 9, 10, 11, 15, 17, 118, 119, 121; see also Kashmir
Alaungpaya, King 76
Ampthill, Lord 147
Anglo-Chinese Convention 1890 140, 145, 146
Anglo-Chinese Convention 1906 121, 125, 147–50, 152, 153; see also Peking Convention 1906
Anglo-Russian Convention of 1907 5, 121, 122, 124, 125, 129, 130, 149, 150, 152, 153, 156; see also St. Petersburg Treaty 1907
Armed Forces Special Powers Act 1958 4, 10, 53; see also AFSPA
Arunachal Pradesh 3, 22–3, 26–7, 34, 36, 49, 52, 70, 73, 88, 110, 111, 116, 119, 132, 150, 159, 162, 189
Assam 1, 3–6, 33–5, 36–45, 46–54, 70, 73, 75, 78–80, 82, 83, 85, 86–91, 93, 95, 100, 102, 108–11, 113, 114, 116, 117, 128–32, 136, 142, 155, 159–79, 180–3, 184–6, 188–90, 197, 199, 200–4, 207

Assam Accord 182, 183; see also Assam agitation
Assam agitation 180, 183; see also Assam Accord
Assam Line System to check Muslim migrants 176, 178, 179
Assam Military Police (AMP) 42; see also Assam Rifles
Assam Rifles 4, 33, 36–45, 46–48, 50, 131, 164
Assam Valley 38, 79, 87, 176, 186; see also Brahmaputra Valley
Ava Kingdom 74, 75
Ayapoorel 98, 99, 100, 101; see also Balaram, Major

backward tracts 34, 79, 109, 162
Balaram, Major 96, 98, 100, 103; see also Ayapoorel
Bangladesh 2, 3, 19, 22, 23, 26, 31, 34, 120, 159, 166, 175, 181–2, 188
Barak valley 19, 42, 70, 108, 160, 176, 181; see also Surma Valley
Bardoloi, Gopinath 174, 177, 178, 179, 180
battle of Imphal 50, 64; see also battle of Kohima
battle of Khonoma 95, 96
battle of Kohima 50, 64; see also battle of Imphal
Bell, Charles 126, 141

215

INDEX

Bengal Eastern Frontier Regulation 1873 78, 88, 109, 111, 141, 163
Bhagat, Prem 2, 54, 138
Bhutan 2, 26, 31, 32, 34, 90, 110, 113, 140, 146, 150, 153, 154–6, 205
Bhutan treaty 1910 154
Bodhchandra, King 205
Bombay Burmah Corporation 101
Brahmaputra 3, 20, 23, 27, 37, 70, 108, 113, 119, 160, 166, 170, 174, 176, 178–9, 186
Brahmaputra valley 70, 111, 113, 160, 160, 166, 172, 174, 176, 178, 179, 186
Bronson, Miles 169
Brooke, Henderson 2
Bruce, Robert 36, 63, 108; see also tea industry
Burma 22, 23–7, 34–8, 41, 43–5, 51, 67, 75–6, 80, 82, 89–91, 92, 93, 98–103, 108, 115, 116, 130, 137, 142, 155, 164, 199, 201–6

Cachar 4, 33, 37, 39–40, 42–3, 51, 74, 91, 92, 95–7, 99, 102, 162, 164, 166, 172–4, 178, 181
Cachar Levy 4, 39, 40, 42, 164; see also Jorhat Militia
Cachari kingdom 74, 96
Caroe, Olaf 114, 129, 130
Chakma 186–90, 203
Chandrakirti King 98, 99
Chiang Kai-shek 115, 137–8
China 2–6, 9–12, 15–17, 22–7, 31–2, 36, 50, 52–4, 77, 80, 88, 90, 115–21, 122–9, 131–2, 135–49, 150–4, 155–6
Chinese forward policy 1910 111, 124, 150–4
Chittagong Hill Tracts 6, 186–90, 193
Christian missionaries 168, 202
Chumbi valley 144, 145, 146, 148, 153

civil militia 4, 36, 39–40, 45, 164
Col. Johnstone see Johnstone, James
Curzon, Lord 11, 77–8, 89–91, 102, 108, 120, 122, 139–40, 145–9, 151–2, 161, 172–3

Dalai Lama 53, 120, 124, 125, 129, 131, 140, 141, 143, 145–6, 151–4, 155
Dalhousie, Lord 94

Eisenhower, David 137, 138
excluded area 35, 109, 162, 189–90, 203; see also partially excluded area

forward policy 54, 111, 121, 124, 126, 150–4

Geneva Conventions 1949 57, 58, 59, 65
Government of India Act 1919 109, 162, 203
Government of India Act 1935 67, 102, 109, 130, 162, 203
Great Game 1, 13, 121, 137, 139, 141, 146, 147, 149
Grow More Food programme 165–8
Gurkha Rifles 14, 41–3, 50, 146, 156, 164

The Hague Conventions 1899 and 1907 57
Haipu Jadonang 75, 104
homeland 7, 76–7, 176, 186, 198, 199
homeland politics 76, 104, 186, 198
human rights 4, 25, 33, 40, 45–6, 49, 54, 55–62

Indian Army 4, 39, 42, 45, 49, 52, 54, 164, 201, 205
India's China War see Maxwell, Neville
Indus valley 18, 19, 119
Indus Water Treaty 1960 3, 20, 21

216

INDEX

Inner Line 5, 34–5, 75, 78–80, 81, 85, 87, 88, 89–91, 93, 95, 108–32, 135–56, 141, 162, 163, 203; see also Outer Line
insurgency 7, 18, 40, 45, 48–9, 202
Ivan (I-fan) Chen 126, 127

Japanese see World War II
Jeevan Reddy Committee 61
John Ardagh Line 1897 17
Johnstone, Col. James 95, 99, 100, 101, 102, 107
Johnstone Boundary Commission 1881 90, 100
Jorhat Militia 39; see also Cachar Levy

Kabaw valley 51, 75, 93, 98, 101, 104; see also Kubo valley
Karakoram see Kashmir
Kashmir 3, 9–15, 17, 18–22, 23
Kendat Expedition 1885 101; see also Bombay Burma Corporation
Khasi 82, 162, 181, 190
Khathing, Ralengnao (Bob) Major 131
Kingdon-Ward, Francis 6, 113, 114–15, 129; see also Tawang
Kissinger, Henry 138
Kohima seige 96
Konbaung dynasty 76
Kookies see Kuki
Kubo valley 51, 101
Kuenlun see Kashmir
Kuki 43, 77, 93, 96, 103, 198, 199
Kuki uprising 43

Laloop system 92
Lhasa 16, 115, 120, 123, 125–8, 131, 140, 144–6, 147–50, 151–6
Lhasa Convention 1904 125, 140, 147–50, 153
Line System for migrants in Assam 176, 178, 179

Look East Policy 26, 38, 51, 142
Lushai 4, 43, 87, 89, 91, 93, 95–100, 102, 111, 189, 200–4
Lushai Duhlian 202, 203
Lushai Expedition 1871–1872 96, 97
Lushai hills see Mizoram

Macartney–Macdonald Line 1899 17
McMahon, Henry 5, 22, 23, 52, 54, 109, 110–14, 117–22, 124–5, 126, 128–32, 141, 148, 159
McMahon Line 5, 22–3, 52, 54, 109, 110–12, 113, 114, 117–19, 120, 121, 122, 124–5, 128–32, 141, 148, 159
McMahon–Shatra notes 128, 130
Manipur 3, 4, 19, 33, 35, 36, 38, 40, 42–3, 45, 49–51, 53, 54, 56, 61, 67, 70–7, 88–90, 91–3, 94–103, 108, 116, 131, 159, 164, 186, 190, 195, 197–9, 203–8
Manipur (Hill Area) Autonomous District Council Act 1971 70, 72
Manipur Merger Agreement 204, 205
Manipur takeover 1891 101, 103
Mao Zedong 137
Maxwell, Col. H.P 101, 102
Maxwell, Neville 2, 54, 131, 138, 148
Meghalaya 49, 70, 91, 159
Meitei 73, 75, 82, 205, 208
Minto, Lord 140, 149, 152, 153
Mizo Accord 195
Mizo National Front 201
Mizoram 4, 43, 49, 67, 70, 91–3, 159, 162, 189, 195, 197, 203, 208
Mongolia 6, 16, 117, 124–6, 136, 140, 146, 149, 150, 151, 155, 200
Morley, Lord 120, 121, 125, 139–40, 149–50, 152, 153, 154, 155

Muslim League 18, 49, 165, 174, 175, 178–80
Myanmar 2, 9, 22, 23–7, 31, 51, 67, 73

Naga hills 4, 38, 43, 53, 54, 70, 74, 89, 91, 93, 94, 95, 96, 102, 116, 198, 199, 200, 201, 202, 203, 204, 207, 208; *see also* Nagaland
Nagaland 4, 38, 43, 45, 49–51, 53, 54, 67, 70–4, 77, 89, 91, 93–6, 102, 116, 159, 162, 195, 197–201, 208
Naga plebiscite 53, 200
Nehru, Jawaharlal 21, 55, 119, 135, 136, 138, 143, 177, 178, 187, 188
Nellie Massacre 183–6
Nixon, Richard 138
Non Aligned Movement (NAM) 138
Northeast 1–7, 8–27, 31–62, 67–103, 108, 109, 115, 116, 119, 120, 121, 128, 131, 135–7, 139, 140, 141, 142, 149, 156, 159, 160, 164, 170, 177, 186, 189, 190, 195–7, 201, 204, 208
NSCN 45–48, 71, 72, 200

Operation Bluebird 47
Outer Line 5, 35, 88, 90, 108, 109, 110–12, 117, 120, 132, 135, 141; *see also* Inner Line

Paddy State 70, 80, 81, 91, 92, 93, 94, 102, 204
Pakistan 4, 6, 18–22, 31, 44, 49, 54, 137, 138, 160, 167, 170, 171, 174, 175, 177, 179, 180, 181, 182, 186, 187, 188, 189, 190
Pamheiba King 75
partially excluded area 35, 109, 162, 189; *see also* excluded area
Partition 3, 4, 6, 18–20, 31, 35, 49, 52, 61, 126, 159–90

Partition of India 3, 4, 6, 18, 19, 20, 31, 35, 49, 52, 61, 159, 160, 166, 170, 171, 172, 173, 174, 175, 177, 179, 181, 185, 187, 189, 190
Patel, Sadar Vallabbhai 143, 177, 187, 188, 204, 205
Peking Convention 1906 125, 149, 150, 152, 153; *see also* Anglo-Chinese Convention 1906
Pemberton Line 93, 98, 100
Phizo 53, 199–200
Posa 5, 75, 80–8, 95, 102, 155
protectorate state 4, 34, 78, 90, 96, 102, 120, 140, 141, 145, 146, 156, 159

Radcliffe Line 22, 49, 159
Rangoon Treaty 1967 102
Reid, Robert 113, 114, 136
Romanes lecture "Frontier" 28, 77, 89, 161
Rushtomji, Nari 35, 131, 190
Russia 5, 6, 10, 12, 13, 15, 16, 17, 26, 77, 78, 90, 120, 121, 122–3, 124, 125, 129, 130, 136, 139, 140, 145, 146, 147, 148, 149, 150, 151, 152, 153, 154, 156

Sadullah, Mohammad 165–6
St. Petersburg Treaty 1907 122, 149, 152; *see also* Anglo-Russian Convention 1907
Salwa Judum 40; *see also* civil militia
Santosh Hegde Commission 61
Sharmila, Irom 55
Shatra, Lonchen 126, 141
Shillong Accord 40, 200
Sikkim 26, 34, 70, 90, 112, 113, 131, 137, 140, 141, 144–5, 146, 150, 153, 155, 156, 159
Sikkim annexation 26
Siliguri corridor 2, 22, 182
Simla Conference 1913–1914 5,

INDEX

109, 113, 114, 117, 120, 121, 122, 123, 124, 125, 126, 128, 131, 141, 148, 150, 156, 159
Simon Commission 198
Slim, William General 50
Sphere of Influence *see* Curzon, Lord
Sphere of Interest *see* Curzon, Lord
Stilwell, Joseph 115
Stilwell Road 116
Sukapha, King 160; *see also* Ahom Kingdom
Surma valley 19, 38, 42, 160, 172, 174, 176, 177; *see also* Barak valley
Sylhet referendum 6, 33, 38, 39, 41, 42, 159, 160, 165–78, 180, 181, 186

Tawang 6, 112–15, 116, 128, 129, 130–2
tea industry 36, 37, 93, 95, 170
Thangal, Major 96, 100, 103
Tibet 2, 5, 6, 10, 11, 12, 14, 15, 16, 21, 22, 23, 26, 27, 34, 50, 52, 53, 77–8, 109–10, 111–15, 116–19, 120–31, 136, 137, 139, 140–56, 159, 201
Tikendrajit, Jubaraj 103
Treaty of Yandaboo 1826 3, 90, 91, 93, 159, 164
Tripura 35, 49, 54, 70, 91, 92, 95, 108, 159, 189, 204
Truman, Harry 137, 138
Tsangpo valley 115

Tularam, King 96; *see also* Cachari Kingdom
Tungoo dynasty 75

Union Territory 72, 203, 206, 207
United Nations 49, 55, 68, 122, 123, 135
USSR 124, 137, 138

Village Defence Force *see* Salwa Judum

Wavell, Lord 165, 166
World War I 4, 42–3, 50, 125, 128–9, 137, 139, 150, 164, 198
World War II 35, 43, 50, 51, 52, 57, 63, 64, 102, 114, 115–16, 117, 137, 165, 199

Yarkand 10, 11, 12, 14, 15, 16, 17, 26, 121; *see also* Kashmir
Yarlung Tsangpo 27
Younghusband, Francis 14, 15, 120, 125, 140, 145, 146, 147, 151, 152, 153, 154, 155
Younghusband Expedition 1904 14, 15, 120, 125, 140, 145, 146, 147, 151, 152, 153, 154, 155; *see also* Younghusband, Francis

Zomia 5, 67, 70, 80–8, 91, 93, 102, 103, 204